Advance Praise for
Rhetoric, Politics, and *Hamilton: An American Musical*

"This edited collection offers engaging analyses of Lin-Manuel Miranda's politically complex and massively popular *Hamilton*, addressing its contributions to and contestations of public memory about the nation-state, cultural discourses about race and gender, and political rhetoric about social movements and change. Foregrounding the pedagogical value of the musical, this book will itself be a valuable resource for scholars and students of rhetoric, performance, and popular culture. Just as the musical mashes up a variety of musical and historical sensibilities, this collection brings together a diverse range of scholarly perspectives including rhetorical, critical race, and intersectional feminist theories and offers close readings of not only lyrics and music but also of a range of historical intertexts that have shaped and been shaped by *Hamilton*. The essays are clear and compelling and will appeal to critics and fans of the musical alike."
—Claire Sisco King, Associate Professor, Vanderbilt University;
Editor, *Women's Studies in Communication*

Rhetoric, Politics, and *Hamilton: An American Musical*

Mitchell S. McKinney and Mary E. Stuckey
General Editors

Vol. 48

The Frontiers in Political Communication series
is part of the Peter Lang Media and Communication list.
Every volume is peer reviewed and meets
the highest quality standards for content and production.

PETER LANG
New York • Bern • Berlin
Brussels • Vienna • Oxford • Warsaw

Rhetoric, Politics, and *Hamilton: An American Musical*

Edited by
Jeffrey P. Mehltretter Drury and
Sara A. Mehltretter Drury

PETER LANG
New York • Bern • Berlin
Brussels • Vienna • Oxford • Warsaw

Library of Congress Cataloging-in-Publication Data

Names: Drury, Jeffrey P. Mehltretter, editor. | Drury, Sara A. Mehltretter, editor.
Title: Rhetoric, politics, and Hamilton : an American musical / Jeffrey P.
Mehltretter Drury, Sara A. Mehltretter Drury [editors].
Description: New York: Peter Lang, 2021.
Series: Frontiers in political communication; vol. 48 | ISSN 1525-9730
Includes bibliographical references and index.
Identifiers: LCCN 2020039341 (print) | LCCN 2020039342 (ebook)
ISBN 978-1-4331-8064-4 (hardback) | ISBN 978-1-4331-8065-1 (paperback)
ISBN 978-1-4331-8066-8 (ebook pdf) | ISBN 978-1-4331-8067-5 (epub)
ISBN 978-1-4331-8068-2 (mobi)
Subjects: LCSH: Miranda, Lin-Manuel, 1980– Hamilton. | Musicals—Political
aspects—United States. | Hamilton, Alexander, 1757–1804. | Persuasion
(Rhetoric)—Political aspects—United States. | Communication in
politics—United States.
Classification: LCC ML410.M67976 R54 2021 (print) | LCC ML410.M67976 (ebook) |
DDC 792.6/42—dc23
LC record available at https://lccn.loc.gov/2020039341
LC ebook record available at https://lccn.loc.gov/2020039342
DOI 10.3726/b16938

Bibliographic information published by **Die Deutsche Nationalbibliothek.**
Die Deutsche Nationalbibliothek lists this publication in the "Deutsche
Nationalbibliografie"; detailed bibliographic data are available
on the Internet at http://dnb.d-nb.de/.

© 2021 Peter Lang Publishing, Inc., New York
80 Broad Street, 5th floor, New York, NY 10004
www.peterlang.com

All rights reserved.
Reprint or reproduction, even partially, in all forms such as microfilm,
xerography, microfiche, microcard, and offset strictly prohibited.

Table of Contents

Acknowledgments vii

Chapter One Introduction: *Hamilton* as Cultural and Rhetorical
    Phenomenon 1
    Sara A. Mehltretter Drury, Jeffrey P. Mehltretter Drury, & Henry Egan

Part One: *Hamilton* and Public Memory 11

Chapter Two The I/Eye of History: Performing Public Memory, Utopia,
    and Critical Nostalgia in *Hamilton* 13
    Jade C. Huell & Lindsay A. Jenkins

Chapter Three *Hamilton* and the Entelechy of the American Dream 31
    Michaelah Reynolds & Ryan Neville-Shepard

Chapter Four Exhibiting *Hamilton:* History, Memory, and Musical Theater 47
    Sara A. Mehltretter Drury & James Anthony Williams Jr.

Part Two: *Hamilton* and Rhetoric of Social Identity 67

Chapter Five *Hamilton* as Cosmogonic Myth 69
  Christopher Bell

Chapter Six *Hamilton* and Public Memory of the Founding Era: Myth, Humanization, and Comforting Whiteness in "Post-Racial" America 87
  John Clyde Russell

Chapter Seven Patriarchy and Power: A Feminist Critique of *Hamilton* 105
  Emily Berg Paup

Part Three: *Hamilton* and Rhetoric of Democracy and Social Change .. 125

Chapter Eight Bondage and Circulation 127
  Brandon Inabinet

Chapter Nine Political Niceties and Rap in *Hamilton* 145
  Jeffrey P. Mehltretter Drury

Chapter Ten Diverse Offerings for Understanding U.S. Politics: Analyzing the Invitational Rhetoric of *Hamilton* and President Barack Obama 163
  Mark P. Orbe

Chapter Eleven The Rhetorical Significance of *Hamilton* in Public Protests 179
  Nancy J. Legge

Note on Contributors 197
Index 201

Acknowledgments

Our work as editors on this volume has been supported and aided by the genius and graciousness of all the authors involved. Reading their work has deepened our understanding and critical evaluation of *Hamilton*. We are especially grateful for the authors' patience and diligence during the spring and summer of 2020. Faced with a pandemic that forced much of our lives into a digital medium, these authors continued to write (non-stop), respond to changes in timelines with grace, and provide their quality rhetorical, communication scholarship. To each of you, thank you; it has been our privilege to serve as your editors on this volume.

We also are appreciative of those who helped bring the volume into fruition. We thank Ryan Neville-Shepard for sparking the project when at a conference he encouraged Jeff to edit a book about *Hamilton*. We are grateful to the editorial team at Peter Lang for their support of the project, specifically to acquisitions editor Erika Hendrix for her guidance and patience and to series editors Mary Stuckey and Mitchell McKinney for their enthusiasm and support, especially for Mary's lightning-fast responses to email inquiries. Our editorial process was aided by Henry Egan, an undergraduate summer intern supported by Wabash College. Wabash College also supported our intellectual and pedagogical development on this project: first, by providing an opportunity for Jeff to teach a first year tutorial on *Hamilton* and the liberal arts, and then generously supporting a trip for Jeff, Sara, their first year students, and Anthony Williams to travel to Chicago to see the musical live.

We applaud Lin-Manuel Miranda for creating a musical that produces so much conversation about our nation's past and how to reflect, critique, and consider what matters most today. We thank the cast and creative teams of *Hamilton*, past and present, who brought and will continue to bring this story to life, fostering renewed appreciation for and debate about U.S. history.

Finally, this book would not have come into being without those who experienced the musical on stage with us, especially Jason L. S. Raia; Joseph and Kathleen Mehltretter; Walter, Kathleen, James, Katherine, and Caroline Novak; Rana Yared, Mark Weaver, Jana Checa Chong, and Philip Ng; and Bridgit Hayes. Thank you for sharing this journey with us.

Jeffrey P. Mehltretter Drury and
Sara A. Mehltretter Drury
December 2020

CHAPTER ONE

Introduction: *Hamilton* as Cultural and Rhetorical Phenomenon

SARA A. MEHLTRETTER DRURY, JEFFREY P. MEHLTRETTER DRURY, AND HENRY EGAN[1]

Hamilton: An American Musical has become a cultural phenomenon since its debut in 2015, amassing both popular and critical fame. The show was nominated for 16 Tony Awards and won 11 of them. On top of that, the musical took home a Grammy and a Pulitzer Prize. The same year *Hamilton* debuted, the musical's 35-year-old writer, Lin-Manuel Miranda, won the MacArthur Genius Grant, which is awarded "to individuals who show exceptional creativity in their work and the prospect for still more in the future."[2] The cast album for the musical was not only the bestselling cast album in fifty years but also shot to number one on the Billboard Rap charts.[3] *Hamilton*'s ticket sales blew away many of the standing records at the time. At its Broadway debut venue, the Richard Rodgers Theatre, *Hamilton* broke the record for highest ever one-week gross (roughly two million dollars in one week). The show also boasts fifty-seven million dollars in advance ticket sales.[4]

Critics have raved about the show as well. In his early review of *Hamilton* on Broadway, famed *New York Times* theater reviewer Ben Brantley began his assessment by saying, "Yes, it really is that good," and later explained that the show's dialogue is a "fervid mix of contemporary street talk, wild and florid declarations of ambition, and, oh yes, elegant phrases from momentous political documents you studied in school, like Washington's Farewell Address."[5] Five years later, *Hamilton* boasted productions in Chicago (ending a three-year run in January 2020), Los Angeles, and London, three U.S. tours, and at the time of this writing, planned to begin a run in Sydney in 2021.[6] The *Hamilton* cast album was the most streamed cast album in the 2010s—with more than four billion listens.[7] On July 3, 2020, the streaming platform Disney+ released *Hamilton: An American Musical*, a recording of the Broadway production with the original cast, bringing the musical into the headlines once more.[8]

A show does not end up with this much press and popularity without amassing a dedicated fanbase. *Hamilton* managed to go beyond typical Broadway fandom to reach people across generational, political, and racial boundaries. Outside of the theater stages, *Hamilton* prompted a phenomenon through public engagement and popular culture, as cast members connected with "HamFans"/"Hamilfans" through social media.[9] When the show's popularity surged on Broadway, Miranda and the cast created #HAM4HAM, a short public show outside the stage doors that ran each day simultaneously with the limited ticket lottery and was filmed and shared through social media by adoring fans.

A fandom such as this is bound to infuse other aspects of people's lives. The show's historical context paired with its intergenerational appeal made it a powerful tool for educators to get their students excited about learning history. As historian Benjamin L. Carp has argued, "It would be too dismissive to argue … that *Hamilton* is merely entertainment and thereby beneath highbrow criticism; popular culture does matter, and it influences popular audiences, including students."[10] In the United States, *Hamilton* has a particularly strong following among youth and has been integrated into the K-12 curriculum in some school districts.[11] The musical tried to deliberately reach beyond the Broadway demographic through the Hamilton Education Program, which greatly discounted midweek ticket prices for public school students taking history classes. Many of these students had never seen a Broadway show before. However, because *Hamilton* offers a more inclusive musical at the level of sound and racial representation, the students became enthusiastically invested.[12]

Hamilton has been connected to politics since its inception. In February 2009, Miranda debuted the opening number from what he was then calling "a concept album about the life of someone I think embodies hip-hop: Treasury Secretary Alexander Hamilton" at the Obama White House arts event, "An Evening of Poetry, Spoken Word, and Music."[13] President Barack Obama and First Lady Michelle Obama praised *Hamilton* for its creativity and attention to history, inviting the cast back to the White House for a concert performance of the musical in March 2016. In his introductory remarks, Obama shared that the musical was "a favorite in the Obama household," and joked that their love of *Hamilton* was "the only thing Dick Cheney and I agree upon."[14]

Thrust into the spotlight for their work, the cast of the musical has engendered political notice and controversy. For example, after a performance of the show on November 18, 2016, Brandon Victor Dixon, the actor who played Aaron Burr at the time, addressed Vice President-elect Mike Pence who was in the audience that evening. Dixon read a pre-planned speech critiquing the Trump administration's policies towards immigration and race, concluding that "We truly hope that this show has inspired you to uphold our American values and to work on behalf of all of us."[15] This act of public protest was spread across social media and stirred up much political controversy on the role of entertainment in public political discourse, as evidenced by numerous chapters in this volume. The 2017 *Hamilton Mixtape* album also served as political commentary, including a variety of remixes of songs and lyrics from the show, including "Immigrants: We Get the Job Done," featuring K'naan, Snow Tha Product, Riz MC, and Residente, which expanded a single *Hamilton* lyric into a critique of President Donald Trump's immigration policy.[16] Four years later, in early 2020, *Hamilton* was in the political news once more when former U.S. National Security Advisor John Bolton titled his memoir of his time in President Trump's administration *The Room Where It Happened*, an homage to a song from the musical.[17]

HAMILTON AS RHETORICAL ARTIFACT

Hamilton is a powerful example of how rhetoric might use history to speak to the conflicts of today, in this case through themes connected to public memory, national and cultural identity, and democracy and social change. The symbolic significance and resonance of this musical is enhanced because of how it addresses civic themes through theatrical entertainment and reaches a broader audience than more traditional forms of political discourse. The show addresses these themes by blending a very canonical musical theatre structure with hip-hop, rap, and R&B composition. Part of *Hamilton*'s vernacular appeal is that it takes the genre of biography and jazzes it up, literally and figuratively. As the musical's dramaturg, Oskar Eustis, explained, "Lin does exactly what Shakespeare does ... he takes the language of the people, and heightens it by making it verse."[18]

The result is that *Hamilton* speaks to national, social, and personal identity in the United States—historically and in the nation's political present.[19] In 2016, President Obama praised *Hamilton*'s relevance, calling it "a quintessentially American story. In the character of Hamilton—a striving immigrant who escaped poverty, made his way to the New World, climbed to the top by sheer force of will and pluck and determination—Lin-Manuel saw something of his own family and every immigrant family."[20] Furthermore, *Hamilton* emerged at a time when there is widespread dispute about historical meaning (e.g., the value of confederate statues, the teaching of Columbus). When *Hamilton* was released on Disney+ in July of 2020, the debate began anew about the historical representation/revisionism in the musical, and particularly whether the musical took seriously the history of slavery in the United States.[21] The summer of 2020 was marked by the intense public response to videos of the murder of George Floyd by police officers in

Minneapolis, Minnesota, and a subsequent surge in public activism with the Black Lives Matter (BLM) movement. The musical, which focuses heavily on the narrative force of history, has a unique relevance to the BLM movement, especially given the importance these protests placed on the toppling of monuments that stood for the United States' racist and imperialistic past.

The foregoing discussion has illustrated how *Hamilton* is a rhetorical text that both reflects and influences culture. With multiple tours bringing the live show to new audiences, its reach continues to grow. This relationality urges scholars to consider the messages within it. No text is beyond the reach of academic criticism even if it has risen to this level of ubiquity. The historic nature of *Hamilton* makes it especially important to critique how it represents or erases aspects of the country's history, politics, and identity. Much of the musical's praise comes from its unconventional and revolutionary juxtaposition of the white founding story with "non-white"[22] bodies on stage and traditionally Black[23] musical motifs. Despite its praises, the show is not immune to academic and political critique. As much as *Hamilton* has been rightly praised for pushing boundaries within musical theater, many people still desire more from it.

This book enters the ongoing conversation about *Hamilton* as a cultural, political, historical, and rhetorical artifact. The chapters in this volume recognize *Hamilton*'s multifaceted nature: as a groundbreaking moment in musical theater history and also a living artifact whose meaning continues to expand and evolve; as a biographical narrative about a historical person and also a contemporary narrative about national culture; as a story about a white male founder but also a story by and about minority cultures; as a production inspired by the past but also a production that inspires the future. *Hamilton*'s numerous layers provide the rich foundation for the chapters that follow.

Communication and rhetorical scholars can provide unique insights into the meaning, function, and implications of *Hamilton* in today's political climate. The chapters in this volume employ rhetorical criticism, a method of research involving textual analysis that probes a rhetorical text's meaning and implications. Through rhetorical criticism, critics argue their own interpretation of the text, often exploring its possible meanings and invitations rather than its effects. The process of rhetorical analysis can take many forms, with a "diversity in results" of interpretation, because rhetorical critics look at the various ways the text or artifact interacts with "time, space, context, the specific audience assembled, and other factors."[24] The interpretive nature of criticism means that critics will often arrive at different conclusions about the same text, as the reader may find in their exploration of this volume. Rhetorical scholar David Zarefsky explains that this is not a flaw in the method of rhetorical criticism but rather each perspective "may offer valuable insight on the case, enabling criticism to proceed additively rather than only by substituting one explanation for another."[25] Moreover, we note that rhetorical criticism considers "text" to be a broad category. The reader will discover that the contributors in this work address a variety of rhetorical texts—from the lyrics, staging, and costumes of the musical itself to the circulation of the lyrics in public discourse to the Exhibition accompanying the musical in Chicago. In all cases, the authors probe the deeper meaning and significance of the musical for public and political life in the United States.

OVERVIEW OF CHAPTERS

The volume is divided into three parts. The first part, "*Hamilton* and Public Memory," considers how *Hamilton* characterizes history. Public memories permeate and are created by the musical, evident in the veneration of the nation's founders to the treatment of slavery, the founding narrative embedded in Act I to the historical dispute between Hamilton and Adams in Act II. Moreover, *Hamilton* explicitly references "narrative" as an agent and driving force of history, recognizing the implications of these narratives for how the audience uses history to make sense of the present world.

In Chapter Two, Jade C. Huell and Lindsay A. Jenkins fixate on a central idea to *Hamilton*: Who tells your story? They utilize the concept of "critical nostalgia" to consider how the musical represents History. By examining the intersection of the audience's assumed previous knowledge of history and *Hamilton*'s representation of history, Huell and Jenkins address how the musical's use of public memory intersects with the Black and Brown bodies on stage as well as the current U.S. immigration crisis.

In Chapter Three, Michaelah Reynolds and Ryan Neville-Shepard explore how *Hamilton* speaks to the myth of the American Dream. Specifically, the authors build on the enduring conflict between two aspects of the American Dream—moralistic and materialistic—to contend that *Hamilton* serves as a cautionary tale for today's polarized political climate because the musical represents the tragic entelechial nature of the materialistic myth.

Sara A. Mehltretter Drury and James Anthony Williams Jr. move beyond the musical in Chapter Four to address Hamilton: The Exhibition, a large, museum-style exhibition built in 2019 and accompanying the Chicago run of *Hamilton*. Drury and Williams argue that the exhibition's dynamic, immersive sets articulate a historical narrative that was designed to include diverse audiences but struggled to transcend public memories of the Founding Fathers, generally, and Hamilton specifically.

The second unit of the volume, "*Hamilton* and Rhetoric of Social Identity," emphasizes the implications of *Hamilton* for understanding group identities. *Hamilton*'s acclaim derives in part from its anachronistic portrayals of racial, gender, class, and national identities. Moreover, *Hamilton* draws attention to these elements at various points, inviting the audience to more critically engage "the story of America then, told by America now."[26]

In Chapter Five, Christopher Bell discusses how founding myths function in *Hamilton* to elevate its titular character to the same mythic level as his fellow Founders. Bell draws parallels between the origin stories of Miranda's Hamilton and superheroes such as Spider-Man. Through this analysis, Bell explains how the musical makes the nation's cosmogonic myth more accessible to all people in the United States, particularly audience members of historically marginalized races.

John Clyde Russell also discusses *Hamilton* and race in Chapter Six, specifically how the musical's portrayal of the nation's white founders through Black and Brown bodies (dis)comforts whiteness. The chapter considers the powerful ways that whiteness influenced and continues to influence the founding myth of the United States, and how that myth is reified in *Hamilton*. Russell contends that *Hamilton*'s multiracial performance humanizes the characters in ways that reinforce the myth of a "post-racial" United States for sympathetic audiences.

Chapter Seven turns from race to gender, as Emily Berg Paup presents a feminist critique of *Hamilton*. She outlines how the musical portrays women of the era in a subservient role to men, with particular attention to Elizabeth Schuyler Hamilton as a model of republican motherhood. Paup contends that this representation of women in the musical, when juxtaposed with *Hamilton*'s more progressive representation of race, reinforces patriarchy in potentially damaging ways for the audience.

The third and final part of the volume studies "*Hamilton* and Rhetoric of Democracy and Social Change." The musical is, to be sure, a cultural production designed to entertain audiences. It is also a democratic intervention in a specific moment in time and, as Miranda envisioned, serves a political function. This section considers the implications of these political messages for the viewing public as they relate to civic education and activism in the public sphere.

In Chapter Eight, Brandon M. Inabinet calls upon the second act of *Hamilton* to examine the role of melodrama in governing and lawmaking. Inabinet highlights the portion of the musical between "Cabinet Battle #1" and "The Room Where It Happens" to show how information shifts from the private to the public sphere—particularly Hamilton's affair with Maria Reynolds becoming public melodrama—helped to push corporate structures and power into the private sphere.

Jeffrey P. Mehltretter Drury considers in Chapter Nine the musical's normative portrayal of political debate. Recognizing that the musical speaks to youth culture, Drury approaches political debates in *Hamilton* from two perspectives: as uncivil argumentation that prevents productive political change and as rap battles designed to confront systems of power. He contends that both perspectives provide insight into the value and limits of civility for change in contemporary society.

Mark P. Orbe addresses *Hamilton*'s potential for social change explicitly in Chapter Ten. Employing the theory of invitational rhetoric, Orbe situates the rhetoric of *Hamilton* within a broader discursive field of invitational rhetoric that includes communication from Lin-Manuel Miranda, President Barack Obama, Brandon Victor Dixon, and others. His analysis demonstrates how these public rhetors have used the musical as a springboard to generate understanding and transcend differences.

Finally, in Chapter Eleven, Nancy J. Legge considers *Hamilton*'s relationship to public protests across the political spectrum. Recognizing the historical connection between theater and participatory democracy, Legge focuses her analysis on how counter-public sphere protestors have used *Hamilton* to resist the Trump administration and to promote equality and justice through long-term social change.

Lin-Manuel Miranda's *Hamilton: An American Musical* is a rhetorically rich text that warrants examination through numerous critical lenses. The musical's unparalleled rise to popularity and penetration into popular culture, homes, and even classrooms makes it crucial that audience members consider *Hamilton* beyond the surface level. This volume enables audience members to do just that through the tools of rhetorical criticism. Our hope is that the chapters that follow offer approachable insights into *Hamilton* for both members of the academic community and fans of the musical.

NOTES

1 Sara A. Mehltretter Drury, Associate Professor, Wabash College, drurys@wabash.edu; Jeffrey P. Mehltretter Drury, Associate Professor, Wabash College, druryj@wabash.edu; Henry Egan, Wabash College, hoegan22@wabash.edu.
2 "Frequently Asked Questions," MacArthur Foundation, 2019, https://www.macfound.org/about/frequently-asked-questions.
3 Marjua Estevez, "'Hamilton' Broadway Album Tops Billboard Rap Chart," *VIBE*, November 18, 2015, https://www.vibe.com/2015/11/lin-manuel-hamilton-broadway-album-no-1-billboard-rap-chart; Andrea Towers, "Hamilton Cast Recording Breaks Records," *Entertainment Weekly*, November 3, 2015, https://ew.com/article/2015/11/03/hamilton-cast-recording-breaks-records.
4 Jack O'Keeffe, "'Hamilton' Has the Most Tonys [sic] Nominations Ever, but that's Far from the Musical's Only Record," *Bustle*, June 12, 2016, https://www.bustle.com/articles/165774-hamilton-has-the-most-tonys-nominations-ever-but-thats-far-from-the-musicals-only-record; Rhian Daly, "'Hamilton' Just Broke Another Record," *NME*, March 6, 2018, https://www.nme.com/news/hamilton-just-broke-another-record-2255970.

5. Ben Brantley, "Review: 'Hamilton,' Young Rebels Changing Musical History and Theater," *New York Times*, August 6, 2015, https://www.nytimes.com/2015/08/07/theater/review-hamilton-young-rebels-changing-history-and-theater.html.
6. *Hamilton: An American Musical*, "Cast and Creative," https://hamiltonmusical.com/new-york/cast.
7. Ruthie Fierbieg, "19 Milestone Broadway Shows of the Decade," *Playbill*, January 6, 2020, http://www.playbill.com/article/19-milestone-broadway-shows-of-the-decade.
8. Todd Spangler, "'Hamilton' Drives Up Disney Plus App Downloads 74% Over the Weekend in U.S.," *Variety*, July 6, 2020, https://variety.com/2020/digital/news/hamilton-disney-plus-premiere-app-downloads-72-percent-1234698795.
9. Jessica Hillman-McCord, "Digital Fandom: *Hamilton* and the Participatory Spectator," in *iBroadway: Musical Theater in a Digital Age*, ed. Jessica Hillman-McCord (Cham, Switzerland: Palgrave Macmillan, 2017), 119–44.
10. Benjamin L. Carp, "World Wide Enough: Historiography, Imagination, and Stagecraft," *Journal of the Early Republic* 37 (2017): 291.
11. Zach Schonfeld, "'Hamilton,' the Biggest Thing on Broadway, Is Being Taught in Classrooms All Over," *Newsweek*, February 9, 2016, http://www.newsweek.com/2016/02/19/hamilton-biggest-thing-broadway-being-taught-classrooms-all-over-424212.html; Michael Paulson, "Students Will Gets Tickets to 'Hamilton,' With Its Hip-Hop-Infused History," *New York Times*, October 27, 2015, https://www.nytimes.com/2015/10/27/theater/students-will-get-tickets-to-hamilton-with-its-hip-hop-infused-history.html.
12. Michael Paulson, "For $10, New York City Students See 'Hamilton' and Rap for Lin-Manual Miranda," *New York Times*, April 13, 2016, https://www.nytimes.com/2016/04/14/theater/hamilton-inspires-students-and-their-takes-on-history.html.
13. Alessandra Codinha, "*Hamilton* at the White House and President Obama's Arts Legacy," *Vogue*, December 12, 2016, https://www.vogue.com/article/hamilton-and-the-legacy-of-president-obama.
14. Barack Obama, "Remarks Prior to a Musical Performance by Members of the Cast of 'Hamilton,'" in *Daily Compilation of Presidential Documents: Administration of Barack Obama*, March 14, 2016, https://www.gpo.gov/fdsys/pkg/DCPD-201600146/pdf/DCPD-201600146.pdf.
15. Christopher Mele and Patrick Healy, "'Hamilton' Had Some Unscripted Lines for Pence. Trump Wasn't Happy," *The New York Times*, November 19, 2016, https://www.nytimes.com/2016/11/19/us/mike-pence-hamilton.html.
16. Sopan Deb, "New 'Hamilton Mixtape' Music Video Takes Aim at Immigration," *New York Times*, June 28, 2017, https://www.nytimes.com/2017/06/28/arts/new-hamilton-mixtape-music-video-takes-aim-at-immigration.html.
17. Ben Brantley, "'Hamilton' Makes a Curious Cameo in Trump Impeachment Trial," *New York Times*, January 29, 2020. https://www.nytimes.com/2020/01/27/theater/bolton-hamilton.html.
18. Oskar Eustis, quoted in *Hamilton: The Revolution*, eds. Lin-Manuel Miranda and Jeremy McCarter (New York: Grand Central Publishing, 2016), 103.
19. Loren Kajikawa, "'Young, Scrappy, and Hungry': *Hamilton*, Hip Hop, and Race," *American Music* 36 (2018): 471.
20. Obama, "Remarks Prior to a Musical Performance."
21. Stephanie Goodman, "Debating 'Hamilton' as It Shifts from Stage to Screen," *New York Times*, July 10, 2020, https://www.nytimes.com/2020/07/10/movies/hamilton-critics-lin-manuel-miranda.html.

22 The official casting call for the Broadway production of *Hamilton* used the adjective "non-white" to describe all the principal cast members except "King George," who was labeled "Caucasian." "HAMILTON–Richard Rodgers Theatre Auditions," *Broadway World*, March 12, 2015, https://www.broadwayworld.com/equity-audition/HAMILTON-Richard-Rodgers-Theatre-2015-10518.

23 As editors of the volume, we have chosen to capitalize "Black" and "Brown" but not "white" when referring to race and we have applied this system of capitalization to each of the chapters in the volume, unless otherwise specified by the author. This decision follows several editorial guides released in 2020, including from the *Chicago Manual of Style*—the style guide for this volume—in its "Shop Talk" statement as well as, among others, the *AP Style Guide* and *Columbia Journalism Review*. "Black and White: A Matter of Capitalization," *Chicago Manual of Style Shop Talk*, June 22, 2020, https://cmosshoptalk.com/2020/06/22/black-and-white-a-matter-of-capitalization; "Race Related Coverage," *AP Style Guide*, accessed July 29, 2020, https://www.apstylebook.com/race-related-coverage; Mike Laws, "Why We Capitalize 'Black' (and Not 'White')," *Columbia Journalism Review*, June 16, 2020, https://www.cjr.org/analysis/capital-b-black-styleguide.php.

24 Whitney Gent, Emily Sauter, and Daniel Cronn-Mills, "Validity and the Art of Rhetorical Criticism," *Annals of the International Communication Association*: 3. Published ahead of print, July 20, 2020, https://doi.org/10.1080/23808985.2020.1792792.

25 David Zarefsky, "Knowledge Claims in Rhetorical Criticism," *Journal of Communication* 58 (2008): 636.

26 Lin-Manuel Miranda has used this phrase in numerous interviews and the advertisements for *Hamilton* in 2015 also included it. See, for example, Hamilton, "'Be There When It Happens'—Hamilton Broadway (Radio Commercial)," YouTube video, 1:00, July 2, 2015, https://youtu.be/C2iDenRGYGY.

PART ONE

Hamilton and Public Memory

CHAPTER TWO

The I/Eye of History: Performing Public Memory, Utopia, and Critical Nostalgia in *Hamilton*

JADE C. HUELL AND LINDSAY A. JENKINS[1]

At the pivotal moment in the musical when Alexander Hamilton is bestowed a commanding post by then General George Washington, the foreshadowing and momentous tune, "History Has Its Eyes on You," echoes across the stage and into the audience. In the song, Washington cautions Hamilton against seeing himself as a martyr and insists that soldiers ultimately "have no control" over "who lives, who dies, who tells your story."[2] However, in this musical, Lin-Manuel Miranda creates a historical and performative version of Hamilton's legacy that interacts with Miranda's lived experience coming from a family of immigrants and is in direct conversation with our current political climate. While the sentiment of "History Has Its Eyes on You" is certainly correct on the historical truths of who lives and who dies on the battlefield of war or on the battlefield of life, who tells the story is the very crux of the rhetorical and performative arguments presented in the musical. In the progression of the plot, History had its eyes on Hamilton, but in the telling of the tale, Lin-Manuel Miranda and the host of professionals that helped to bring the show to fruition had their eyes keenly fixed on History itself. The representation of which bears fruit in the analysis of public memory practice in the area of live performance.

The song "History Has Its Eyes on You" personifies History, casting it as a character in the show and defining it as having a perspective. This character interacts with, speaks to, and ultimately defines each of the characters in the musical; and for this reason we have made the choice to capitalize History when it's used in this way. Our intention is to prompt a conversation about agency and self-actualization with respect to historical representation. It is clear that Miranda is not only concerned with history, but the writing of history. As Philip Goldfarb Styrt asserts, "*Hamilton* makes clear its awareness of both history and historiography as active forces in its reception, as well as the reception of its story and character."[3] The title of this chapter, "The I/Eye of History" evokes the rhetorical slippage between the "I," meaning the self, and the "eye," connoting the ocular, the vision, the view. Dickinson, Ott, and Aoki deploy a similar usage in their analysis of the Plains Indian Museum in Cody, Wyoming.[4] Their analysis reveals that the museum's experiential landscape creates a "dream reality," which, along with other factors, works to absolve white Americans of their guilt by cultivating a feeling of reverence, or "a double articulation, evoking both a profound sense of respect and a distanced, observational gaze."[5] In their work, the "eye" of history becomes distanced from the "I," separating the observer from the history that they are observing. We, however, utilize this slippage in order to bring into focus the ways in which history is a negotiation with the self in context, the ways the individual (self or I)—always already the product of culture—must envision (interpret or see) what history means. To be a minority in this country is to grapple with a perspective of history that is often poorly contextualized or leaves out the minoritarian viewpoints all together. This dynamic necessitates the cultivation of a creative and imaginative relationship with the past.

In this chapter, we are occupied with the rhetorical and aesthetic approaches utilized in the performance of history. Concurrently, we are interested in the narrative and sociohistorical significance of not only the direction of the "eye," or historical perspective, involved, but also the quality and composition of the "I," asking questions about the subjective experiences being illustrated, noting the impact on the insistence of historical personhood, and foregrounding practices of identity inextricable from representations of public memory and history. While some may wrestle with the effectiveness of Miranda's historical representation, we argue that the performative approaches to history in the musical reveal novel dynamics unearthed through practices of critical memory, utopia, and ultimately, critical nostalgia. By describing and analyzing these practices throughout the musical we not only uncover *Hamilton*'s rhetorical and representational politics, but we also explore how the performance of public memory in *Hamilton* can stimulate critical nostalgia by juxtaposing utopian hope and critical historical reflexivity. In the present chapter, we take a multimethodological approach, practicing textual, visual, and performance analysis to first outline the historically imaginative enterprises at work in *Hamilton*, next, describe the utopian and nostalgic performances evident in the musical, and finally, explore the potential in the utilization of strategies and practices advanced in *Hamilton* by closing the chapter with a reading of the current U.S. immigration crisis.

PERFORMANCES OF CRITICAL MEMORY: UTOPIA AND NOSTALGIA

In his book, *Embodying Black Experience*, Harvey Young explains that rather than recalling specific and identical experiences, critical memory instead "acknowledg[es] that related histories create experiential overlap."[6] He applies this concept to Black identity, understanding that Blackness is both a creation and a representation; it isdirectly tied to historical performances inherited from one generation to another and it is influenced by cultural depiction. Thinking of critical memory in this way, Young makes room for a variety of intersecting histories placed within, and contributing to, Black experience. Young writes that "critical memory assists the process of identifying similarities—shared experiences and attributes of being and becoming."[7] It is our belief that America's identity works in a similar fashion. What is America? It is just as much the historical record of the founding of our country as it is the individual experiences and histories that contribute to larger ideas of life, liberty, and the pursuit of happiness.

In addition to Young's theory, we accord with Jill Dolan's characterization of theater and performance, that it "can articulate a common future, one that's more just and equitable, one in which we can all participate more equally, with more chances to live fully and contribute to the making of culture."[8] The very idea that theater can evoke utopian futures is utopian in itself. Dolan points out that theater and performance need not explicitly prescribe behaviors, but instead, can offer small gestures, emotional impact, and community dynamics in support of a better world. Miranda's perspective on the founding of America is one that is inclusive and passionate. By portraying America in this way from its inception, the musical illustrates possibilities for its future. "Theatre can move us toward understanding the possibility of something better, can train our imaginations, inspire our dreams, and fuel our desires in ways that might lead to incremental cultural change."[9] Dolan describes the "utopian performative" as the way "utopia can be imagined or experienced affectively, through feelings in small, incremental moments that performance can provide."[10] *Hamilton* activates critical memory in audiences by enacting utopian ideals of what America could be. Additionally, and concurrently, *Hamilton* juxtaposes these ideals to the materiality of Black and Brown bodies and all that they signify in American culture, allowing for both the pleasures and pains of U.S. history to be represented. Thus, the audience is denied neither historical critique nor utopian sentiment, making space for a more complex sense of nostalgia.

Originally conceptualized by medical professionals as the root cause of certain physical ailments, nostalgia has slowly changed in usage, evolving from a physical concern, to a psychological condition, and finally to an emotional state usually wrapped up in the context of memory or the act of remembering. Nostalgia, as it is commonly used, is generally treated as a "style of dealing with, or writing about the past."[11] Whether the consequence of colloquial usage (which typically reduces nostalgia to a descriptor of kitschy knick-knacks, classic television, or feelings about childhood) or the passage of time, nostalgia appears in academic conversations mainly as a critique of wistful remembrances or as a memory practice employed to pave over the psychosocial damage of modernity. Jade C. Huell argues instead that "the etymology and history of the term nostalgia give weight to its critical power" and by focusing on the corporal aspects of nostalgia, Huell returns "to a theory of nostalgia that features the body, a body theorized and realized in performance."[12] One of the key etymological components of nostalgia is that it was originally interchangeable with "homesickness." Huell posits the possibilities for reconceptualizing the performance of nostalgia as an active and body-focused practice of critical memory inextricable from its associations with the concept of past-home. The notion of past-home constitutes a memory experience in which not *only* the past or an idea of *home* is expressed, but rather both. Home, here, connotes a place connected to origin, ancestry, and belonging. Past-home speaks to origin, identity, and roots, going beyond a physical, or even temporal definition and into evocative sense of longing; a place where identity can be anchored.

Critical nostalgia aligns history and memory with not only the past (that which is temporally located before the present moment) but also home (that which is expressed through a material or conceptual attachment, a sense of belonging, origin, or family for example).[13] In our reading of the musical *Hamilton*, we explore movement toward the subjunctive or imaginative experience of public memory, and draw on concepts of utopia in theater and critical memory to articulate and specify what Huell has come to call "critical nostalgia," a critical memory practice characterized by the simultaneous appreciation *and* analytical evaluation of phenomena related to a person or group of persons' past-home.[14] Huell argues that "the physical body is a site where home is recalled and created," therefore her approach identifies nostalgia as an embodied practice, performing a return home.[15] A notable example of critical nostalgia can be seen in the artwork of Kehinde Wiley, a contemporary portrait painter who often calls upon the signs and symbols of historical opulence readily available in traditional Western portraiture portraying homelife (which is often displayed in moneyed homes).[16] Against this historical background, Wiley often takes realistic Black urban bodies as subjects of his portraits, thus creating evocative visual critiques suggesting imaginative reflection on the ways in which Black bodies, as complex and fully human subjects, have been historically misrepresented in (and missing from) traditional painting. Wiley, through his art, then, performs a return home; returning Blackness to Western representation.

The return home of which we speak is more or less material and concrete. For example, one might long to feel "at home," settled, wanted even, in a particular environment. As Miranda has articulated, his creative team was determined to find a home for bodies of color within the context of both American history and Broadway. He does this by treating History in a way that simultaneously scans past, present, and future, creates morally righteous figures represented by the typically unrepresented, and lays bare a longing for home that resonates with America's diverse population.[17] Black and Brown Americans, too, have a yearning to belong in the U.S. founding story beyond the narrative and legacy of chattel slavery.

HISTORY/MEMORY, REPRESENTATION/IMAGINATION

Sparked by the Black Lives Matter protests of the Summer of 2020, which erupted after the violent killing of George Floyd at the hands of law enforcement, individuals and groups have honed in on the importance of historical representation, especially as related to white male figures that loom large in our American imaginary. Statues of colonizers, confederate officers, and racist historical figures are being toppled all over the country, and we are contemplating the ways that history presents itself in our daily lives, in our subconscious, and in our performances. Street signs, statues, building names all attest to what and whose histories remain in our public memory and cultural imaginaries as we move through our days busily occupying the spaces that were formerly occupied by those who came before us. However, when we go to the theater, we have set aside daily life to experience, for one or two hours, the heightened and purposeful imaginary of a very specific group of writers, directors, actors, and technicians. The undertaking of this artistic group is to enable audiences to escape the rapid progression of events that we call "the present," to reckon with the past, and to imagine a future. Yes, indeed, everything that is seen on *any* stage is historical. All potential scenes originate from someone's notion of human action, and are then rehearsed over and over, perfected in time and space, and then presented to each audience as new. And it is. Both new and old simultaneously. The simultaneity and historicity inherent to theatrical experience is particularly relevant and complex when examining performances that explicitly take for a subject the presentation of historical events.

In the case of *Hamilton*, History is a driving force in the plot, while simultaneously speaking to the current political climate as history in the making, all while the production itself makes history in terms of style, sales, and overall saturation. Though it is a period piece on the founding of America, *Hamilton* is contemporary in its intention and its messaging. Writer and star Lin-Manuel Miranda confronts this reality directly, saying, "this is a story about America then, told by America now," Miranda explains, "and we want to eliminate any distance between a contemporary audience and this story."[18] It is with this intention that Miranda makes it evident that the eye of History in *Hamilton* is not strictly turned to the past, but also fixed on the present and future. It is historiographical, explicitly concerned with "who lives, who dies, who tells your story."[19] In an instance of temporal shaping, Alexander Hamilton warns the audience, "Don't be shocked when your history book mentions me."[20] *Hamilton* manipulates the eye of History, shifting toward critical memory, guiding the audience not by laser focusing on a particular moment in the past, but instead, by scanning through the past, present, and future seamlessly. For example, just before Alexander Hamilton and the Marquis de Lafayette go into the Battle of Yorktown, they take a moment to declare, in unison, breaking the fourth wall to briefly direct to the audience, "Immigrants: We get the job done!"[21] By making this statement, in this way, Miranda scans history: indicating the past, nodding toward the present, and introducing a future where immigrants are recognized for the vital role they play(ed) in building America. As Styrt writes, "deploying the audience's previous awareness of early American history in its favor, and carefully choosing how and when to challenge that awareness, *Hamilton* is able to make a radical point about the nature of American history largely without resistance" or extensive temporal framing.[22]

Part of the reason Miranda is able to cast History in this way—as shifting yet knowable—is his dependence on a familiar understanding of history already present in the minds of his audience. Styrt argues that, "the history in which *Hamilton* is so invested is not, primarily, that of university history departments and academic journals; rather, it is the kind of popular, common, and familiar history typical of public monuments, textbooks, and mass-market biography."[23] He goes on to contend that the musical "benefits from being able to reproduce and reawaken its audience's historical awareness rather than producing it for the first time."[24] In other words, rather than spend the limited time available recounting an already told version of events, Miranda activates, relies on, and performs the common sense and critical memory of his audience. Even audiences in London, where the show opened, would have certain existing knowledge (as the show points to explicitly through decrees and vignettes from the King of England) because the American Revolution is a part of that audience's history, too.

Some scholars of history and politics critique *Hamilton* for its willful lack of adherence to a static interpretation of history. According to Nancy Isenberg, "history should be about dislodging misconceptions, not entertaining students."[25] She goes on to ask, "at what point do we surrender to popular culture and reinforce the irrelevance of professional history?"[26] However, those who are more concerned with a normative notion of history (one ultimately indebted to white supremacist patriarchal academic elitism) neglect to acknowledge that the revisioning of Alexander Hamilton's story is one of many strategies deployed to emphasize the future while acknowledging the past. Most of *Hamilton*'s audience will have pre-existing knowledge of America's Founding Fathers, the good, the bad, and the ugly. Though men like George Washington, Thomas Jefferson, and James Madison are often synonymous with freedom, equality, and justice, they were all slaveholders, building monetary and political capital from the unpaid labor of Black Americans. While historically these men have been elevated to mythical status, their personal histories make them less than ideal heroes to contemporary audiences who are prone to "cancel" well-known figures when what is done in the dark comes to light.

Though he appears on the $10 bill, Hamilton's full story is arguably less known than the other Founding Fathers. According to the musical, Hamilton did not personally own slaves and, in fact, wrote against the practice of slavery. He was an immigrant and a member of the working class who had to fight to achieve a better station in life. He called out Jefferson's dependence on slavery and fought for American ideals of freedom, equality, and justice, three ideals inherent to conceptions of American identity. These concepts are purportedly the grounds on which the country was founded, and have been used as catalysts in many internal American revolutions, namely for enfranchisement, civil rights, and marriage equality. Miranda emphasizes these ideals by remixing the narrative, making Jefferson and Washington secondary characters and pushing Alexander Hamilton, an "arrogant immigrant" as Aaron Burr refers to him, to the forefront.[27] Miranda's Alexander Hamilton is thus an imaginative interplay between memory and history, giving audiences a figure to look up to and to aspire to, a utopian figure representing the combined hopes of American reconciliation: fully overcoming slavery, immigrant equality, and an inclusive origin story.

It is in this strategy of aspirational and historical reconstruction of affect we see critical nostalgia functioning as mode of thinking, as an engaged memory practice, as a way to represent past-homes, and as a style of performance. Audiences are allowed their place in the origin story of homeland *through* rather than despite known and felt realities of America's complex and often violent past. Critical nostalgia, like critical memory, "grants access to past experiences ... At the same time, it does not blind us to their (or our) present reality."[28] The production, therefore, enacts a kind of critical memory and nostalgia that does not ask the audience to erase or deny their own historical memory, but instead asks them to identify with a different aspect of what they know.

To expedite this shift in what is explored, the musical exercises selective memory and romanticism in its depiction of Hamilton's life. Dolan builds on Richard Dyer's notion that romanticism "gives us a glimpse of what it means to live at the height of our emotional and our experiential capacities."[29] In the musical, this heightened affective state is embodied by a revised and reenvisaged Alexander Hamilton made materially more complex through the Brown body of Lin-Manuel Miranda. Though born in the Caribbean, Alexander Hamilton was still a white man and an American citizen at the time the U.S. Constitution was written. And though he did not own enslaved persons himself, he did negotiate slave deals for his in-laws the Schuylers. Interestingly, it is romance, Hamilton's marital relations, that seemed to have compelled him to participate in the brokerage of human flesh despite his recorded objections to the institution of slavery. Hamilton was imperfect and deeply flawed even as his personal history is more in-line with ideal, and therefore utopic, ideas of American history than some of his contemporaries. His underdog story of immigration, triumph despite circumstance, and willingness to die for what he believed in paints a picture of a compassionate and inclusive Founding Father. "This intense, utopic romanticism is what creates those moments of magic and communion in performance."[30] By romanticizing the past, Miranda spins an origin story that reinforces what we as citizens consider ideal American values, as discussed later in this volume by Christopher Bell. Dolan writes,

> ... in order to pretend, to enact an ideal future, a culture has to move farther and farther away from the real into a kind of performative, in which the utterance, in this case, doesn't necessarily make it so but inspires perhaps other more local "doings" that sketch out the potential in those feignings.[31]

Much of *Hamilton* is an illustration of what we as citizens should hope for out of our government and out of the individuals that represent us in that government. The utopic reimaginings in the musical often center performance traditions and stylistic proclivities of people of color. For example, Miranda remixes congressional debates by staging them as highly stylized rap battles, giving the audience a glimpse of what an impassioned political process could look like while, at the same time, illustrating the active and intentional cultural inclusion of people of color. Like many moments in *Hamilton*, the "Cabinet Battles" between Thomas Jefferson and Alexander Hamilton use historical moments to speak to current times. Lin-Manuel Miranda points out,

> The fights that I wrote between me and Jefferson, you could put them in the mouths of candidates on MSNBC ... these are all conversations we're still having, and I think it's a comfort to know that they're just a part of the more perfect union we're always working towards, or try to work towards, and that we're always working on them.[32]

This is a dynamic understanding of America that rejects the notion of a static past origin story in exchange for a vision of the country that is ever-changing, ever-evolving and is, therefore, full of possibilities.

The "Cabinet Battles" subvert the typical form of the Socratic debate in exchange for a model that inspires more rhetorical urgency, personality, and style from both participants and observers. Performing History in this way favors politicians who fight for what they believe in rather than follow the shifting political winds. The civically enlivened battle scenes provide a clear opposition to the politically ambiguous performance embodied by Aaron Burr. To have politicians in office who are deep thinkers, fiery orators, and empathetic activists is a utopian imagining of American government. We want to believe that our representatives not only have our interests at heart, but are enthusiastically fighting for them in Congress. In many tales outstanding and heroic figures like Alexander Hamilton are portrayed as outsiders. But the "Cabinet Battles" are a clear example of a more utopian American performance, one where History is portrayed as the whole of government working in this inclusive, impassioned, and expedient way. Not only does the show allow us to envision what a fully engaged government could look like, it also gives hope to individuals that their voices can be heard no matter what that voice might sound like. Starry-eyed activists, hopeful optimists, and underserved underdogs are inspired to believe that there is a place for them in government, a place for them in history. *Hamilton* inspires emotional sentiment and affective investment around what might typically be viewed as the banality (and whiteness) of the legislative process. This sentiment "can spur emotion, and being moved emotionally is a necessary precursor to political movement."[33] Though Dolan yearns for a utopia and a political movement that "takes place now," she acknowledges that many definitions of utopia "point to the future, to imaginative territories that map themselves over the real."[34]

The spatiotemporal mapping that Dolan describes aligns with the process of historical scanning that we outlined earlier in this chapter. The plot, the characters, and the embodied movement displayed on stage are all key in guiding the audience's and History's eye back and forth, seamlessly, through time. Not only does the direction of History's eye look forward, toward a new and better future, in *Hamilton*, History is also overdetermined, always aware of itself, and always reflecting or looking back. This backwards looking modality of memory might be best recognized as nostalgia.

Susan Stewart, in her study of nostalgia, would assert that nostalgia glorifies the past, overlooking prevalent issues like racism and class. Indeed, there are some facets of society that long for "good ole days" where sexism and xenophobia were not just the standard, but the goal. But as Huell writes, "a productive function of nostalgia is its ability to create positive versions of a communal identity in contrast to those indelibly marked by racism and discrimination."[35] Marvin McAllister agrees, quoting Aja Romano's defense of "*Hamilton* as 'a postmodern meta-textual piece of fanfic' which does not simply celebrate the founding fathers, but argues with American history to reclaim it for 'the dismissed and devalued.'"[36] The casting choices of *Hamilton* function in this way, intentionally layering contemporary Black and Brown bodies over historically white stories in order to find agency in the performance of history and fulfill a longing for a past-home.

The casting of *Hamilton* has been met with criticism—Ishmael Reed, for example, and his salaciously titled article, "'Hamilton: The Musical': Black Actors Dress Up like Slave Traders ... and It's Not Halloween."[37] Why cast Black and

Brown bodies to tell white stories, and completely erase real historical characters that made real contributions? While we don't disagree with the critique, our rhetorical analysis is concerned with what is there, and not what we wish was there. Especially since it is impossible to predict whether or not a musical about Sally Hemings would have received the same funding, development, and reception that *Hamilton* did. The disparities of Broadway are a topic for another time. What is important to note, however, is that the creation of America is better represented by the various ethnicities in the cast of *Hamilton* than the portraits of white men that hang in the Capitol. Each of the Brown bodies on the *Hamilton* stage carries its own history: an amalgamation of personal experiences, shared cultural memories, and familial inheritance. Miranda tasks these bodies to the work of not only performing, but re-framing the critical memory of America. In doing so, he is able to make a contemporary rhetorical argument about the lack of representation in history and on Broadway. *Hamilton*'s creative team viewed the project as "two revolutions: the eighteenth-century American Revolution and a contemporary revolution in how Broadway looks, sounds, and moves."[38]

The twin revolutions articulated in the above quote suggest an upsetting of the historical apple cart. Revolutions only come to fruition through a combination of present material, action, or performance, a movement away from the past, and an imagined vision of the future. In this way, much of the sentiment around the musical is a conflation of nostalgia and utopia. Though *Hamilton* is a historical performance, its diversity, passion, and patriotism speak to a need in the present for a hopeful, utopian future. *Hamilton* activates in audiences utopian ideals of what America could be by performing critical memory of our founding that elevates morally righteous historical figures, illustrates a government that is full of passion and just ideals, and inspires a sense of patriotism from Americans of every race and background without, once again, rehearsing the violent subjugation of Black bodies. In the space of the musical, Blackness and Brownness are not erased, they are materially and visually present. What is missing is the imposed abjection onto these bodies as the "correct" representation of minorities in American history.

McAllister compares the casting choices in *Hamilton* to William Brown and the African Company's all-Black performances of *Richard III* at the turn of the century to illustrate the way that "racebending" inserts bodies of color into narratives never intended for them, allowing them to reinsert themselves into the narrative.[39] The color-conscious casting in *Hamilton* allows the musical to stay true enough to history while simultaneously giving us visuals that hint at the present and allow us to imagine a future where people of color are passionately involved in shaping the country. As McAllister writes, "the optics of *Hamilton* proffer an idealized America resting just outside of history, an aspirational vision of what the nation could be."[40] The moment the audience sees that white men, slaveholders, are portrayed by people of color, we are asked to suspend our disbelief, as we always do in theater, in order to contextualize the musical within its larger place in society. Washington, Jefferson, and Madison each became rich and powerful off the labor of enslaved Black men and women. In essence, their historical significance is inextricable from the shared cultural memory of the Black men who portray them. Thus, the Black actors reclaim their role in history every time they take on the performance of these historically white figures. McAllister points out:

> The ideology driving *Hamilton* embraces an exciting idealization of America, rather than a full accounting of what America was, and in many respects still is. Through this ambitious and aspirational musical, minority actors and audiences get to feel more "American" than they have ever felt before, because *Hamilton* places them "in the room where it happens." Yet even as this ridiculously successfully project elevates hip hop, reinvents color-conscious casting on Broadway, and moves colored bodies from margins to center, the price is leaving certain stories behind.[41]

McAllister highlights how certain stories are left behind. For example, the musical heavily features the efforts of another immigrant, Hercules Mulligan, an Irish spy and a member of the Sons of Liberty. Though his contributions to the American Revolution cannot be denied, they also would not have been possible without assistance from an enslaved Black man named Cato.[42] When Hercules Mulligan finds out that the British are about to capture George Washington, it is Cato who warns the Americans. Cato and Mulligan acted as a pair, a duo, with Mulligan gathering information and Cato dispersing it. Despite this, the annals of history have neglected to celebrate, or even fully identify Cato. This historical figure, who was pivotal to the founding of the country, disappears from historical record after the Revolutionary War, and he is never once mentioned in the musical. This is the case for many disenfranchised communities. Often times we are overlooked and when included the record is often incomplete. However, McAllister overlooks the idea that, "performance has a historical consciousness, although a performer may not be aware of it and a performance may not call attention to it."[43] *Hamilton* casts a Black man in the role of Hercules Mulligan. Again, the double entendre is employed as the actor performs the history of Mulligan from a perspective that is influenced by a cultural history he shares with Cato and others like him who have been erased from history. Though Miranda could be criticized for not mentioning Cato by name, it is not entirely true that his story is completely left behind. "The shared goal of performing whiteness, in all its iterations and functions, is not to simply get beyond color or build careers, but to create representational and rhetorical room," and it is through this spatiotemporal room-making employed through utopia and nostalgia that a critical imagination is able to thrive.[44]

From the outset of the musical, *Hamilton* establishes itself as nostalgic in nature, but critically so. For our purposes, we define critical as appreciating both the possibilities *and* the problematics of memory practices. The critical nostalgia evident in the musical is both reflective (concerned with the past) and reflexive (concerned with an understanding of what that past means today). Not only is the audience contemplating the shaping of America, a place many of them may call home, the concept of home is also broadly explored across the time-space of the show. George Washington, for example, has an entire song dedicated to his desire to "go home."[45] After telling Alexander Hamilton that he intends to step down as President, Hamilton is once again concerned about the optics ("They'll say you're weak"[46]). Washington, however, insists that it is important that the nation learn to say goodbye so it can outlive him and so that he can go back to Virginia and enjoy the nation he has helped create. This reveals a concern for the future, while also longing for a past-home: "I want to sit under my own vine and fig tree, a moment alone in the shade. At home in this nation we made." As the song comes to an end the chorus repeats, "Washington's going home" and just before it ends, Christopher Jackson, the Black actor playing Washington, reminds us once again, "History has its eyes on you."[47] This song, "One Last Time," along with Eliza's contention that she is erasing herself "from the narrative,"[48] and Burr's obsession with being "in the room where [history] happens"[49] are just a few examples of the overdetermined and nostalgic sentiment of the musical, the characters standing in relation to (or outside of) history, looking back, longing to find their home in the historical narrative, and hyper aware of the consequences of that home. The entire vision for the musical is an affective, reflexive/reflective, and overdetermined look back at various iterations of past-home.

This longing for past-home is most clearly evidenced in Lin-Manuel Miranda's performance of Alexander Hamilton. The opening song of Miranda's musical functions as a prologue, a long-standing theatrical device, which in this case works to set up the nostalgic undercurrents that run throughout the remainder of the show. Prologues not only set the scene, but also reveal events that happen much later in the story. Miranda uses Shakespearian prologue, the ability of rhyme to deliver a condensed version of events that gives the audience context, as well as reveals the ending of the show. This choice primes the audience for non-linear storytelling from the top of the show. As an audience, we are aware that this prologue is happening outside of the main dramatic action because the actors we know will go on to play important roles are nameless and out of context in this scene. They, along with the ensemble, act as a chorus, singing the origin story of a "bastard" son from the West Indies who came from nothing and worked tirelessly to have something. "Got a lot farther by working a lot harder; By being a lot smarter; By being a self-starter."[50]

The prologue is told omnipotently, from the outside, without using any names. It is the very ambiguity of the narrative that invites the audience to imagine themselves as the hardworking self-starter. Those of us who have had lived experiences similar enough to relate are able to recall our own origin stories and our own past-homes, evoking a sense of nostalgia and a longing to find ourselves in the American story from the very beginning of the show. The opening song continues, slow and concentrated. The actors tell the story of Hamilton's childhood efficiently with minimal musical accompaniment. A calm before the storm. The song is slow and intentional, introducing the audience to the story of a hurricane making landfall. The lights emerge creating large circles on the stage floor and the music begins to swell. Leslie Odom Jr. appears, as Hamilton's rival and opening narrator Aaron Burr, illustrating through song and movement how a group of businessmen collected enough money to send a young man, one of their own, away to get a better education. It is in this moment of the opening number that the tense switches from past to present and from third person to second person. Odom sings that they "sent him" to the mainland, then turns directly to the audience and says "get your education, don't forget from whence you came."[51] Though we know we are witnessing a performance of history, we are brought into the present by the direct address. Odom concludes with a prophecy and a question: "And the world's going to know your name; What's your name, man?"[52] Miranda is now revealed at center stage, taking his place in the spotlight. His character's name is uttered for the first time. Alexander Hamilton, and the crowd erupts into applause. Perhaps not for 1770s Alexander Hamilton, but for 2010s Lin-Manuel Miranda. Though born on the island of Nevis in 1755 (or 1757), Alexander Hamilton's legacy is created in this contemporary moment onstage. Similar to "hip-hop emcees or lyricists" who, as McAllister points out, often "write themselves into existence by crafting originary myths or histories," Miranda uses the power of the pen to craft a new origin story for Hamilton, and as a Caribbean immigrant, it is only appropriate that this story begins with a hurricane.[53]

Hurricanes are very much ingrained in the histories, experiences, and identities of Caribbean natives. They activate transformation, creating liminal spaces where hierarchies are destroyed and community is established. They are inevitable and cyclical, and are also experienced as ritual. Cultural and economic ramifications of hurricanes are performed and re-performed on islands' past, present, and future. In her essay entitled, "The Political Ecology of Storms in Caribbean Literature," Sharae Deckard describes the function of hurricanes in Caribbean literature as embodying, "something like the revolutionary opening up of historical time suggested by Marx, which disturbs the repetitive, cyclical, seemingly 'timeless' homogeneity of capitalism."[54] This disruption in hierarchy and capitalism is the opportunity Hamilton needs to escape an alternate future and the time to reflect on his past-home. Deckard describes this as *kairos*, or a "fleeting rhetorical moment when appropriately chosen words could have the most power to temper a course of events which previously seemed immutable."[55] It is the opportunity of the hurricane that allows Hamilton to write his "way out":[56] "Then a hurricane came, and devastation reigned; Our man saw his future drip, dripping down the drain; Put a pencil to his temple, connected it to his brain; And he wrote his first refrain, a testament to his pain."[57] Miranda's use of the hurricane as the foundation for Hamilton's origin story speaks to a self-awareness of History, a scanning of the eye of History, fueled by both utopia and nostalgia.

Bringing "the past is prologue" to fruition, as the opening number comes to a close, the characters introduce themselves, the last performer plays Aaron Burr, and reveals the ending within the first ten minutes of the show: "And I'm the damn fool that shot him."[58] The opening number ends with 19-year-old Hamilton ready to build his legacy. But a storm begins to brew late in the second act when he reveals the details of his sordid affair to Jefferson, Madison, and Burr. When his legacy (future) is threatened, he seeks refuge in History, yearning for his past-home. He makes his way to the eye of the stage, the eye of the storm. The lights on the stage go dim. A single piano chord rings out. "In the eye of the hurricane there is quiet; For just a moment; a yellow sky."[59] As these words ring out, the actors utilize slow motion movement to freeze time for the audience, to suspend the rapid progression of events, in order to pause for a moment and reflexively/reflectively reveal the importance of the act of remembering one's own past-home. The story is bittersweet; it is tender and painful. The hurricane washes everything away but also signifies a new beginning. And eventually, hierarchies of power reassert themselves in the rebuilding. We as audience members caught "in the eye of the hurricane" are able to reckon and identify with the tensions of home and past. He turns his eye to History in search of motivation to move forward.

Huell describes one of the functions of nostalgia as, "a mental journey, a shift in time and place that for some functions to disconnect them from the present and reconnect them with the past."[60] She goes on to write that "much of the scholarship concerned with this mode of thinking focuses on the effect of the cognitive shift in time and place on the present."[61] The performance of the song "Hurricane" is a brilliant double entendre that illustrates the meaning of critical nostalgia, which Huell describes as "a method of scholarly inquiry, as an active practice of personal and cultural memory, as a tool for representing memories of past-homes, and as a compositional aesthetic."[62] "Hurricane" speaks to Alexander Hamilton's experiences, while evoking critical memories from Lin-Manuel Miranda of his own family's origin story of immigration from the Caribbean and how he was also able to write his way out through the creation of the musical. Miranda dives further into this performance of critical nostalgia by returning to the role of Alexander Hamilton in 2019 for the Puerto Rican premiere of *Hamilton* in the midst of Hurricane Maria recovery efforts:

> With his body draped in the Puerto Rican flag, his emotions struggling to get through the song titled "Hurricane" and his presence celebrated all across San Juan, "Hamilton" creator Lin-Manuel Miranda returned to the role of Alexander Hamilton on Friday night on the

island of his beloved father's birth, revealing stronger vocal technique and deeper on-stage emotions.[63]

The "deeper on-stage emotions" show Miranda's connection and reverence for his past-home of Puerto Rico, birthplace of his parents. "I just love this island so much," Miranda states, "and I want it to be proud of me."[64] In his personification of both his own History and the history he is tasked with performing, Miranda dexterously engages and evokes a critically nostalgic Alexander Hamilton.

PERFORMING IMMIGRANT, A CONCLUSION

As with Alexander Hamilton's tale, immigration stories are often told in the past tense. A person or group of people, by necessity, by force, or by choice, leave their homes and relocate to another place and time. *Hamilton* is also an origin story of the United States of America. Origin stories, often full of mythic features, organize historical chaos into a narrative that we—as audiences, individuals, and Americans—may lay some claim to and have an affective relationship with. To emigrate is to originate; movement across space and time requires new life experience, new understanding of our past selves and homes, and a new way of casting History.

As we write this chapter, countless immigrants from various places in South America sit incarcerated in poorly run detention centers. They are held in limbo, "in the eye of a hurricane," surrounded by chaos, disease, and uncertainty about their futures.[65] The Trump administration seems to be maliciously bent on telling the tale of these immigrants, casting them as illegal and undesirable, unbefitting of a place in American society. In the space of *Hamilton: An American Musical*, a Latinx cultural icon is cast as a white Founding Father and is met with some minor resistance including being called an "arrogant immigrant," but ultimately, he "writes [his] way out" of much of the oppression he faces.[66] When we think about the situation at the Southern U.S. border, it is hard for us to be utopian, hard to apply *Hamilton*'s bootstrap narrative, hard to be hopeful for a future when these immigrants are valued and appropriately storied. To do so would mean to deny the severe reality of the present moment on the ground. The potential of *Hamilton* is not its accuracy, nor in its ability to write us past challenging beginnings, the actions of nefarious governments, or the indifference of bureaucratic systems. Rather, *Hamilton*'s import is in its capacity to utilize critical practices of memory, and in so doing, the musical illustrates subjunctive and imaginative strategies that move toward holding, in tension, the utopic and nostalgic contradictions, the critical nostalgia in the body of History.

NOTES

1. Jade C. Huell, Assistant Professor, California State University, Northridge, jade.huell@csun.edu; Lindsay A. Jenkins, Independent Scholar, info@maroonarts.com.
2. Lin-Manuel Miranda and Jeremy McCarter, *Hamilton: The Revolution* (New York, NY: Grand Central Publishing, 2016), 120, 280.
3. Philip Goldfarb Styrt, "Toward a Historicism of Setting: *Hamilton* and American History," *Modern Drama* 61 (2018): 2.
4. Greg Dickinson, Brian L. Ott, and Eric Aoki, "Spaces of Remembering and Forgetting: The Reverent Eye/I at the Great Plains Indian Museum," *Communication and Critical/Cultural Studies* 3 (2006): 27–47.
5. Dickinson, Ott, and Aoki, "Spaces of Remembering and Forgetting," 28.
6. Harvey Young, *Embodying Black Experience: Stillness, Critical Memory, and the Black Body* (Ann Arbor: University of Michigan Press, 2010), 18.
7. Young, *Embodying Black Experience*, 18.
8. Jill Dolan, "Performance, Utopia, and the 'Utopian Performative,'" *Theatre Journal* 53 (2001): 455.
9. Dolan, "Performance, Utopia, and the 'Utopian Performative,'" 460.
10. Dolan, "Performance, Utopia, and the 'Utopian Performative,'" 460.
11. Jade C. Huell, "Performing Nostalgia: Body, Memory, and the Aesthetics of Past-Home" (PhD diss., Louisiana State University, 2012), 2.
12. Huell, "Performing Nostalgia," 2.
13. Huell, "Performing Nostalgia," 49.
14. Huell, "Performing Nostalgia," 9–11.
15. Huell, "Performing Nostalgia," 10.
16. Kehinde Wiley, Kehinde Wiley Studio, accessed June 25, 2020, https://kehindewiley.com/.
17. Miranda and McCarter, *Hamilton: The Revolution*, 116. "When the Battle of Yorktown sequence ended that day [referring to an early performance in May 2014], the largely [B]lack and Latino cast (singing a song written by a Puerto Rican composer, wearing costumes selected by an African-American designer) climbed on top of boxes and chairs to celebrate having done the impossible."
18. Edward Delman, "How Lin-Manuel Miranda Shapes History," *The Atlantic*, September 29, 2015, https://www.theatlantic.com/entertainment/archive/2015/09/lin-manuel-miranda-hamilton/408019.
19. Miranda and McCarter, *Hamilton: The Revolution*, 120, 280.
20. Miranda and McCarter, *Hamilton: The Revolution*, 26.
21. Miranda and McCarter, *Hamilton: The Revolution*, 121.
22. Styrt, "Toward a Historicism of Setting," 7.
23. Styrt, "Toward a Historicism of Setting," 3.
24. Styrt, "Toward a Historicism of Setting," 7.
25. Nancy Isenberg, "'Make 'em Laugh': Why History Cannot Be Reduced to Song and Dance," *Journal of the Early Republic* 37 (2017): 302.
26. Isenberg, "'Make 'em Laugh,'" 302.
27. Miranda and McCarter, *Hamilton: The Revolution*, 266.
28. Young, *Embodying Black Experience*, 19.
29. Dyer qtd. in Dolan, "Performance, Utopia, and the 'Utopian Performative,'" 472.
30. Dolan, "Performance, Utopia, and the 'Utopian Performative,'" 472.

31 Dolan, "Performance, Utopia, and the 'Utopian Performative,'" 457.
32 Delman, "How Lin-Manuel Miranda Shapes History."
33 Dolan, "Performance, Utopia, and the 'Utopian Performative,'" 459.
34 Dolan, "Performance, Utopia, and the 'Utopian Performative,'" 457.
35 Huell, "Performing Nostalgia," 7.
36 Marvin McAllister, "Toward a More Perfect Hamilton," *Journal of the Early Republic* 37 (2017): 282.
37 Ishmael Reed, "'Hamilton: The Musical': Black Actors Dress Up Like Slave Traders ... and It's Not Halloween," *Counter Punch*, August 21, 2015, https://www.counterpunch.org/2015/08/21/hamilton-the-musical-black-actors-dress-up-like-slave-tradersand-its-not-halloween.
38 McAllister, "Toward a More Perfect Hamilton," 281.
39 McAllister, "Toward a More Perfect Hamilton," 282–83.
40 McAllister, "Toward a More Perfect Hamilton," 283.
41 McAllister, "Toward a More Perfect Hamilton," 288.
42 "The Legend of Hercules Mulligan," Central Intelligence Agency Feature Story Archive, last updated July 7, 2016, https://www.cia.gov/news-information/featured-story-archive/2016-featured-story-archive/the-legend-of-hercules-mulligan.html.
43 Huell, "Performing Nostalgia," 17–18.
44 McAllister, "Toward a More Perfect Hamilton," 282.
45 Miranda and McCarter, *Hamilton: The Revolution*, 209–11.
46 Miranda and McCarter, *Hamilton: The Revolution*, 209.
47 Miranda and McCarter, *Hamilton: The Revolution*, 209–11.
48 Miranda and McCarter, *Hamilton: The Revolution*, 238.
49 Miranda and McCarter, *Hamilton: The Revolution*, 186.
50 Miranda and McCarter, *Hamilton: The Revolution*, 16.
51 Miranda and McCarter, *Hamilton: The Revolution*, 16.
52 Miranda and McCarter, *Hamilton: The Revolution*, 16.
53 McAllister, "Toward a More Perfect Hamilton," 280.
54 Sharae Deckard, "The Political Ecology of Storms in Caribbean Literature," in *The Caribbean: Aesthetics, World-Ecology, Politics*, eds. Chris Campbell and Michael Niblett (Liverpool: Liverpool University Press, 2016), 26.
55 Deckard, "The Political Ecology of Storms in Caribbean Literature," 25.
56 Miranda and McCarter, *Hamilton: The Revolution*, 233.
57 Miranda and McCarter, *Hamilton: The Revolution*, 16.
58 William Shakespeare, *The Tempest: With New Dramatic Criticism and an Updated Bibliography*, ed. Robert Woodrow Langbaum (New York: Signet Classic, 1987), 72; Miranda and McCarter, *Hamilton: The Revolution*, 17.
59 Miranda and McCarter, *Hamilton: The Revolution*, 232.
60 Huell, "Performing Nostalgia," 6.
61 Huell, "Performing Nostalgia," 6.
62 Huell, "Performing Nostalgia," v.
63 Chris Jones, "'Hamilton' Opens in Puerto Rico with Emotional Performance by Lin-Manuel Miranda: 'I Just Love This Island So Much,'" *The Chicago Tribune*, January 12, 2019.
64 Jones, "'Hamilton' Opens in Puerto Rico."
65 Miranda and McCarter, *Hamilton: The Revolution*, 232. For further reading on the humanitarian crisis at the border, see the following sources: "Southern Border Humanitarian Crisis." Center for

Disaster Philanthropy, June 2, 2020, https://disasterphilanthropy.org/disaster/southern-border-humanitarian-crisis; Eugene Robinson, "This Is the reality of Trump's America," *The Washington Post*, June 24, 2019, https://www.washingtonpost.com/opinions/this-is-a-humanitarian-crisis-of-trumps-making/2019/06/24/431262f8-96c3-11e9-8d0a-5edd7e2025b1_story.html; Caitlin Dickerson, "Border at 'Breaking Point' as More Than 76,000 Unauthorized Migrants Cross in a Month," *New York Times*, March 5, 2019, https://www.nytimes.com/2019/03/05/us/border-crossing-increase.html.

66 Miranda and McCarter, *Hamilton: The Revolution*, 266, 233.

CHAPTER THREE

Hamilton and the Entelechy of the American Dream

MICHAELAH REYNOLDS AND RYAN NEVILLE-SHEPARD[1]

Audiences have frequently pointed to the myth of the American Dream to explain the powerful feelings created by Lin-Manuel Miranda's *Hamilton: An American Musical*. Cultural critic Kate Maltby of *The Financial Times* summarized that the narrative of a "penniless immigrant from the Caribbean ... epitomizes the American [myth]," and that Hamilton represents a "liberal of the old school" in the way he defends civil rights against "more patrician colleagues."[2] Similarly, others have suggested Hamilton's immigrant status and opposition to slavery in the musical make him a progressive defender of multiculturalism.[3] Beyond identifying themes of inclusion, audiences also claim the show is "as American as it gets" in depicting the classic bootstrap myth, portraying Hamilton as someone who works nonstop to "rise up" in society.[4] Along those lines, President Barack Obama called it a "quintessentially American story" of a "striving immigrant who escaped poverty ...[and] climbed to the top by sheer force of will, and pluck, and determination."[5] Collectively, these responses point to how *Hamilton* simultaneously appeals to different strains of the American Dream, and thus to people across the political spectrum, from President Obama and Secretary of State Hillary Clinton, to former House Speaker Paul Ryan and Vice President Mike Pence. For this reason, music scholar Elizabeth Titrington Craft has argued the musical has a "complex, multivalent nature" as it "seeks to lay full claim to U.S. history, identity, and belonging."[6] Similarly, music scholar Loren Kajikawa summarized that *"Hamilton*'s politics depend upon who is watching and listening."[7] Agreeing that "people on all sides of the political spectrum can project what they want onto *Hamilton*," Miranda himself summarized for *Rolling Stone*, "It's a Rorschach test."[8]

This chapter resists the claim that *Hamilton*'s depiction of the American Dream is endlessly polysemic, however. As many other scholars have pointed out, Miranda's rhetorical choices mean that his musical is hardly an open text. For instance, although Miranda based *Hamilton* on Ron Chernow's bestselling book, and professed that he wanted "historians to take this seriously,"[9] many historians have regarded it as a creative form of fan fiction. Historian and Alexander Hamilton expert Joanne Freeman of Yale University argued that Miranda mischaracterized Hamilton's influence on the 1800 election, incorrectly claimed that the election led to the duel with Burr, and placed both men on a collision course even though "they didn't bump up against each other as often or as meaningfully as the play suggests."[10] Historian Lyra Monteiro also noted that meetings between many characters "could never have happened" while "other events are transposed in time."[11] Others argue Miranda offers a "shockingly rose-colored depiction of Hamilton's immigrant identity" that overlooks his nativist politics and avid support of the Alien and Sedition Acts.[12] Many race scholars also criticize the show for focusing on the lives of "great white men" while erasing Black people who shaped history during the same era.[13]

That Miranda's "historical" show is not very historical should not be surprising, though. As music scholar Elissa Harbert wrote about history musicals, "when they are examined critically, it becomes clear that . . . [they] are never solely about history; they are also vehicles for cultural commentary relevant to the present day."[14] More specifically, *Vox*'s Aja Romano contended that Miranda not only "uses his text to . . . have fun with and celebrate U.S. history but to critique everything about that history," ultimately representing a "fanfic [that] interrogates the mythos of the American dream" by transforming history and reclaiming it for "[B]lack, Latino, and Asian actors who were excluded from it."[15] In other words, if the Alexander Hamilton of the musical is not exactly the real historical figure, it is because he is a symbolic vessel for a larger critique of important American myths. In this sense, Freeman—who observed that different versions of the memory of Hamilton have been invoked throughout history—contends that Miranda's Hamilton is the "embodiment of a folk hero" pursuing the "American Way" as someone who is "sometimes admirable and sometimes reprehensible,"[16] who perhaps just like his country starts his journey with noble goals but takes a tragic turn.

Building off Freeman's observation, we contend that *Hamilton* illustrates the battle between what communication scholar Walter Fisher called the moralistic and materialistic versions of the American Dream, and ultimately frames American individualism as a possible existential threat.[17] As many scholars of political rhetoric have described the myths of the American Dream as forming a complicated dialectic,[18] resulting in tension that is eventually resolved through compromise or competition,[19] we argue that *Hamilton* provides a cautionary tale in an increasingly polarized political environment by focusing on the entelechial nature of American mythology. As Kenneth Burke defined the concept of entelechy, symbol systems are often defined by perfectionist tendencies that lead people to "carry out the implications of their worldviews even if they 'contain the risks of destroying the world.'"[20] While the musical affirms both versions of the American Dream at times, which accounts for its bipartisan following, we suggest Alexander Hamilton's personal story illustrates how the "non-stop"[21] competition inherent in the materialistic myth is loaded with the potential to end tragically. In this sense, our reading of *Hamilton* clashes not only with those critics who suggest anything can be read into the show depending on the audience, we also see the musical as a cultural intervention into America's most important civic myth. As we conclude the chapter, we suggest that while so many see a show that is built on hope, we see it as a warning about the extremes of American identity, particularly the extremes of individualism.

THE AMERICAN DREAM AND ITS EXTREMES

The most common definition of the American Dream is that anyone can rise from their place in society if they have enough gumption to succeed. However, Walter Fisher revealed that the myth actually comes in two forms. The materialistic myth "is grounded on the puritan work ethic and relates to the values of effort, persistence, 'playing the game,' initiative, self-reliance, achievement, and success." Alternatively, the moralistic myth's values are more collectivistic, involving "the values of tolerance, charity, compassion, and true regard for the dignity and worth of each and every individual."[22] With the materialistic version grounded in individualism and the moralistic in collectivism, both civic myths exist in a natural tension with one another, serving as an ongoing point of contention in both politics and popular culture.[23]

While both versions of the American Dream have mass appeal, the country usually swings toward one or the other in any given moment. The moralistic myth carried significant weight during the Johnson administration, but the materialistic myth has been the focal point for American identity since the early days of the Reagan presidency.[24] As presidential rhetoric scholar Martin Medhurst explained, for Reagan the key to this materialistic myth was "that Americans were to better their own lives through their own creative efforts, not wait for the government to ride to their rescue or provide taxpayer-funded benefits."[25] Thus, Reagan redefined the American Dream by using the "romantic narrative at the center" and creating a "scene embodying the opportunity to create a better life."[26] It was, many agree, a key victory for the conservative movement. That success, however, was challenged by Barack Obama, who stormed the political arena in 2004 with a message that the American Dream was in crisis. Providing a different path from Bush-era individualism, Obama stressed a communitarian version of the American Dream, suggesting that the country was a "whole" that needed to be lifted as one.[27]

Though these myths are in constant tension, that tension can be alleviated when both myths are affirmed through a form of "dialectical synthesis." Defining this appeal, rhetorical scholars Janice Hocker Rushing and Thomas Frentz explained "the old is not merely replaced with the new, but rather an integration of the old with the new is formed in such a way that the relationship among the participants is reaffirmed."[28] In other words, dialectical synthesis is a way for audiences to feel a sense of resolution in the battle between the ideologies that make up both myths of the American Dream. Beyond Rushing and Frentz's analysis of how the film *Rocky* provides a "renewal of hope," dialectical synthesis has been described by others seeking similar models in popular culture. For instance, Martha Solomon described dialectical synthesis in the plot of *Chariots of Fire*, a film focusing on two competitive runners who embody both myths. Instead of one ideology prevailing over the other, *Chariots of Fire* relieves the tension by validating both myths and "[diminishing] the schizophrenic struggle within an American viewer."[29]

Like so many other scholars and cultural critics, we locate the myth of the American Dream at the heart of *Hamilton*, but we suggest that the moral of Miranda's story is a bit more limited. In particular, we contend that *Hamilton* is a cautionary tale about the entelechial potential of the American Dream, reflecting a deep sense of cynicism about the materialistic myth by portraying it as a possible existential threat to self and society. Entelechy is a concept borrowed from Aristotle, but redefined by Kenneth Burke as "the human tendency to define 'an essence in terms of the end.'"[30] In other words, people have an inclination to take a symbol system, and the beliefs it represents, to the "end of the line." While Aristotle grounded entelechy in philosophy, Burke extended the term by describing it as one of the defining features of humans as symbol-using creatures. Burke explained, "there is a principle of perfection implicit in the nature of symbol systems" that "[humans are] moved by," clarifying that the entelechial principal of perfection leads to humans becoming "'rotten' with perfection."[31] In short, humans tend to follow an ideology to the point where it can have dangerous implications, representing a tendency that makes polarized approaches to the myth of the American Dream especially dangerous. Walter Fisher hinted at this danger, stating that "in naked form, the materialistic myth is compassionless and self-centered; it encourages manipulation and leads to exploitation."[32] This entelechial approach to competition means one's opponents must be destroyed, while the individual ends up alone. This, we suggest, is *Hamilton*'s lesson for its American audience. Even when one is drawn to community and the desire to lift up others, the impulse of selfish individualism and competitive confrontation is too strong, often leading one down the path of mutual destruction and tragedy.

THE AMERICAN DREAM AND MYTHIC ENTELECHY IN *HAMILTON*

Hamilton portrays the entelechial potential of the American Dream, but its target is mainly rampant individualism that ends tragically when unchecked. Rather than offering a historical perspective of Hamilton and Burr, Miranda fictionalizes many aspects of their lives to describe them as inevitably and tragically clashing, but attributing their decline and demise specifically to their ideologies. In this chapter, we have conducted a close rhetorical analysis of the musical's messages about the American Dream specifically. We examined both the stage production of the musical, as well as the recorded album and written lyrics. In addition to an inductive analysis of the lyrics, we paid careful attention to the visual and sonic components of the musical and how they influenced the meaning of the ideologies of the main characters. In this section, our analysis of the central role of the American Dream in Miranda's musical evolves over three parts. First, we describe how the visual rhetoric in *Hamilton* serves as an introduction of both the materialistic and moralistic versions of the American myth, pitting them and their representative characters at odds with one another. Second, we show how musical motifs and lyrics represent the individualistic nature of Hamilton, despite his desire for communitarian (or Federalist) projects like the Bank of the United States, and how such musical elements set up both Hamilton and Burr to ultimately throw away their shots in the spirit of competition. Finally, we analyze the duel at the end of the musical to show how Miranda's message is a critique of the potential existential crisis of American individualism.

Visual Representations of the American Dream

The visual rhetoric in *Hamilton* allows the audience to see the conflict between individualism and collectivism early on, especially in the show's costuming. In this sense, the ideological clash begins with the first song's contrast between Hamilton and Burr. As the show starts, Burr steps out in a dark maroon coat over a beige colored outfit. It does not seem out of the ordinary until the other characters come out on stage in just the beige costumes, including Hamilton himself. This becomes an important perspective during the opening, as others who play equally important people in Hamilton's story have this monochrome costume. As they all come to the front of the stage in a straight line in the title song, Burr stands out as the one spot of color in a wall of beige, indicating his important status, and perhaps something to be achieved by other characters as the story unfolds. At the same time, the monochrome costumes of other characters show the audience that a clean slate is given for the others to grow, just as one ideally has a clean slate in America, emphasized by lyrics that suggest one can "be a new man" in the country.[33] The symbolism smacks of the American Dream, putting collectivism in conflict with individualism. By having the majority of the cast in the cream costumes, it not only signifies the uniformity among them and the collectivism that allows individual citizens to rise up, but also solidifies Burr's individualism against the rest of the pack, alluding to the conflict he will have as others rise to challenge his superior status.

If the colors are not enough to indicate this meaning, several lines hint at the clash between the ideologies represented in these visual motifs. While Hamilton immigrates to a land of opportunity, he ultimately gets "a lot farther by working a lot harder; By being a lot smarter; By being a self-starter."[34] With both versions of the American Dream at work, and Hamilton stepping from the shadows by declaring his name, he is also introduced as a man who would "never back down" and "never learned to take [his] time," marking the possibly tragic trajectory of individualism. As the maroon coated Burr announces in his final line in the opening song that he is the "damn fool that shot" Hamilton,[35] there is yet another hint that the differences between the beige outfits and those with color are not inconsequential; to embrace one's own ambition may clash with another's individual pursuits. Thus, from the start of the show, Burr is shown through his mistake of acting on his ideology despite its cost to others, and before the audience begins to understand his obsession with Hamilton's success, the audience is drawn to rank, order, and the value of social climbing. He is the sympathetic villain, denounced for killing an American hero, but introduced as the embodiment of the materialistic myth.

The show's costumes change as the characters evolve in their competitive trajectories, further setting them on a collision course through subtle hints of their unchecked individualism. Hamilton's costume starts off in the cream color until the ensemble sings "in New York, you can be a new man."[36] As Hamilton is alluding to how he can be an influencer in establishing a new country, Burr takes off Hamilton's cream coat while a woman, who we eventually learn is Hamilton's future wife, Eliza, gives him a new dark tan jacket that sets him apart from the others on stage. This references the next song, "Aaron Burr, Sir," when Burr and Hamilton meet for the first time, and subsequently spark Hamilton's political prospects and career. This also sets up how Burr's entelechial individualism will eventually drag Hamilton down with him in his destruction. Though the musical focuses on the life of Alexander Hamilton, Miranda shows clearly that Burr had his own side of the story that led to him being the "villain in [our] history" from the famous duel.[37] As each man seeks to leave his mark on his country and history itself, the costuming visually represents Burr's trajectory of embracing a blinding ideology, one where there could be only one "winner" in his intertwined existence with Hamilton. And as Hamilton steps from beige into color, he indicates a willingness to embrace that competition.

While the costumes indicate the narrative dominance of the materialistic myth, Miranda's use of color-blind casting allows the collectivistic theme to be carried on throughout the show. In other words, *Hamilton* makes clear that there are alternatives to individualism, without which the story would not be as tragic. As Miranda maintains "this is a story about America then, told by America now,"[38] the aesthetic of his cast is immediately disruptive to one's expectations. Specifically, Miranda's choice of selecting only people of color to play the white Founding Fathers shows that he has a vision for what the country should be: a melting pot of identities held together by mutual respect and common sacrifice. The aesthetics are made clearer by the musical's choice of hip-hop style, subverting traditions of the Broadway musical genre, and reaching out to audiences spanning a variety of ages and races. As Elizabeth Titrington Craft summarized, the show's aesthetics are about affirming "cultural citizenship," celebrating an artistic form "with roots in minority communities rather than assimilating to a predominately white so-called mainstream."[39] Audiences rarely miss this distinguishing characteristic of the show. David Horsey of the *Los Angeles Times*, for instance, wrote that the "rap and hip-hop sounds that drive the musical, [and] the social sensibilities of the characters are very much of our time," showing how Miranda highlights "commonalities between the founding generation and today's upcoming generations."[40] Moreover, he writes, the musical's tendency to make the racial diversity of its actors "irrelevant" means that the audience, "especially the non-white, youthful segment of his audience," can "connect with the story of America's creation" through "hip-hop instead of harpsichords and diversity instead of literal representation." The musical's style is welcoming to a diverse audience, and as other chapters explain elsewhere in this volume, the story sees community and diversity as important objectives in retelling American history. Yet the musical conveys that each American is haunted by the quest for pure individualism, a mission that spoils the good that can be accomplished by selfless citizenship.

Individualism through Musical Themes

Musicals use lyrics and musical motifs to speak for characters, often in place of actual dialogue. In particular, composers often give a character a certain melody to signify important moments in that character's arc. That melody becomes their mark on the entire narrative, but the way it evolves indicates a character's evolution as well. Miranda uses both of these aspects of music to build the conflict between individualism and collectivism at the beginning of the show and continues it further through Burr's adoption of a dangerous version of the materialistic myth. In other words, Hamilton and Burr's musical motifs are a vital part of the show that display their conflicting ideologies, stressing not just a story of flawed men, but a dark quality of an American myth that so often woos audiences.

In the first song, "Alexander Hamilton," Miranda briefly describes how Hamilton was able to come to America from his native island, Nevis. The song introduces a unique melody to Hamilton's name that then reappears several times throughout the show. Introduced in a song that makes his immigrant status a central aspect of his identity and mission to rise up, the melody helps Hamilton stand out individually among the other characters, as it centers the musical on him. In songs appearing later in the show, he meets different characters, such as Angelica Schuyler and Thomas Jefferson, all appearing in their own introductory songs. However, rather than going along with the established melody of these songs, he still uses his personal melody for his name to introduce himself. While this does not necessarily interrupt the songs, Hamilton forces himself and his history into the context of whatever is being sung, further emphasizing the importance of his individual pursuit to rise up and be noticed. While the musical is about the collective America, and is composed of a collection of songs, Hamilton has his own tune that separates him from others and foregrounds his story. By itself, this rhetorical maneuver does not represent the entelechialization of individualism, especially since a few other characters get their own melodies. For Hamilton, though, the melody is a central part of the musical, emphasizing his personal ambition, and his desire to rise above his station. However, like the acorn that could become a tree, it is the seed of Hamilton's selfishness and competitive spirit.

While Hamilton's story as an outsider coming to America to make a better life has roots in both the moralistic and materialistic myths, the focus on immigrants tends to highlight their sense of belonging based on their respect for the Puritan work ethic. Miranda includes several lyrics about immigrants, such as "another immigrant coming up from the bottom" and "immigrants: we get the job done."[41] Hamilton's belief that only he can bring himself up in society is further impressed into the audience through the song, "My Shot," which highlights the tragic trajectory of his competitive spirit. Being his first solo song of the show, "My Shot" allows Hamilton to discuss his goals for self-actualization. This follows Burr telling John Laurens, Hercules Mulligan, and the Marquis de Lafayette that they should keep quiet about their opinions on the war. Though he does not know these men, Hamilton butts in asking, "if you stand for nothing, Burr, what'll you fall for?"[42] This sets up the conflict between Hamilton and Burr as Hamilton spends a majority of the show mocking Burr for not taking initiative for his place in life. From there, Hamilton launches into his explanation of how he plans to "rise up" in society. This starts with the lyric: "Rise up!; When you're living on your knees, you rise up; Tell your brother that he's gotta rise up; Tell your sister that she's gotta rise up."[43] The lyrics embody both collectivistic and individualistic themes, representing a blended form of politics that define Hamilton for much of the musical. It is in this song that Hamilton stresses that individuals are responsible for improving their own lives by working hard to improve their status. While he is singing about creating a legacy in the colonies, and even the obligation of other citizens to join the movement to claim "our promised land,"[44] "My Shot" also becomes the anthem for Hamilton's materialistic myth, and undoubtedly the source of conservative identification with his character. The nation's story becomes intertwined with his individual pursuit of influence. Because it appears early in the musical and stresses both the materialistic and moralistic myths, it speaks of the possibilities of dialectical synthesis, and previews how a literal shot will shatter the possibilities of a shared community.

While aspects of Hamilton's politics represented the moralistic myth, his personal drive did not; oddly, while Burr's politics represented the materialistic myth, his personal drive was inherently collectivistic, at least at first. Burr's musical motif, introduced in the song "Wait For It," describes his philosophy about life and paints him as a classic conservative who rises up patiently. We are shown from the beginning how headstrong Hamilton is to make his opinion known, but this is the first opportunity we have to truly see what Burr is thinking. Immediately, the type of song, being slower and seemingly more thought out than Hamilton's quick witty lines, shows their differences by contrasting Hamilton's strong individualism and Burr's refusal to show his ambition or ideological leanings. Not only does the musical phrase "wait for it" accompany Burr's ideology through the rest of the show, but it is used for Hamilton to confront their differences.[45] When sung by Burr, the line is more of a reassurance of what he *ought* to do, but will ultimately ignore in his tragic competition with Hamilton. And when the line is sung by Hamilton, it is mocking in nature, baiting Burr to stumble and fueling his competitive drive.

Burr starts to abandon his philosophy of waiting in the fifth song of the second act, "The Room Where It Happens." In this pivotal moment for Burr, he decides he will no longer "wait for it," or seek the blessing of those around him, and instead decides to go after what he desires.[46] Burr's turn is inspired by competition and individualism, but also a drive not only to defeat Hamilton but to replace him entirely. As Hamilton sings about how he convinced Thomas Jefferson and James Madison to give him the votes for the national bank, he sings to Burr that "you get nothing if you wait for it," then asks, "what do you want Burr?" Burr, sparked by Hamilton's ambition, states that he wants "to be in the room where it happens,"[47] kick starting his political career by doing whatever he needs to do to enhance his status. This begins his dangerous path to their destruction as Burr's rise in the political world begins the central conflict between the two in the show. As they both embrace individualism, the audience sees that this switch is ultimately what causes the tragic duel because Hamilton "throw[s] away [his] shot"[48] and Burr does not "wait for it."[49] Burr's motif then becomes ironic, as he is not remembered for what he repeatedly says throughout the musical, but is instead remembered for the one time he did not wait. Burr's transition to Hamilton's ideology clearly shows that instead of just embracing the materialistic ideology, Burr fatalistically pursues the entelechial trajectory of individualism by driving the competitive nature of his conflict with Hamilton to a life or death situation. As he summarizes in "The World Was Wide Enough," "They won't teach you this in your classes; But look it up, Hamilton was wearing his glasses; Why? If not to take deadly aim?; It's him or me, the world will never be the same."[50]

The Duel and the Entelechial Dangers of Individualism

Consistent with how the American Dream has been explored in previous forms of popular culture, *Hamilton*'s main characters seem to be a synthesis of the moralistic and materialistic myths; this synthesis could account for the vastly different reactions that audiences have to the show. However, a commitment to a polysemic reading of the musical fails to acknowledge the entelechy that Miranda sees specifically in the materialistic myth. At first, Hamilton's personification of the myth is harmless. He is hailed as a penniless illegitimate child who was orphaned by the death of his mother, so beloved by his community that they raised money to send him to the mainland to receive a proper education, and who worked and wrote like he was "running out of time" to eventually become the "ten-dollar founding father."[51] This, to be clear, inspires audiences, but the best of Hamilton happens before he is transformed by the entelechial nature of individualism. Like a spell, the Puritan work ethic he exhibited transforms into a competitive drive that became tragic, as this extreme version of the American Dream leaves little room for others to succeed as well.

It is in Burr, however, that the entelechial nature of individualism is most obvious, which is likely why he is conveniently portrayed as the reluctant villain. His early advice that Hamilton should "talk less [and] smile more" sets the tone for how Burr views others who are competing in the political realm, and how little space there is for others to succeed around him.[52] The culmination of his growing conflict with Hamilton is witnessed in the song, "The Election of 1800," which describes Hamilton endorsing Thomas Jefferson over Burr for president because at least "Jefferson [had] beliefs, Burr [had] none."[53] Despite his tendency to "wait for it,"[54] Burr is moved by his passions, his desire to persevere over his enemies, and his yearning to put Hamilton in his place. In the world they create together, there is no room for mutual success, as there must be a winner and loser, and losers in this tragic competition must be eliminated. Only one person may stand honorably.

By bringing their conflict to a duel, both Burr and Hamilton follow the entelechial trajectory of the materialistic myth. In this sense, the story lacks a clear villain, despite Burr's announcement in the opening number that he is the man who shot Hamilton. Both are simultaneously victims, controlled by the spell of individualism. As shown in the song, "The World Was Wide Enough," Burr states that although Hamilton died, he is the one that "survived, but ... paid for" the consequences of the duel.[55] While he technically won the shooting match, the duel triggered the end of his political career, and all of his accomplishments were cruelly wiped clean as he would be forever remembered for the ten paces that cut down his fellow Founding Father. However, the need for competition not only brings Burr down, but Hamilton along with it. Hamilton is hardly a perfect victim by that point. Though his character arguably represented collectivistic ideas that benefited Americans more broadly, Hamilton, too, falls to his selfishness and competitive spirit. As early as his assistance with the duel between John Laurens and Charles Lee, continuing with his constant battle with Thomas Jefferson in the second act, Hamilton shows a tendency to fall into competition with no real end. Rather than letting the conflict go and working past differences, Hamilton participates in the duel, despite knowing from his own son's death that such a battle for one's honor has no happy ending. Having already broken his wife's heart after a very public and embarrassing love affair, Hamilton took additional actions that would eventually leave her widowed. At best, both Hamilton and Burr are tragic heroes, with their accomplishments and legacies—some of which are listed in "Who Lives, Who Dies, Who Tells Your Story"—becoming overshadowed by the stubbornness of their competitive spirits.

CONCLUSION

This chapter has explored how the American Dream manifests in *Hamilton: An American Musical*. We aim to describe the more nuanced ways that the American Dream is featured in the musical, and also how it serves a dual purpose of not just uniting audiences but warning everyone about taking the materialistic myth to the end of the line. We have described three ways the musical advances this message, particularly in how its visual rhetoric foregrounds the men's drive to individualism or collectivism, how Miranda furthermore uses lyrics and musical motifs to build the conflict between these ideologies, and how the duel represents the entelechial implications of following the materialistic myth too far.

Our reading of *Hamilton* clashes specifically with the countless critiques suggesting the musical is overly hopeful, and another Broadway act that plays loose with history to portray the country's white founders as forward-looking men to be forever revered. For instance, historians David Waldstreicher and Jeffrey Pasley recently argued that the show "[rescues] and [renews] an embarrassingly patriotic, partisan, and partial version of early American history." In doing so, they argue, *Hamilton* embraces "Founders Chic" by making "its hero into a great white hope for the founding, spinning a neo-Federalist, anti-slavery past that is myth, not history."[56] Although the musical ends tragically, Waldstreicher and Pasley suggest that it leaves Hamilton looking like a "quasi-'gangsta'" who modern Americans can perceive as "an unproblematic outsider, regarding him with no more ambivalence than we devote to any tragic hero—and, if we are honest, just as much admiration."[57] Our reading differs, and we think while *Hamilton*'s selection and deflection of history is problematic, its promise is in how it attempts to complicate civic myths in the United States.

Drawing large audiences, *Hamilton* serves to educate and influence shared narratives that form national identity. Scholarly discussion of its influence on civic myths has thus far been limited to its focus on founding myths and American exceptionalism. Like other critics, historian Renee Romano notes that *Hamilton* pushes a traditional civic myth that "[emphasizes] American exceptionalism, [portrays] the United States as committed to ideals of liberty and equality, and [valorizes] the founders and the Constitution as vital to cultivating a proud civic identity."[58] Yet we suggest that the hopefulness of the American Dream is stymied by the lessons of entelechy. If there is a new civic myth in *Hamilton*, it is one that recognizes the American Dream is potentially flawed, especially when one's individual pursuits are emphasized before the community's best interests, or when individualism is stubbornly taken to the end of the line. It is perhaps why—as the chapters by Mark P. Orbe and Nancy J. Legge will discuss further in this volume—Vice President-elect Mike Pence was confronted a week after the 2016 election when actor Brandon Victor Dixon spoke of a "diverse America" that was "alarmed and anxious that [the Trump] administration will not protect us, our planet, our children, our parents, or defend us and uphold our inalienable rights."[59] And it is also probably why Lin-Manuel Miranda tweeted that Trump would go "straight to hell" for abandoning Puerto Rico after Hurricane Maria, accusing the president of playing golf while San Juan's mayor and many others worked to repair communities.[60] And the lessons of entelechial individualism might also explain why Dictionary.com named "existential" the Word of the Year for 2019, describing the "sense of grappling with the survival—literally and figuratively—of our planet, our loved ones, our ways of life."[61]

NOTES

1 Michaelah Reynolds, Marketing and Publicity Account Assistant, Bond Theatrical Group, mar020@uark.edu; Ryan Neville-Shepard, Assistant Professor, University of Arkansas, rnevshep@uark.edu.

2 Kate Maltby, "'Hamilton' Hype Highlights Our Transatlantic Differences," *Financial Times*, January 27, 2017, https://www.ft.com/content/a412b7dc-e479-11e6-9645-c9357a75844a.
3 Ronald J. Granieri, "Alexander Hamilton and the American Dream," *Foreign Policy Research Institute*, April 13, 2016, https://www.fpri.org/article/2016/04/alexander-hamilton-american-dream.
4 Kevin O'Keeffe, "After a Year of Dominance, 'Hamilton' Has Forever Changed What Musical Theater Can Be," *Mic*, December 2, 2015, https://www.mic.com/articles/129323/after-a-year-of-dominance-hamilton-has-forever-changed-what-musical-theater-can-be.
5 Caroline Framke, "Watch Live: The Cast of Broadway's Hamilton Performs at the White House," *Vox*, March 14, 2016, https://www.vox.com/2016/3/14/11225074/hamilton-white-house-livestream.
6 Elizabeth Titrington Craft, "Headfirst into an Abyss: The Politics and Political Reception of Hamilton," *American Music* 36 (2018): 435, https://www.muse.jhu.edu/article/715970.
7 Loren Kajikawa, "'Young, Scrappy, and Hungry': Hamilton, Hip Hop, and Race," *American Music* 36 (2018): 478, https://www.muse.jhu.edu/article/715972.
8 Mark Binelli, "'Hamilton' Creator Lin-Manuel Miranda: The *Rolling Stone* Interview," *Rolling Stone*, June 1, 2016, https://www.rollingstone.com/culture/culture-news/hamilton-creator-lin-manuel-miranda-the-rolling-stone-interview-42607.
9 Janice C. Simpson, "The Man Who First Brought Us *Hamilton*—Ron Chernow on Serving as Lin-Manuel Miranda's 'Right Hand Man,'" *Playbill*, January 12, 2016, http://www.playbill.com/article/the-man-who-first-brought-us-hamilton-u2014-ron-chernow-on-serving-as-lin-manuel-mirandas-right-hand-man.
10 Joanne B. Freeman, "Will the Real Alexander Hamilton Please Stand Up?" *Journal of the Early Republic* 37 (2017): 256, https://doi.org/10.1353/jer.2017.0021. See also: Joanne B. Freeman, "'Can We Get Back to Politics? Please?': Hamilton's Missing Politics in *Hamilton*," in *Historians on Hamilton: How a Blockbuster Musical Is Restaging America's Past*, eds. Renee C. Romano and Claire Bond Potter (New Brunswick, NJ: Rutgers University Press, 2018), 42–57.
11 Lyra D. Monteiro, "Race-Conscious Casting and the Erasure of the Black Past in Lin-Manuel Miranda's Hamilton," *The Public Historian* 38 (2016): 90–91, https://doi.org/10.1525/tph.2016.38.1.89.
12 Phillip W. Magness, "Alexander Hamilton as Immigrant: Musical Mythology Meets Federalist Reality," *The Independent Review* 21 (2017): 498.
13 For instance, see: Marvin McAllister, "Toward a More Perfect *Hamilton*," *Journal of the Early Republic* 37 (2017): 279–88, https://doi.org/10.1353/jer.2017.0024; Monteiro, "Race-Conscious Casting and the Erasure of the Black Past," 93–96; Billy G. Smith, "Alexander Hamilton: The Wrong Hero for Our Age," *The Independent Review* 21 (2017): 519–22.
14 Elissa Harbert, "*Hamilton* and History Musicals," *American Music* 36 (2018): 414, https://www.muse.jhu.edu/article/715969.
15 Aja Romano, "Hamilton Is Fanfic, and Its Historical Critics Are Totally Missing the Point," *Vox*, April 14, 2014, https://www.vox.com/2016/4/14/11418672/hamilton-is-fanfic-not-historically-inaccurate.
16 Freeman, "Will the Real Alexander Hamilton Please Stand Up?" 251–60.
17 Walter R. Fisher, "Reaffirmation and Subversion of the American Dream," *Quarterly Journal of Speech* 59 (1973): 160–67, https://doi.org/10.1080/00335637309383164.
18 For instance, see: Martin J. Medhurst, "LBJ, Reagan, and the American Dream: Competing Visions of Liberty," *Presidential Studies Quarterly* 46 (2016): 98–124, https://doi.org/10.1111/psq.12253; Ryan Neville-Shepard, "Constrained by Duality: Third-Party Master Narratives in

the 2016 Presidential Election," *American Behavioral Scientist* 61 (2017): 414–27, https://doi.org/10.1177/0002764217709042; Kurt W. Ritter, "American Political Rhetoric and the Jeremiad Tradition: Presidential Nomination Acceptance Addresses, 1960–1976," *Central States Speech Journal* 31 (1980): 153–71, https://doi.org/10.1080/10510978009368054; Robert C. Rowland and John M. Jones, "Recasting the American Dream and American Politics: Barack Obamas Keynote Address to the 2004 Democratic National Convention," *Quarterly Journal of Speech* 93 (2007): 425–48, https://doi.org/10.1080/00335630701593675.

19 For more, see: Wayne J. McMullen, "Reconstruction of the Frontier Myth in Witness," *Southern Communication Journal* 62 (1996): 31–41, https://doi.org/10.1080/10417949609373037; Janice Hocker Rushing and Thomas S. Frentz, "The Rhetoric of 'Rocky': A Social Value Model of Criticism," *Western Journal of Speech Communication* 42 (1978): 63–72, https://doi.org/10.1080/10570317809373925; Martha Solomon, "Villainless Quest: Myth, Metaphor, and Dream in 'Chariots of Fire,'" *Communication Quarterly* 31 (1983): 274–81, https://doi.org/10.1080/01463378309369516.

20 Robert C. Rowland and John Jones, "Entelechial and Reformative Symbolic Trajectories in Contemporary Conservatism: A Case Study of Reagan and Buchanan in Houston and Beyond," *Rhetoric & Public Affairs* 4 (2001): 56–57, https://doi.org/10.1353/rap.2001.0010.

21 Lin-Manuel Miranda and Jeremy McCarter, *Hamilton: The Revolution* (New York, NY: Grand Central Publishing, 2016), 137.

22 Fisher, "Reaffirmation and Subversion of the American Dream," 161.

23 Renee C. Romano, "*Hamilton*: A New Civic Myth," in *Historians on Hamilton: How a Blockbuster Musical Is Restaging America's Past*, eds. Renee C. Romano and Claire Bond Potter (New Brunswick, NJ: Rutgers University Press, 2018), 300.

24 Rowland and Jones, "Recasting the American Dream and American Politics," 432–33. See also: Medhurst, "LBJ, Reagan, and the American Dream."

25 Medhurst, "LBJ, Reagan, and the American Dream," 107.

26 Rowland and Jones, "Recasting the American Dream and American Politics," 430.

27 Keith B. Jenkins and Grant Cos, "A Time for Change and a Candidate's Voice: Pragmatism and the Rhetoric of Inclusion in Barack Obama's 2008 Presidential Campaign," *American Behavioral Scientist* 54 (2010): 184–202, https://doi.org/10.1177/0002764210381706.

28 Rushing and Frentz, "The Rhetoric of 'Rocky,'" 70–71.

29 Solomon, "Villainless Quest," 277.

30 Rowland and Jones, "Entelechial and Reformative Symbolic Trajectories in Contemporary Conservatism," 56–57.

31 Kenneth Burke, "Definition of Man," *The Hudson Review* 16 (1963): 508–9, https://doi.org/10.2307/3848123.

32 Fisher, "Reaffirmation and Subversion of the American Dream," 161.

33 Miranda and McCarter, *Hamilton: The Revolution*, 17.

34 Miranda and McCarter, *Hamilton: The Revolution*, 16.

35 Miranda and McCarter, *Hamilton: The Revolution*, 17.

36 Miranda and McCarter, *Hamilton: The Revolution*, 17.

37 Miranda and McCarter, *Hamilton: The Revolution*, 275.

38 Miranda and McCarter, *Hamilton: The Revolution*, 33.

39 Craft, "Headfirst into an Abyss," 430.

40 David Horsey, "'Hamilton' Gets Past Race by Imagining Founding Fathers with Black and Brown Faces," *Los Angeles Times*, September 18, 2017, https://www.latimes.com/opinion/topoftheticket/la-na-tt-hamilton-jefferson-20170916-story.html.

41 Miranda and McCarter, *Hamilton: The Revolution*, 17, 121.
42 Miranda and McCarter, *Hamilton: The Revolution*, 25.
43 Miranda and McCarter, *Hamilton: The Revolution*, 28.
44 Miranda and McCarter, *Hamilton: The Revolution*, 29.
45 Miranda and McCarter, *Hamilton: The Revolution*, 91.
46 Miranda and McCarter, *Hamilton: The Revolution*, 91.
47 Miranda and McCarter, *Hamilton: The Revolution*, 188–89.
48 Miranda and McCarter, *Hamilton: The Revolution*, 26.
49 Miranda and McCarter, *Hamilton: The Revolution*, 91.
50 Miranda and McCarter, *Hamilton: The Revolution*, 272.
51 Miranda and McCarter, *Hamilton: The Revolution*, 137, 16.
52 Miranda and McCarter, *Hamilton: The Revolution*, 23.
53 Miranda and McCarter, *Hamilton: The Revolution*, 261.
54 Miranda and McCarter, *Hamilton: The Revolution*, 272.
55 Miranda and McCarter, *Hamilton: The Revolution*, 275.
56 David Waldstreicher and Jeffrey L. Pasley, "*Hamilton* as Founders Chic: A New-Federalist, Antislavery, Usable Past?" in *Historians on Hamilton: How a Blockbuster Musical Is Restaging America's Past*, eds. Renee C. Romano and Claire Bond Potter (New Brunswick, NJ: Rutgers University Press, 2018), 140.
57 Waldstreicher and Pasley, "*Hamilton* as Founders Chic," 149.
58 Romano, "*Hamilton*: A New Civic Myth," 304.
59 Christopher Mele and Patrick Healy, "'Hamilton' Had Some Unscripted Lines for Pence. Trump Wasn't Happy," *New York Times*, November 19, 2016, https://www.nytimes.com/2016/11/19/us/mike-pence-hamilton.html.
60 Constance Grady, "Hamilton Composer Lin-Manuel Miranda to Donald Trump: You Are Going Straight to Hell," October 2, 2017, https://www.vox.com/culture/2017/10/2/16400388/hamilton-composer-lin-manuel-miranda-donald-trump-going-straight-to-hell.
61 Li Cohen, "'Existential' Is Dictionary.com's Word of the Year," *CBS News*, December 2, 2019, https://www.cbsnews.com/news/word-of-the-year-existential-is-the-word-of-the-year-dictionary-dot-com.

CHAPTER FOUR

Exhibiting *Hamilton*: History, Memory, and Musical Theater

SARA A. MEHLTRETTER DRURY AND JAMES ANTHONY WILLIAMS JR.[1]

A central theme of *Hamilton* is the refrain "who lives, who dies, who tells your story," which functions first as advice to a young Alexander Hamilton from Commander George Washington, and then as a testament to Eliza Hamilton's efforts to preserve Hamilton's legacy.[2] Open from April 2019 to August 2019 in Chicago, Illinois, Hamilton: The Exhibition curates a legacy for *Hamilton: An American Musical* and the historical period of Hamilton's life, 1757–1804. Costing more than $13 million, the exhibition was presented as a temporary, immersive museum-style experience, located on Chicago's Northerly Island.[3] *Hamilton* producer Jeffrey Seller oversaw the creation of the stand-alone exhibition, with *Hamilton* set designer David Korins creating 35,000 square feet across twenty-two rooms and three theatrical presentations, and narrations from creator Lin-Manuel Miranda, original cast members Phillipa Soo and Chris Jackson, as well as academics Joanne Freeman and Annette Gordon Reed.[4] The exhibition was pitched as the ultimate experience for Hamilfans, but also represented an opportunity for people to explore the history of Hamilton's life and the events he experienced in the Revolutionary War and early U.S. history.

As a text, Hamilton: The Exhibition represented, expanded, and in some cases, corrected the musical. The exhibition's rooms roughly follow the timeline of the musical, and the audionarration featured a new orchestral recording of the show.[5] Outside of this experience, the rooms are inspired by moments in the show's narrative, and expanded to incorporate a greater social, economic, and cultural history of the early United States. That history, at times, contradicts the musical. At the beginning of the exhibition, Miranda tells visitors that there are small white placards throughout that correct a variety of historical inaccuracies in the musical; for improving the musical's story, Miranda took a few liberties and "made things up," as he confesses to visitors in the exhibition's audionarration.[6]

In seeking to expand the historical presentation made by the musical, Hamilton: The Exhibition offers a revised narrative of Hamilton as historical figure and of the history and culture of the founding period of the United States. Like other scholars of rhetoric, our argument here relies on rhetorical theory and on our subject positions experiencing the exhibition.[7] As a rhetorical text of public memory, Hamilton: The Exhibition set an expectation for a retelling of the U.S. founding as history created of, by, and for everyone. Hamilton: The Exhibition recognized and recovered a broad set of voices from early U.S. history, but at times struggled to uphold its own stated promise of America as a story shared and celebrated by all.

This essay begins by exploring the significance of studying museums and memorials from a rhetorical perspective, and explains our methodology of rhetorical autoethnography for this analysis. Next, we analyze the exhibition, demonstrating the opportunities and challenges of acknowledging diverse perspectives. We explain how the exhibition retained a driving narrative focus on celebrating *Hamilton*, Alexander Hamilton as historical figure, and the founding period, even as it sought to broaden the scope of history. Finally, we offer concluding thoughts on the enduring legacies of *Hamilton: An American Musical* and Hamilton: The Exhibition for U.S. public memory of the late eighteenth and early nineteenth centuries.

MUSEUMS AS EXPERIENTIAL LANDSCAPES

Scholars of rhetoric have analyzed museums as contested sites of history, memory, and identity. In display, museums make constructed appeals to a "shared past" and to "collective identities,"[8] and become locations of "partial, partisan, and thus frequently contested" discourses.[9] Museums are more than repositories for artifacts, more than displays and sets, and more than a presentation of historical record. Museums *curate*, and by that act, construct meaning for visitors. They create "spaces of attention," which "rhetorically invoke a collective sense of civic and cultural understanding"[10] and exist as "ongoing site[s] of rhetorical contestation and struggle."[11]

Museums *are visited*, therefore materiality is critical to understanding how museums enact meaning—and ask "what does a text or artifact do/what are the consequences beyond the [author]'s goals?"[12] In their research on reading museums as experiential landscapes, Greg Dickinson, Brian L. Ott, and Eric Aoki advise that museum "spaces of memory" should be analyzed "as diffuse texts" rather than discrete and isolated ones, that museums may engage in activating a "dreamscape," or a cognitive landscape activated by the physical landscape of the museum, and that such experiential museums invite "visitors to assume (to occupy) particular subject positions."[13] In analyzing the material rhetoric of a museum—or, in this case, an exhibition—the critic therefore should consider these three factors and how they contribute to the meaning(s) created by the space. Museums proclaim and interpret histories for visitors, contextualizing and selecting elements for a narrative. This meaning-making—or, recognizing the experiences of different audiences and visitors, meanings-making—enables museums to serve as sites of civic identities, displaying—or forgetting—narratives of community, history, and culture. The material rhetorics of museums may, as Tamar Katriel notes, "both utilize and dissolve claims to factuality."[14] Museums connect particular histories to broader individual and shared landscapes of understanding, memory, and identity.

Rhetorical scholars have paid close attention to the various ways that museums and memorials present the history of U.S. civil rights and race,[15] despite the tendency Roger Aden notes of a "near-absence of African American history from the commemorative landscape" as "one part of a larger pattern of the historical exclusion of [B]lack Americans from public places."[16] Spaces of Black public memory may recover or draw on a painful, difficult past—of slavery and systemic racism—while also memorializing the struggles and triumphs of Black men and women who fought for justice. Such spaces can offer pathways of influence for recovering marginalized voices of history.[17] In her study of Black history museums, Patricia Davis examines how such sites exhibit a highly contested past, advancing a "cultivation" of Black culture while recovering events, places, and persons.[18] Victoria J. Gallagher demonstrates that such spaces of public memory "enact a dialectical tension between reconciliation and amnesia, conflicts resolved and conflicts simply reconfigured."[19] Museums and sites of commemoration make choices about who and what to display, and in so doing, may exhibit in ways that replicate injustice and privilege.[20]

Such sites are relevant to an analysis of Hamilton: The Exhibition, because the exhibition invites memory-making that is more inclusive of Black, Indigenous, and female identities in two ways. First, the exhibition necessarily connects with the various ways that *Hamilton* engages historical, public, and racial memory, as discussed throughout this volume. The musical is as much source material for the exhibition as are historical documents, dates, and figures. Second, the exhibition begins with an explicit invitation in the opening video that grounds what the visitor is about to experience as an authentic, true history, and as a history for all "Americans." Speaking to visitors through the audionarration, Lin-Manuel Miranda proclaims, "the story of America is your story too—history has its eyes on you."[21] This analysis therefore seeks to consider the exhibition both as an extension of the musical's historical education and as a site of public memory of early U.S. history and politics.

ANALYZING HAMILTON: THE EXHIBITION AS A RHETORIC OF SPACE, PLACE, AND MEMORY

A reading of the exhibition could be done in a variety of ways, even with the particular focus on museum studies and public memory. Given the context of *Hamilton* as a hip-hop musical, as a musical about an American past, performed by people who look like the America of today, autoethnography emerged as an appropriate methodology to capture what animated our conversations about the text: namely, our own positions and experiences of the exhibition. Autoethnography, according to Robin M. Boylorn and Mark P. Orbe, is a "cultural analysis through personal narrative," and represents a "critical lens" alongside an "introspective and outward one, to make sense of who we are in the context of cultural communities."[22] In an overview of rhetorical autoethnography, Brett Lunceford suggests that rhetorical ethnography "draws on theory to help illuminate some aspect of rhetoric," while simultaneously drawing "on the critic's experiences with the rhetorical transaction in question."[23] The autoethnographic element has been explored by other scholars of space and place, particularly in sites that connect museums to tourism, and in moments when the critic's own awareness and experiences lend understanding to the materiality of the text.[24] Furthermore, autoethnography fits with the analysis of spaces of public history and memory suggested by Aden in his definition of understanding "meanings generated by *persons-with/in-places*." This perspective acknowledges that "physical site[s]" hold "a rich collection of symbolic representations of the past," which then interact with "those of us who visit the site" and our "own assemblages of understandings and expectations about how the past should be remembered and used."[25]

Our study of Hamilton: The Exhibition takes into account both our identities and experiences with the broader *Hamilton* phenomenon. Drury is a white, female faculty member in her thirties, with a background in rhetoric, politics, and civic education; Williams is a Black, male in his twenties, who at the time of researching this article, was a fourth-year student at Wabash College. We represented two different audiences for the exhibition—those who visited after viewing the show, as Hamilfans (Drury), and those who visited without prior knowledge or viewing of the musical (Williams). Drury visited the exhibition twice, first as part of a personal trip to see *Hamilton* in Chicago and second with Williams as a critical research trip for this essay. Due to the unexpected early closure of the exhibition,[26] Williams saw the exhibition before we both returned to Chicago two weeks later to see the musical.

During our visit, we individually took pictures and notes of each room. Additionally, during her second visit, Drury transcribed parts of the audionarration. We individually identified elements that stood out to us and why—drawing on both the cognitive and physical "dreamscapes" of early U.S. history (as we "remembered" and invoked them), and of the musical's interaction with the exhibition. These individual elements then broadened to a discussion between us, with consideration of the scholarship on the rhetoric of museums, space, and place. Finally, we developed the analysis and its implications together.

In addition to enabling us to explore some of the differences in our reactions to the text, autoethnography seemed appropriate for this text because Hamilton: The Exhibition was an oddly personal, isolated experience. Because the exhibition is set up as an immersive, audionarrated experience, visitors are preoccupied with listening to the narration and music. Visitors—even those who come in groups—do not seem to interact with one another. Drury found that to be true for both visits (in her first trip, she attended with a group of seven; in her second, her and Williams); she observed very little talking amongst groups of visitors, including her own. We largely experienced the exhibition individually, and then collectively shared after our time working through the various rooms and interactive displays. The exhibition, to build on Lunceford, engaged a "mixture of thoughts, feelings, history, beliefs, viewpoints, and training" in each of us, prompting us to reflect on how the displays connected to our understandings of culture and history.[27] This process gave us an entryway into understanding the struggles of Hamilton: The Exhibition to articulate cohesive stories for all visitors.

EXPERIENCING HAMILTON: THE EXHIBITION

From its first audio-visual narration through the final room's 3D video of the opening number from the musical, touring Hamilton: The Exhibition felt like walking through a combination of a Broadway show and a multimedia museum. Before experiencing the exhibition's 25,000 square feet of viewing space, however, visitors had to get there. Constructed in a largely open park on a peninsula jutting out into Lake Michigan, the location felt isolated.[28] To get there, visitors had to board a trolley (playing songs from the musical) that loaded at parking lots up to a mile away, or arrive via taxi or rideshare. Then, visitors walked through a park, up entrance stairs into the massive hanger, and checked in using pre-purchased tickets. Once inside, this entrance room was minimalist, with black walls and floors. To the right was a small café, gift shop, and facilities. After being checked in, visitors picked up their headsets, and while in line to enter the exhibit, listened to the first audionarration (included with admission, headphones provided). The visit was guided by the Broadway stars of *Hamilton*, namely creator Lin-Manuel Miranda, Phillippa Soo (who originated the role of Eliza Hamilton), Chris Jackson (who originated the role of George Washington), and historian Joanne Freeman. The Spanish narration was provided by actress Olga Merediz (who performed with Miranda in *In the Heights*).[29]

As we waited in line to enter the exhibition, the audionarration began. We were told to think of the exhibition less as an extension of the musical, and more as an opportunity to learn about the history of the period. Historian Joanne Freeman contributed throughout this opening narration, reminding visitors that while the word "Founding" often associated with this era "makes you think it was inevitable," in fact, "it was a period full of question marks."[30] While listening and traveling through four rows of back-and-forth queuing, the attention of the visitor would likely be drawn to the only decoration in the area: a large, accordion art installation overhead, three-dimensional and brightly colored. When viewed from the right, the visitor would see the iconic *Hamilton* silhouette images of characters from the musical (Aaron Burr, the three Schuyler sisters, Alexander Hamilton, George Washington, King George III, John Laurens, and the Marquis de Lafayette). From the left side, the visitor would see historical painted portraits of those same figures. Since the queue was largely on the left side of the building, we saw more of the historic images, and recognized the musical's icons primarily from the yellow color and black silhouettes similar to *Hamilton*'s publicity materials. Paired with the audionarration, the visitor's view of the display suggests that the focus here is on the historical, rather than the musical.

While emphasizing history, the exhibition's physical form often relied on the musical. The exhibition unfolded in a series of 22 rooms of set designs, artifacts, and images; three of those rooms featured theatrical/multimedia presentations. The rooms were nothing short of spectacularly staged. The aesthetic echoed the musical's set pieces; when it varied from that source material, the result was still nothing short of spectacular (e.g., a room focusing on King George III uses bright pink neon lighting to convey the opulence—and a bit of the ridiculousness—of the monarchy, harkening to the character portrayal in the show).

The rooms were immersive, resulting in a feeling of being part of the set rather than looking at it. At one point, visitors walked through a small officers cabin (depicting Hamilton's time serving in the Continental Army during the Revolutionary War), and then exited that room only to walk *around* the cabin, feet landing in the "snow" on the floor, to learn about the broader historical campaign and the experiences of Continental and British soldiers. Another room depicted the winter's ball from the musical when Alexander met Eliza, and had life-sized bronze statues of historical figures (both characters in the musical and beyond). In each room, the electronic device automatically sensed when visitors entered and played a narration. Some rooms were linear, with a clear pathway; others had displays and interactive elements that could be encountered in various orders, or skipped altogether. In most rooms, in addition to the automatically played audionarration, there were displays tagged with "click to hear more" and an image of a speaker that could be accessed by the visitor pointing their personal narration device at the icon.

The rooms combined interactive elements (both digital and physical) with more static displays of maps, images, portraits, and written information.

Unlike many museums, authentic documents were not the focus, but rather, curation and replication into a dynamic experience of Hamilton's historical timeline.[31] While there were a number of cases with historical documents—largely pamphlets and letters—the exhibition used almost exclusively reproductions. The exhibition also interplayed with the musical, with each room displaying a lyric in a designated font used only for the show's lyrics throughout. The lyrics were on dark backgrounds and lit from behind, drawing the eye and keeping the visitor within the musical's framing. All the while, the soundtrack played; it may have been possible to find a quiet spot, but in our experience, we were always seeing and hearing Hamilton—the person and the musical—around us.

In this way, the audio, visual, and physical experience oscillated back and forth between a stated historical focus on the "real" events, and reliance on the theatrical staging of Hamilton's life as a connection point for visitors to experience those events. This duality of perspective directly related to our experiences visiting, and our arguments that the exhibition provokes tensions through its presentation of U.S. history and public memory.

ANALYZING HAMILTON: THE EXHIBITION

One of the most quoted lines about the framing of the musical is from creator Miranda: "This is a story about America then, told by America now," a reference to the diverse casting and musical styles in the show.[32] The exhibition picked up that line of thinking—it works to convey that the American history of *then* belongs to everyone in America *now*. This message first became apparent in the opening multimedia display. Delivered via a large, movie screen-like panel with historical images and words as well as appearances from Miranda and Soo, the video introduced the exhibition, the narrators, and the framing for visitors. This narration invited the visitor to see an inclusive creation of the United States—referred to both as "America" and the "United States" throughout the exhibition. Speaking to visitors, Miranda noted, "it took creativity, compromise, and passionate debate" to create this nation, and the narration listed groups involved in this founding story: enslaved persons, natives, working people, immigrants, and women. Miranda told visitors, "The story of America is your story, too … History has its eyes on you." After this opening video, the exhibition explored Hamilton's life, the Revolution, and quest to create a representative government "from scratch." This opening framing invited visitors to consider a more diverse history, while still celebrating the journey of Hamilton, a singular "great man" of history.

As we moved through the exhibition, we reflected on how these two narratives unfolded, with an emphasis on inclusive history early on, and a stronger focus on Hamilton and political leadership in the early nineteenth century. Early rooms—especially the "St. Croix" and "A Winter's Ball" rooms—focused on broadening and correcting historical narratives inspired by the musical's depiction. Later rooms, however, leaned more heavily on institutions and political leaders, and less on social history.

Acknowledging Slavery in the St. Croix Room

After the opening video's upbeat message, visitors moved down a dark hallway to the "St. Croix" room. This room confronted the realities of early economics and slavery in the American colonies by merging Hamilton's participation in the system of slavery with additional information about enslaved persons and the injustices suffered in this economic system. The room was dominated by a larger-than-life set of scales: the left with a bed and small possessions, and the right with a single barrel. The audionarration explained that the single barrel of sugar was worth more than all of a young Alexander Hamilton's possessions. As we beheld the massive scale, easily more than 12 feet high, the narration explained that Hamilton's young life was connected to the system of enslavement in the Americas. Underneath the scales, closer inspection revealed rum casks sunk into a water-filled opening in the floor. The casks offered brief information about slavery when flash-lit for a few seconds at a time: "At least 10 million Africans were shipped by force to the New World," "The unpaid labor of millions of [enslaved persons] created the Caribbean economic power-house of the 1700s," and excerpts of laws punishing enslaved persons. These flashes invited visitors to see this history as hidden, murky, and needing to be uncovered with the light of truth. Hamilton's world, we learn from a large placard, was controlled by white Europeans although the majority of people were Black Africans: "The mass of population—roughly nine out of every ten people—consist[ed] of enslaved Africans. A tiny percentage escaped to nearby Spanish-administered Puerto Rico where they formed free communities though they faced dire punishment if caught." Around the room, which is set as a storehouse, the walls have reproduced images of drawings and paintings from St. Croix and the Caribbean of enslaved persons working, and of newspaper clippings advertising punishments for those who resisted and fled.

While the autoplayed narration largely focused on Hamilton, the additional narrations available to visitors added recognition to the horrors of slavery on African lives and culture. For example, a narration by Jackson and Soo explained how those who owned Africans considered them "replaceable," and "worked them to death," and that enslavement "robbed" people of "identity and culture." Another narration accompanied a digital map that lit up to show "exchange and movement of goods, products, and people between Europe, Africa, the Caribbean, and America." The narration began with a description of the "new world" as accessible to anyone who made the journey, but the end contained a description of how eighteenth-century science wrongly justified beliefs of racism (white over Black) and sexism (men over women), meaning that "anyone" was, in fact, exclusionary.

The opening room is worth reviewing in such detail because, as the first impressive set-filled room, it set expectations for what visitors would encounter in terms of the visual depiction, the audio narration guiding us through the rooms, and the optional narrations and displays to examine. For Drury, the first room displayed the rhetorical interplay of *Hamilton* the musical and Alexander Hamilton in U.S. history that also featured in subsequent rooms throughout the exhibition. In the audionarration, Miranda reminded visitors that throughout the exhibition there are small framed facts about the real-life people and places of *Hamilton*. These placards were set in plain wood frames, a stark white paper with black text, in a font similar to courier. In the St. Croix room, the placard read, "The real Hamilton wasn't an abolitionist, but he did oppose slavery. Being anti-slavery served as a common cause with his closest friend, John Laurens." Across the room, a sign discussing "Slavery and Resistance" noted that Rachel Faucette, Hamilton's mother, "was a slave owner." It proceeded to say that Hamilton was "never an aggressive anti-slavery advocate," but rather "like a number of the wealthy white American founders, he favored a very gradual emancipation of the enslaved." Here, the exhibition corrected the historical record of the musical, introducing Hamilton's record on slavery alongside his origin story in St. Croix. The interplay of audio guidance to history with Miranda's framed "corrections" sprinkled throughout the exhibition prompted visitors to engage in critical reflection about the ways the musical glossed over or even ignored history.

No other room in the exhibition focused so extensively on the experiences of enslavement. Unlike many of the other rooms that would follow, in the "St. Croix" room, Williams felt a connection. He explained, *This room functioned to acknowledge, but not display, the horrors of slavery inflicted upon enslaved Africans. This was important because the St. Croix room was the primary means of conveying the history and lives of millions of African Americans, through words on placards, through phrases lighting up under murky water for a few seconds, or through a document of enslaved persons laying on a reproduction of a merchant's desk.* Williams reflected that he wanted to see the realities of slavery, because *for myself and many others, slavery could not be defined in those few quick words under murky water; slavery was people's lives, culture, and my history.*

Experiencing Social History

Some rooms openly provoked a tension between the materiality of walking through what seemed inspired by the musical's set design and the broader social history. For example, in the third room focusing on New York City just prior to the Revolution, Miranda invited us to "join" him in walking down the wooden structure from the ship into New York City—just like he does every night in the show, as he reminded us. Visitors lingered at this stage, with many arranging photographs of themselves, and resulting in the only human traffic jam that Drury experienced in her two visits to the exhibition. This physical experience was all about the musical, the staging, and putting ourselves into the role of Alexander Hamilton. However, the larger room portrayed a more diverse and vibrant history of New York City and early America. Bright blue walls were crowded with replicated portraits, paintings, and pamphlets of the period—beginning as you enter with a portrait of King George III, then proceeding to include images of well-known figures such as John Adams, Abigail Adams, and Benjamin Franklin, as well as figures depicted in the musical such as James Madison, Samuel Seabury, and Aaron Burr. Other portraits depict people that would be familiar to those studying the revolutionary period, but perhaps less well known: Son of Liberty Sam Adams, Hamilton's mentors William Livingston and Elias Boudinot, president of King's College Myles Cooper, and Loyalist James Revington who published Hamilton's *The Farmer Refuted* pamphlet in 1775. Each wall also had one or two portraits of a white woman, a Black man, and/or a Black woman. The three portraits of white women documented their political voices, whether Penelope Barker's "first known political demonstration by American women" boycotting British tea, or the political opinions and writings of Abigail Adams and Mercy Otis Warren. The descriptions of the three Black portraits in the room drew attention to slavery and its impact on participation in public life: Crispus Attucks, a "formerly enslaved man who had liberated himself 20 years earlier," Peter Williams Sr, an "enslaved New Yorker" who joined the Continental Army, was "sold" to members of the John Street Methodist Episcopal Church, and then had to buy his own freedom, and Phillis Wheatley, an enslaved woman who is celebrated in the description for her book of poems, "praised on both sides of the Atlantic."

While these portraits and placards offer a breadth of perspectives, the presentation takes time to engage. The room decor is crowded, with the portraits, paintings, replications of documents, and placards stacked in columns on tall walls. In our observations, few visitors stopped to read all of the placards or portraits. Furthermore, in order to read the material, a visitor had to stop listening to the narrated guide. Even with the "traffic jam" mentioned due to the physical exhibition structure, the narration still took time. Then, most people visiting seemed in awe of the room, glancing around at the various images of portraits, paintings depicting the conflicts leading up to the Revolutionary War, and historical timeline markers of the classic pre-revolution acts—the Stamp Act, Sugar Act, Tea Act, and Intolerable Acts featured in U.S. history textbooks. For Drury, this part of the exhibition felt rushed and overwhelming: *With the narration playing, it was hard to take time to read placards and not feel like I was holding up the line. I was torn between enjoying Miranda's references to the musical and experiencing the room from my Hamilfan perspective, and absorbing the images, placards, and models in the room. The first time I visited, I felt rushed, maybe because it was a room that was crowded. People around me seemed to struggle with how to process the different information sources—the placards, multiple audionarrations, and even mediated touch screens at the far side of the room. It did not seem like many people took enough time to read and listen to everything. The second time I visited, I ignored the recordings and more closely read the placards, but I had the experience of feeling like I was holding others up as they stepped around me.* An unfortunate consequence of the many display points throughout the room is that a visitor could easily miss the diverse voices (for example, a profile on Thayendanegea, an Indigenous Mohawk military leader, had to be accessed through a media screen on the side of the room).

As we traveled through the exhibition, we found ourselves drawn to acts of inclusion and recovery that interplayed the Hamilton narrative with broader representation. For example, in the room depicting George Washington's military headquarters, Williams immediately noticed the backlit portrait of Washington, which displayed a Black man, in a red headcovering, on a horse standing behind Washington's shoulder. This portrait drew our eyes, perhaps because of the lyric above it proclaiming "Here comes the general!" But it also drew our further attention because the Black man was not identified in the audio guide, nor discussed in a placard like the portraits in New York.

This became a powerful moment in the exhibition for our experiences thinking about what histories were presented and explained. Williams reflected, *When I saw that kid, with the first President of the United States, I immediately had to find out who he was and what he was doing there. To be honest, I have never seen George Washington pictured with any African Americans, especially a young African slave boy. I wanted to know this boy's name, his origin, his story, but then it kind of made me think of the many Black stories that are not told and have been lost.* Based on our later research, we learned that the portrait was a replication of John Trumbell's 1780 depiction of Washington and William Lee, an enslaved "valet, groom, and military aide."[33] Although Lee would later be depicted in the ballroom scene, this seemed a lost opportunity to tell his story alongside that of the military men of the musical—Washington, Hamilton, John Laurens, and the Marquis de Lafayette. The celebration of telling the story of the men in the musical seemed to dominate the rooms of the exhibition focused on Washington and the Continental Army.

The fulsome focus on social history and diverse perspectives was also created in the "A Winter's Ball" scene. The audionarration informed us that this was a fictional scene, but we were invited to meet the "real people who inspired" the characters in the musical. Inside the room, bronze, life-size statues were arranged in small circles of guests. The statues of Hamilton and Washington were most crowded, with visitors stopping to take selfies and photographs.

A compelling example of how the exhibition created opportunities for inclusion was the first figure that visitors would encounter if they entered the room and turned to their left. This figure was a Black woman, labeled "Unknown," and holding a serving tray. After pointing to the "Unknown" label, the audionarration questioned, "Who was this young woman? Was she born in New York, or kidnapped in Africa, sold in the Caribbean, and then again in New York?" It went on to cite statistics on slavery, such as that one in every five Americans in this period was enslaved, a total of half a million people, "their lives stolen, their identities lost." As Rachel Cristine Woody noted in *The Public Historian*

> In place of where her story should be (had it been kept) the audio uses known historical details of the time to create a composite sketch ... there are known historical accounts from those who experienced being enslaved during this time curators might have used, but the composite approach prompts visitors to consider how historians use sources to write history.[34]

The story of "Unknown" in this room confronted us to recall the earlier scenes, like the room of "St. Croix," and made Williams wonder again about the Black man pictured earlier with Washington. While we did not know it at the time, we later put together that this room contained a statue of Lee, the man depicted in Trumbull's painting. In the ballroom, Lee stands near Washington, and his story is available to be heard. Williams explained how the exhibition missed an opportunity to tell Lee's story more fully in both places: *After researching Trumbull's painting and connecting it to Lee's statue, it was exciting to realize there was a minor Black perspective storyline throughout the exhibition. But in reflection, I wish Lee's story had been told in more than one place; I believe many others (particularly those not looking for Lee's story or representation) may have missed out on a major part of American history.*

The ballroom was a compelling interplay of histories, but because of the many narrations in the room, visitors could—and likely did—miss some of the presentations. The narrations of several characters centralized the social and economic systems of slavery. If one were not to select the "Unknown" woman as the first audionarration of choice in the room, one might turn to one of two men that you would encounter next. These figures also drew attention to the ways that the wealth and comfort of a ball like this one would have relied on the unpaid labor of enslaved persons: The narration of Philip Schuyler noted that he made his fortune "on the backs" of those enslaved and John Laurens' narration discussed his commitment to antislavery. But like the "New York City" room, visitors needed a substantial amount of time to experience the more than a dozen narrations. This room seemed designed to have a variable amount of time for visitors, since it was a holding room for the subsequent tabletop performance of the battle of Yorktown. Since that performance was timed, visitors had to be called by a staff member to enter. We mention that because this room contained the largest number of optional audionarrations, many of which offered a fuller look at social history. It is unfortunate that many visitors seemed to take a photograph with a prominent figure, listen to a narration, and then be called to move on. Despite the variance in visitor experience, the ballroom's individual statute narrations used historical figures to deepen understandings of race (through the Unknown, Lee, Schuyler, and Laurens statues) and gender (through Martha Washington and the Schuylers statues) alongside the biographies of figures like Washington and Hamilton.

The Exhibition's Institutional Turn

After establishing the most robust social and cultural history that led to the Revolution in these early rooms of the exhibition, subsequent rooms coalesced around an increasingly institutional and Hamilton-centric narrative. After the Revolutionary War, the rooms focused on the Constitutional Convention, federalist debates, and early U.S. government, with the later rooms focusing on the rivalry and duel between Hamilton and Burr. The institutional narrative of the exhibition functioned to downplay individual voices, which in many ways created a jarring experience from the social-political narratives in the early part of the exhibition.

This institutional history narrative became apparent after visitors experienced a live, table-top model of the battle of Yorktown, and traveled through the aforementioned King George III neon pink room to arrive in a room focusing on the founding of the U.S. government. The musical's references to the Constitutional Convention were briefly contained in the song "Non-Stop," with a section on Hamilton's proposal of "his own form of government" while talking for "six hours," and then an interlude about the *Federalist Papers*.[35] The "American Experiment" was a long rectangular room, with wall displays depicting gears and industry as representations of the states' struggle to form a nation that worked together. Along the walls were also placards, portraits, and a few cases with replicated documents. The room was full of small movements symbolizing a nation at work to build institutions of government—for example, the center floorboard was glass, with two ropes that slowly moved in the direction of visitor traffic, with black brick-style placards featuring key events and dates chronologically laid to mark the tumultuous years before the adoption of the U.S. Constitution. Along the walls, gears turned, ropes moved, and a map of the "disunited states" separated and came together along political and trade alliances.

The social history of earlier rooms was relegated to small placard and portrait displays in this room. The perspectives of those outside leadership were present, although the vibrant and moving design of the rest of the room deemphasized small displays on contributions of women, Indigenous persons, and Black Americans. Perhaps most notably, a single placard, titled "The Three-Fifths Compromise," discussed the debate over slavery with a description that swept broadly over Black history in the United States:

> The infamous Three-Fifths Compromise treated the enslaved as a combination of property and human being . . . Neither the word 'slavery' or 'slave' appears in the Constitution. In the 1860s, slavery led to the breakup of the Union and a bloody, traumatizing Civil War. A century later, the Civil Rights Movement struggled to resolve these profound divisions. Today, the same fundamental fault lines are visible in the systemic racism faced by people of color.

Having just a single placard on a side wall deemphasized the history of and debate over slavery in the founding. Unlike the "St. Croix" room at the beginning, it also largely left out the lived horrors of slavery. A more fulsome account could have included, for example, words and examples from Black Americans at that time. Another perspective would have been to include the debate over slavery as a more prominent part of the Constitutional Convention. The narration could have drawn on the words of those who protested against provisions in the Constitution to protect slavery, such as abolitionist and anti-Federalist Samuel Bryan, whose writing is cited in Nikole Hannah-Jones' 1619 Project in the *New York Times*: "These words are dark and ambiguous; such as no plain man of common sense would have used, [and] are evidently chosen to conceal from Europe, that in this enlightened country, the practice of slavery has its advocates among men in the highest stations."[36]

In rooms depicting the early U.S. government's policies, the institutional narrative even suggested that the nation was less based on principles, or political debate and compromise, but instead a game of chance and luck. The lyric "Winning was Easy, Governing's Harder" transitioned visitors from viewing the Federalist debates into the work of governing the new nation. In a room that was extremely busy—and popular with younger children for its interactivity—the impacts of early government policies were depicted in carnival style games of chance, such as a wheel of fortune for "where to put the capital" and a disc drop game that demonstrated how citizens would struggle to redeem government-issued money and bonds as they experienced speculation and economic depression. In the room focusing on the banking system, the audionarration explained that visitors could turn cranks at "a branch" of the national bank to purchase stock; turning the crank raised and released a ball into a complex metal maze that ultimately deposited the ball into the economic center of the room. Given the "game" style displays, we as visitors found ourselves focusing less on historical lessons in this section, as Drury explained: *This is the part of the exhibit where young people seem the most engaged, but* not in absorbing historical, political information. The displays depict government as a game. Even the fact that one of the drop disc games was broken both times I visited contributes to it seeming like governance is frivolous, and that this system was not reliable. There seemed a missed opportunity here to expand the scope of early U.S. government away from Hamilton, bringing in other leaders and voices.

Like the end of the musical, the end of the exhibition largely focused on the events leading up to Hamilton's death and therefore represent more of a leadership-focused history without much attention to groups outside of Hamilton and his associates. The final room is an incredible visual display—bronze statues of Hamilton and Burr stand, guns drawn at one another (and yes, Hamilton is "wearing his glasses"[37]). The room's primary textual display was a timeline of Hamilton's final 32 hours, and Burr's 32 years of life after the duel. While a moving and historically fascinating display, the end of the exhibition drew things together with an emphasis on Hamilton's death and legacy.

As the exhibition moved through the timeline of the Revolution to the founding of the U.S. government, there was a shift in focus. In the earliest rooms, there was more of an emphasis on Black and female voices of history, including the horrors of the system of slavery. Later rooms of the exhibition, however, replaced these voices by an institutional focus on creating systems of governance. It is perhaps a testament to the exhibition's inclusion that we, after visiting, found ourselves researching various figures from history unfamiliar to us, such as William Lee and Peter Williams Sr. At the beginning of the exhibition, the narration proclaimed to visitors that this is *our* history—it is, but it is also a history presented in pathways for the visitor, with opportunities to engage or bypass, to discover or miss.

LOSING AND FINDING OURSELVES IN THE EXHIBITION'S STORY OF AMERICA

From its initial staging, *Hamilton* has provoked a tension of honoring and celebrating a group of Founding Fathers while (largely) ignoring the histories of marginalized people, particularly in the system of slavery in the American colonies and United States. Historian Patricia Herrera captured this tension writing about her experiences with the show, that the music "allowed" her as a "Latinx woman, to see a sliver of myself in the nation's origin story" while simultaneously drawing concern about using the genre of hip-hop "to narrate a founding story that doesn't, in fact, fully grapple with the legacies of slavery and racism."[38] The release of *Hamilton: An American Musical* on July 3, 2020, on the streaming platform Disney+ occurred after weeks of what might be the "largest movement in history" and national protests in support of Black Lives Matter.[39] We mention this widescale release of the streaming musical because the subsequent discussion about the legacy and implications of *Hamilton* reflects a similar controversy over whether to celebrate a work of art that celebrates the vision of the U.S. government, a vision that offered liberty and representative government to white men while continuing a system that enslaved thousands of Africans.[40]

Hamilton: The Exhibition invited this tension by its own framing of America's story as created by and for everyone. For fans of the musical or those interested in the Revolution and founding period, the exhibition corrected changes in the musical and offered a greater understanding, supported by historians, replicated documents, and diverse voices. But it also struggled to connect the founding to contemporary culture and diversity. After seeing the musical in Chicago, Williams reflected, *Experiencing the musical was different than experiencing the exhibition. The musical connects and resembles Black attributes, physically and culturally. I felt like the musical was familiar, relating to many factors, because elements resembled my own culture, especially in music (3 part female harmonies that I have heard in Black church), performance (African American style dancing), and in appearance of characters (particularly with natural Black hair). All of these are celebrations of Black success, and there were points in the musical when I wanted to cheer seeing it onstage.* When compared to the exhibition, Black history seemed the exception, and Williams felt excluded, nonexistent in the narrative. One of Drury's reflections took stock of how Hamilfans may have experienced the exhibition, separating an appreciation for the musical from a more critical look at historical presentation: *For fans, the musical soundtrack connected to a broader history, inviting visitors to think critically about Hamilton and other leaders in the founding. The historical correction placards were a "find them all" sort of game throughout the exhibition. But like the musical, the exhibition too makes choices on what to include, what to acknowledge, and what to celebrate.*

The penultimate room asked visitors to participate in leaving their legacy (the final room is a video presentation of the opening number of *Hamilton*, starring Miranda in the title role but not with the original Broadway cast). The "Legacy" room featured an early nineteenth century writing desk and chair, and an artistic rendering of large, scrolled paper that began behind the desk and ascended upward in a swirling pattern. On the far wall were three large ink-blot shaped designs, covered with post-it notes, that asked the questions "What would you improve about America?" "What is your wish for America?" and "How can democracy do better?" Historian Freeman's narration stressed to visitors that a central legacy of Hamilton is that Hamilton and those around him in the founding are an example of the importance of robust debate, clash, and creating "better" outcomes. The final line of the audionarration is Chris Jackson, channeling his own line as Washington from the musical to "Pick up a pen, start writing—add *your* ideas to *our* story." This last theme of the exhibition emphasized carrying each visitor's ideas forward, changing with each day as post-it notes were removed and replenished by visitors. In adding visitor ideas to "our" story, Hamilton: The Exhibition ended by writing legacies of an American experiment in politics, one that did not always include "everyone" in the past, but opened possibilities for such inclusion in our future.

NOTES

1 Sara A. Mehltretter Drury, Associate Professor, Wabash College, drurys@wabash.edu; James Anthony Williams Jr., graduate, Wabash College, jawillia20@wabash.edu.
2 Lin-Manuel Miranda and Jeremy McCarter, *Hamilton: The Revolution* (New York, NY: Grand Central Publishing, 2016), 120.
3 Chris Jones, "Did It Fail Us or Did We Fail It? Why 'Hamilton: The Exhibition' Is Closing Early in Chicago," *Chicago Tribune*, July 30, 2019, https://www.chicagotribune.com/entertainment/theater/chris-jones/ct-ent-hamilton-exhibit-closes-why-jones-0804-20190731-sxuddwbtyvajzljlqlxjvhrhy4-story.html.
4 Michael Paulson, "A New Kind of 'Hamilton' Show, This Time on Lake Michigan," *New York Times*, April 29, 2019. https://www.nytimes.com/2019/04/29/theater/hamilton-exhibition-chicago.html; Ryan McPhee, "*Hamilton* Exhibition Launches in Chicago on April 27," *Playbill*, April 27, 2019, https://www.playbill.com/article/hamilton-exhibit-launches-in-chicago-april-27.
5 Kris Vire, "The *Hamilton* Exhibition Was Doomed from the Start," *Chicago Magazine*, July 31, 2019, http://www.chicagomag.com/arts-culture/August-2019/The-Hamilton-Exhibition-Was-Doomed-From-The-Start.
6 Quotation from the audionarration of Hamilton: The Exhibition, transcribed by Sara A. Mehltretter Drury. See also Paulson, "A New Kind of 'Hamilton' Show."
7 Carole Blair and Neil Michel, "Commemorating in the Theme Park Zone: Reading the Astronauts Memorial," in *At the Intersection: Cultural Studies and Rhetorical Studies*, ed. Thomas Rosteck (New York: Guilford Press, 1999), 29–83; Phaedra C. Pezzullo, "Touring 'Cancer Alley,' Louisiana: Performances of Community and Memory for Environmental Justice," *Text and Performance Quarterly* 23 (2003): 226–52, https://doi.org/10.1080/10462930310001635295; Phaedra C. Pezzullo, "Tourists and/as Disasters: Rebuilding, Remembering, and Responsibility in New Orleans," *Tourist Studies* 9 (2009): 23–41, https://doi.org/10.1177%2F1468797609360591; Ellen W. Gorsevski, Raymond I. Schuk, and Canchu Lin, "The Rhetorical Plasticity of the Dead in Museum Displays: A Biocritique of Missing Intercultural Awareness," *Western Journal of Communication* 76 (2012): 314–22, https://doi.org/10.1080/10570314.2012.654888; Andre E. Johnson, "Teaching in Ferguson: A Rhetorical Autoethnography from a Scholar/Activist," *Southern Communication Journal* 81 (2016): 267–69.
8 Greg Dickinson, Brian L. Ott, and Eric Aoki, "Spaces of Remembering and Forgetting: The Reverent Eye/I at the Plains Indian Museum," *Communication and Critical/Cultural Studies* 3 (2006): 29.
9 Carole Blair, Greg Dickinson, and Brian L. Ott, "Introduction: Rhetoric/Memory/Place," in *Places of Public Memory*, eds. Greg Dickinson, Carole Blair, and Brian L. Ott (Tuscaloosa: The University of Alabama Press, 2010), 9.
10 Kenneth S. Zagacki and Victoria J. Gallagher, "Rhetoric and Materiality in the Museum Park at the North Carolina Museum of Art," *Quarterly Journal of Speech* 95 (2009): 171–72, https://doi.org/10.1080/00335630902842087.

11 Brian L. Ott, "Editor's Introduction," *Western Journal of Communication* 74 (2010): 127, https://doi.org/10.1080/10570311003617198.
12 Zagacki and Gallagher, "Rhetoric and Materiality in the Museum Park at the North Carolina Museum of Art," 172. See also Carole Blair, "Contemporary U.S. Memorial Sites as Exemplars of Rhetoric's Materiality," in *Rhetorical Bodies*, eds. Jack Selzer and Sharon Crowley (Madison: University of Wisconsin Press, 1999), 16–57.
13 Dickinson, Ott, and Aoki, "Spaces of Remembering and Forgetting," 29–30.
14 Tamar Katriel, "Sites of Memory: Discourses of the Past in Israeli Pioneering Settlements," *Quarterly Journal of Speech* 80 (1994): 17.
15 Bernard J. Armada, "Memorial Agon: An Interpretative Tour of the National Civil Rights Museum," *Southern Journal of Communication* 63 (1998): 235–43, https://doi.org/10.1080/10417949809373096; Carole Blair and Neil Michel, "Reproducing Civil Rights Tactics: The Rhetorical Performances of the Civil Rights Memorial," *Rhetoric Society Quarterly* 30 (2000): 31–55; Deborah F. Atwater and Sandra L. Hernon, "Cultural Space and Race: The National Civil Rights Museum and MuseumAfrica," *Howard Journal of Communication* 14 (2003): 15–28.
16 Roger C. Aden, *Upon the Ruins of Liberty: Slavery, the President's House at Independence National Historical Park, and Public Memory* (Philadelphia, PA: Temple University Press, 2015), 6.
17 Atwater and Herndon, "Cultural Space and Race," 15–28.
18 Patricia Davis, "Memoryscapes in Transition: Black History Museums, New South Narratives, and Urban Regeneration," *Southern Communication Journal* 78 (2013): 108, https://doi.org/10.1080/1041794X.2012.729125.
19 Victoria J. Gallagher, "Memory and Reconciliation in the Birmingham Civil Rights Institute," *Rhetoric & Public Affairs* 2 (1999): 304.
20 Megan Irene Fitzmaurice, "Commemorative Privilege in National Statuary Hall: Spatial Constructions of Racial Citizenship," *Southern Communication Journal* 81 (2016): 253.
21 Quotation from the opening video at Hamilton: The Exhibition, transcribed by Sara A. Mehltretter Drury.
22 Robin M. Boylorn and Mark P. Orbe, "Introduction: Critical Autoethnography as Method of Choice," in *Critical Autoethnography: Intersecting Cultural Identities in Everyday Life*, eds. Robin M. Boylorn and Mark P. Orbe (Walnut Creek, CA: Left Coast Press, 2014), 17. See also Brenda J. Allen, Mark P. Orbe, and Margarita Refugia Olivas, "The Complexity of Our Tears: Dis/enchantment and (In)Difference in the Academy," *Communication Theory* 9 (1999): 402–29.
23 Brett Lunceford, "Rhetorical Ethnography," *Journal of Contemporary Rhetoric* 5 (2015): 17.
24 Blair and Michel, "Commemorating in the Theme Park Zone"; Johnson, "Teaching in Ferguson," 267–69.
25 Aden, *Upon the Ruins of Libery*, 14–15.
26 Vire, "The *Hamilton* Exhibition was Doomed from the Start."
27 Lunceford, "Rhetorical Ethnography," 20.
28 "Hamilton: The Exhibition FAQ," *The Hamilton Exhibition*, accessed July 5, 2020, https://hamiltonexhibition.com/faq.
29 "Staff for Hamilton: The Exhibition" [placard]. Presented at Hamilton: The Exhibition, visited August 25, 2019.
30 This quotation and subsequent audionarrations are from Hamilton: The Exhibition, transcribed by Sara A. Mehltretter Drury.
31 Rachael Cristine Woody noted for a review in *Public Historian* that "the historical items on display . . . are reproductions," going on to suggest that the hope was to stabilize the HVAC of the

facility enough to have historical documents present, but that this did not occur. Rachael Cristine Woody, "Exhibit Review: *Hamilton: The Exhibition*," *Public Historian* 42 (2020): 126–32.

32 Edward Delman, "How Lin-Manuel Miranda Shapes History," *The Atlantic*, September 29, 2015, https://www.theatlantic.com/entertainment/archive/2015/09/lin-manuel-miranda-hamilton/408019.

33 "George Washington and William Lee," The Metropolitan Museum of Art, accessed July 10, 2020, https://www.metmuseum.org/art/collection/search/12822.

34 Woody, "Exhibit Review: *Hamilton: The Exhibition*," 132.

35 Miranda and McCarter, *Hamilton: The Revolution*, 138.

36 Nikole Hannah-Jones, "Our Democracy's Founding Ideals Were False When They Were Written. Black Americans Have Fought to Make Them True," 1619 Project, *New York Times*, August 14, 2019, https://www.nytimes.com/interactive/2019/08/14/magazine/black-history-american-democracy.html.

37 Miranda and McCarter, *Hamilton: The Revolution*, 272.

38 Patricia Herrera, "Reckoning with America's Racial Past, Present, and Future in *Hamilton*," in *Historians on Hamilton: How a Blockbuster Musical Is Restaging America's Past*, eds. Renee C. Romano and Claire Bond Potter (New Brunswick, NJ: Rutgers University Press, 2018), 260–62.

39 According to the *New York Times*, more than half a million people protested on June 6; estimates of the total number of people who participated in a protest ranges from 15–26 million. See Larry Buchanan, Quoctrung Bui, and Jugal K. Patel, "Black Lives Matter May Be the Largest Protest Movement in U.S. History," *New York Times*, July 3, 2020, https://www.nytimes.com/interactive/2020/07/03/us/george-floyd-protests-crowd-size.html.

40 Terry Gross, "The Past Isn't Done with Us," June 29, 2020, in *Fresh Air*, produced by Lauren Krenzel and Seth Kelley, radio show and podcast, NPR, https://www.npr.org/2020/06/29/884592985/the-past-isn-t-done-with-us-says-hamilton-creator-lin-manuel-miranda. See also Aja Romano, "Why *Hamilton* Is as Frustrating as It Is Brilliant—And Impossible to Pin Down," *Vox*, July 3, 2020, https://www.vox.com/culture/21305967/hamilton-debate-controversy-historical-accuracy-explained.

PART TWO

Hamilton and Rhetoric of Social Identity

CHAPTER FIVE

Hamilton as Cosmogonic Myth

CHRISTOPHER BELL[1]

It has been said that "God made man because He loves stories."[2] Myth lies at the core of everything that might be considered "civilization"; the stories that are told within any culture that explain the nature of life and death, of love, and war may vary from one nation to the next, but the social function of those stories is relatively universal. Myths are designed to provide meaning, structure, and explanation to the world in which we live. Myths tell us who we are, who we should be, and why.

American culture is as steeped in myth as any other civilization. Take, for example, the case of Alexander Hamilton. As a person, Hamilton's achievements are certainly impressive and delineated in great detail elsewhere in this volume; from serving in the first Continental Congress to drafting far more than his fair share of *The Federalist Papers* to founding the U.S. Mint and the first national bank as the inaugural Secretary of the Treasury, Hamilton's legacy can be qualified as nearly unmatched. Still, despite founding institutions from the U.S. Coast Guard to the *New York Post*, for many Americans Alexander Hamilton has been recognized as little more than "that guy on the ten dollar bill."

This is peculiar, as there may be no more favorite myth of the American people than that of the "Founding Fathers." This myth, full of legendary characters and their seemingly infallible, timeless wisdom and heroic actions, is at the core of how we, as a people, understand the history of the country. The stories of these men, often referred to collectively as the American Monomyth, are full of "monomythic heroes that best personif[y] the way Americans wish to see themselves—youthful, physically vigorous, morally upright."³ Robert Jewett and John Shelton Lawrence define the narrative of American Monomyth:

> A community in a harmonious paradise is threatened by evil. Normal institutions fail to contend with this threat. A selfless hero emerges to renounce temptations and carry out the redemptive task, and, aided by fate, his decisive victory restores the community to its paradisal condition. The superhero then recedes into obscurity.⁴

In these monomythic stories, "the hero's struggle [is] one of vertical mobility, raising himself from humble beginnings until he had forced society to recognize him as a successful individual."⁵ Alexander Hamilton seems to fit this mold nicely. Lin-Manuel Miranda saw the potential in telling Hamilton's monomythic story, launching *Hamilton: An American Musical* in 2015. The story of the lone hero rising up through his own ingenuity and perseverance is a *very* familiar touchstone for the American people. This fact will figure heavily into the rest of this chapter. The main point here is that we, as a people, are very well connected to the American Monomyth. This American Monomyth has been distributed throughout our culture, from history classes to The History Channel, through a process that James Loewen refers to as *heroification*: "a degenerative process (much like calcification) that makes people over into heroes. Through this process, our educational media turn flesh-and-blood individuals into pious, perfect creatures without conflicts, pain, credibility, or human interest."⁶

Intuitively, one might think that there is no way on Earth that this show should have been successful. *A Broadway hip-hopera based on the life of America's first Secretary of the Treasury, written by a Puerto Rican, starring almost exclusively people of color?* When placed into those terms, it seems patently ridiculous. And yet, by tapping into the relationship between the American people and the centralizing mythos of our civilization, then humanizing and universalizing our most familiar monomythic characters as flawed, nuanced, even occasionally petty, Miranda was able to connect Alexander Hamilton to a distinct lineage previously removed from that centralizing mythos: that of the American immigrant. In an age of unimaginable animosity by the dying embers of a xenophobic right wing ideology toward the immigrant experience in America, Miranda's musical made a bold claim: if not for the savvy and sacrifice of the country's first immigrant hero, there would be no United States over which to fret.

I argue that the central myth upon which all of American society is predicated—that of the "Founding Fathers"—is intrinsically exclusionary for people of color, but that Miranda deftly breaks a hole in that barrier with *Hamilton* in several ways: through casting, through musical stylings, and through humanizing our culture's most sacred folk patrons. Miranda is able to perform this rhetorical reconfiguration by invoking the most unlikely of sources: the superhero story. *Hamilton* is far less of an exercise in historical accuracy and far more a classic superhero origin story. The story of *Hamilton* is a myth, but it is a myth in a very specific way. In this chapter, I will explore the way in which *Hamilton* functions as the entry point, particularly for Black and Brown people, into a complex mythos by serving as one of American culture's most basic and central discourse points: the superheroic origin story.[7]

MYTH

The term "myth" is a diminutive of the Greek word "mythos," which Aristotle defined as, "a story about the legendary past,"[8] or, more specifically, "the organization of the events" of the legendary past.[9] Embedded within the term is an underlying pejorative; myth is "used frequently to describe a popular misconception; a bubble waiting to be burst."[10] It is not that a myth is a lie, per se; a myth "is not a falsehood. Rather, a myth is a sophisticated social representation; a complex relationship between history, reality, culture, imagination, and identity."[11] A myth is a values discourse, a conversation about the enduring, persistent principles, philosophies, and standards shared by the members of a civilization regarding that which is desirable or undesirable, right or wrong, good or bad. A myth is a qualitative assessment and explanation of human thought, nature, and behavior. Think about the story of Medusa. The myth begins not with the heroism of Perseus or even some treacherous action by Medusa. The myth begins with Poseidon's infatuation with the beautiful, radiant Medusa, and her disinterest in his attention. As punishment for "spurning" Poseidon's unwanted sexual advances, Medusa (and her two sisters, for good measure) is "punished" by Poseidon—her hair is turned to snakes, her body is turned monstrous, and she is allowed to keep her beautiful face, but anyone who looks at it turns to stone. In other versions of the story, Medusa is worshipping at the temple of Athena, and Poseidon is so overcome with his attraction to her that he rapes her. In this version of the story, Athena (the virgin Goddess) is so enraged by this action that she punishes ... Medusa. Not Poseidon. There is an embedded values discourse of Greek society in both versions of the story about the place occupied by women, who should hold the power in a relationship, and what happens to women who fail to acquiesce to a powerful man. Myths serve to explain desirable and undesirable human behavior within a culture. The Medusa myth is a story of one's behavior and how to conduct one's self in the world—a story with horrific implications in modern times that would have been understood as culturally acceptable at the time of its creation.

Some myths are *cosmogonic* in nature. That is to say, some myths are designed to explain the creation of order within worlds—they are an offshoot of *creation myths*. The cosmogonic myth "is the myth which establishes the order of the world and thus has important social, material, and economic ramifications as well as deep religious significance."[12] Cosmogonies are a specific type of creation myth, one which expands beyond a mere account of the creation of the world into an expression of the relative structure of the world. It is not a simple demonstration of how the world came to be, but a careful elucidation of why things are the way that they are. A cosmogonic myth is a deeply sacred story, set in the past, in other worlds or other parts of the world, featuring superhuman, inhuman, or heroic characters. "The Big Bang" is a creation story, for example, but it is not a cosmogonic myth, as it lacks an agentic actor; the story has no characters. The cosmogonic myth is designed to explain to us the creation of the world, and our place in the universe.[13] Eliade and Halperin offer, "Man progressively occupies increasingly vast areas of the planet and 'cosmocizes' them in accordance with the model revealed by the cosmogonical myth. Thanks to this myth, man also becomes a creator."[14]

Our cosmogonies are creation myths that explain how we transitioned from the abyss of nothingness into the existence of the civilized world. Classic cosmogonies range from the story of Adam and Eve to the ritual sacrifice of Prometheus to Theodore Roosevelt's mythic frontiersmanship.[15] In modern days, we bear witness to cosmogonies all the time; we simply refer to them with a different label: A child is placed in a vessel in order to save him from the death of his planet, and he is jettisoned into space where he slumbers until he crashes on the planet Earth, is rescued by farmers, and raised in Kansas as "Clark Kent"; Peter Parker is bitten by a radioactive spider, gains the relative strength and abilities of the spider, and then makes a decision to use his powers for good following the death of his Uncle Ben due to Peter's own negligence. Both of these stories are cosmogonic in nature; they are the stories that order the worlds in which those stories take place. A reader understands the parameters of the alternate universe in which the *Superman* mythos takes place by the end of *Action Comics #1*. Similarly, the cosmogony of the *Spider-Man* universe is laid out in full detail in *Amazing Fantasy #15*.

I refer to these stories as cosmogonies, but in the world of superhero narratives, we also call these *origin stories*. They serve the same function within those specific story universes as cosmogonies serve in ours. Superheroes, after all, are our own idealized exemplars of justice, serving as both role models and inspirations. Their origin stories definitionally contain the same elements: superhuman characters, set in the past (not always our past, as the reader, but the character's past) and in other worlds (alternate universes), and held sacred by those who revere the mythos. Hatfield, Heer, and Worcester define a superhero origin story as, "a bedrock account of the transformative events that set the protagonist apart from ordinary humanity ...[a story about] transformation, about identity, about difference, and about the tension between psychological rigidity and a flexible and fluid sense of human nature."[16] In this sense, the origin story is the tale that gives order and structure to the universe in which the story takes place; it is inherently cosmogonic.[17] We read Wonder Woman's origin story, and we understand the rules and structure of the universe in which that story takes place: Diana is gifted the power of several Greek gods and demigods, wins the trials of her mother in order to take possession of the magic girdle, bracelets, and lasso that give her many of her skills, and is sent away from Amazonia[18] to gain understanding of the world of men. That cosmogonic story contains everything we need to know: that gods are real in this universe, that there is magic, that Amazonia exists, and so on. We are readily able to connect to popular cultural cosmogonies because we are well versed in how to spot an origin story. We have been doing it, as a civilization, for a very, very long time.

It therefore makes sense that American cultural connection to the founding of the country serves as our own cosmogony: this sacred story from our past of a group of superheroic men who came together to create the basis for our civilization. Their names are mythical to us: Benjamin Franklin, Thomas Jefferson, Paul Revere, George Washington. We are culturally instructed to picture these men in very specific ways, as demonstrated by the paintings of John Trumbull. In Trumbull's paintings, very well-mannered white men sit and stand together in harmony to decide how great this country is going to be for the next nearly 400 years. I would argue that, in contemporary times, the "Founders" are no longer real, historical people; instead, we now experience them as largely fictional characters in the cosmogonic myth of the founding of America. The reality of these people is that many of them intensely disliked, even hated, each other; they were mean to each other, and made up lies about each other, and bore very little resemblance to Trumbull's paintings. In fact, Lin-Manuel Miranda included a song in early drafts of *Hamilton* titled "No John Trumbull," in which he makes this same point.[19]

To insinuate the "Founding Fathers" as somehow monolithic or in complete agreement on the nature of the republic they were creating for the future is to totally ignore historicity. Some at the Constitutional Convention, for example, found the idea of an armed citizenry to be dangerous and ridiculous, despite the eventual adoption of the Second Amendment. Hamilton himself argued against presidential terms, proposing that the president serve for life. But contemporary retellings of the "Founding Fathers" story are not intended to be historical; they are intended to be mythological. They are the cosmogonic mythos of the country's superheroic origin story.

SUPERHEROES AND ORIGINS

The "Founders" are easily connected to classic superhero tropes and narratives because of the nature of myth, particularly cosmogonic myth. As previously stated, cosmogonies require superheroic characters, whether those characters be Clark Kent or Alexander Hamilton. A superhero is, by definition:

> Superhero (soo'per hîr'o) *n., pl.* -roes. 1. A heroic character with a universal, selfless, prosocial mission; who possesses superpowers—extraordinary abilities, advanced technology, or highly developed physical, mental, or mystical skills; who has a superhero identity embodied in a codename and iconic costume, which typically express their biography or character, powers, and origin (transformation from ordinary person to superhero); and who is generically distinct, i.e. can be distinguished from characters of related genres (fantasy, science fiction, detective, etc.) by a preponderance of generic conventions. Often superheroes have dual identities, the ordinary one of which is usually a closely guarded secret—**superheroic,** *adj.* Also **super hero, super-hero.**[20]

Much of the American mythos is designed to port these qualities directly onto the "Founders," particularly men like George Washington. One can easily access imagery of Washington in his "iconic costume": blue and gold military jacket, white ruffled cravat, powdered wig, and tri-cornered hat. Washington is imbued by historical legend with near superhuman strategic, diplomatic, and organizational abilities, and a strength of character unmatched by even his contemporaries. He is not just a historical superhero; for America, he is *the* historical superhero—definitionally.

Every superhero requires an origin story, that narrative staple which establishes the rules of the superhero's universe, the nature and extent of the hero's powers, and the important relationships by which the hero will navigate his or her story. "The spectacle of witnessing a character's origin or primal scene is strong in the superhero narrative"[21] because of the establishing principles—if one understands the origin story, then one understands the nature of the superhero at hand. These origin stories are often tied to Joseph Campbell's classical monomyth, but not always (although the monomyth certainly provides a particular saliency for some types of superhero origins, including those of the "Founders"). The origin story is the most important piece of superhero fiction, as it "and its 'consequences' establish the diegetic world [of the hero] once and for all."[22] In any superhero narrative, the origin story is the foundational touchstone; it "is revived again and again in order to underscore its mythical status, reinforce the stability of an otherwise chaotic diegetic universe, and, oddly enough, to present the origin as perennially new ... the origin story itself becomes infinite."[23] *Hamilton* accomplishes the incredible feat of presenting concurrent origin stories: that of Alexander Hamilton as a superheroic character, and the birth of the United States, the world's national Superman (in the eyes of its own people, at least).

Culturally, possibly because of our deep connection to cosmogonies, we tend to "demonstrate an almost obsessional preoccupation with origin stories."[24] In recent years, the nature of origin stories has taken a distinct turn toward the tragic. The nature of our relationship to our cultural cosmogonies has also shifted away from squeaky clean "I cannot tell a lie" Washington-and-the-apple-tree stories toward darker, grittier narratives in a way that can almost surely be traced to 9/11: "The traumatic origin story resonates because it reflects a shift in national consciousness following 9/11: the illusions of invulnerability and safety were shattered, and in the aftermath nationalist rhetoric reconfigured itself around concepts of resolve, revenge, and steadfastness."[25]

For example, witness the escalation of the simple origin story of Batman, from the three-panel "parents shot in a dark alleyway" 1939 original to the tortured, near-horrific displays of violence and trauma of 2019's retelling of the story in Todd Phillips' *Joker*. *Hamilton* possibly (maybe even probably) would have been successful as a Broadway musical at any time in our contemporary history; it is not as though we just started enjoying cosmogonic mythos. However, this post-9/11 turn toward infatuation with the tragic makes this historical moment especially fertile ground in which *Hamilton* could thrive. The traumatic backstory of Alexander Hamilton, with his childhood full of sickness and death, the losses of John Laurens and Phillip Hamilton, and his own demise at the hand of Aaron Burr, seems to fit directly into the historical context described by Horton. Hamilton's origin story has been stripped of the invulnerability typically afforded to "Founding Father" cosmogonies; he is flawed, and his story becomes one of, as Horton stated, both steadfastness and resolve. In Miranda's telling of the tale, Alexander Hamilton literally wills himself into prominence, through his own superheroic hard work and charisma.

RITUAL

Myths in any society are deeply tied to *ritual*. Rituals are formally ordered sets of naturalized behaviors. Myths can be performative and didactic; myths often dictate the behaviors that are expected in the transmission and perpetuation of those myths. For example, there is an entire set of ritualized behaviors that are inextricably attached to the playing of the national anthem: one is directed to stand, to remove one's hat, to face the flag, to put one's hand over one's heart (or to salute, or to stand with the hands at the sides or behind the back, depending on one's status, service, or ability), to sing-along, and so forth. Failure to perform any part of the ritual while in public is sure to draw, at the least, disapproving looks, or even commentary from others nearby. Purposely disrupting the ritual (by kneeling during the anthem, for instance) is a legitimate, rhetorical display (the song itself is one of our core cosmogonies, detailing the survival of the flag—and by extension, the country—through a battle during the War of 1812; disrupting the ritualized group remembrance of the cosmogony is often seen as a rejection of the story, the flag, and thereby, the nation itself).

Rituals are further extended by the introduction of media. Couldry offers that "Media ritual, in broad terms, refers to the whole range of situations where media themselves 'stand in' for something wider, something to do with the fundamental organizational level on which we are, or imagine ourselves to be, connected as members of a society."[26] Theater has been a ritualized conduit for mythos for millennia. Theater "serve[s] to sustain and/or mobilize collective sentiments and solidarities on the basis of symbolization and a subjunctive orientation to what should or ought to be,"[27] and therefore is a media ritual that suggests all sorts of ritualized behaviors. The theater itself is a ritual space; the altar is placed at the front and center of the space, and the congregants are seated in concentric rows that fan out from the altar and are occupied in accordance with one's purchasing power. Those at the very back can still participate to some extent, but not nearly to the level of those with the financial ability (or lottery luck) to sit in the front. The ritual happens in very specific ways, much like the playing of the National Anthem: Going to the theater is an *experience*—one is meant to treat it as a special event, one should dress up (not in costume, rather, in nice clothes—which serve as their own form of costuming, if we are being honest), one is expressly neither allowed to recite the lines aloud with the actors nor to sing-along (when the tickets are $290 each, nobody wants to hear anyone else's sing-along rendition of the show). Mediated ritual behaviors go along with being in the ritual space that reinforce the ritualized nature of the event.[28]

The role of the media ritual event (the combination of the ritual and the ritual space) is to facilitate "integrating society, affirming its common values, legitimating its institutions, and reconciling different sectional elements."[29] It is quite easy to see how media ritual events are perfectly positioned for the transference of cosmogonic mythos. In many ways, theater is the most immediate form of media ritual event. Unlike television, film, or books, the ritual participants occupy the same physical space as the ritualized story. The storytellers share in the same immediate energy as the ritual participants, and the participants can have a direct effect on the story itself (an inadvertent cell phone ring, for instance, or audience laughter at an inappropriate part of the story). As Harbert points out:

> People flock to live theater in general for this very reason: the corporeality of the performers makes the experience feel real and immediate ... these musicals allow the audience not only to witness historical figures' famous actions but to hear, see, and feel their emotions.[30]

Much as Euripides spoke to the common values and institutions of ancient Athens through the media ritual of theater, and Shakespeare spoke to the beliefs and attitudes of Elizabethan England through the media ritual of theater, so too does Miranda capture contemporary standards and ideals through the media ritual of theater. Where better to access our most central of cosmogonies than in a space specifically socially conditioned for ritualized mediation?

HAMILTON AS COSMOGONIC SUPERHERO ORIGIN STORY

It is into this confluence of media ritual and cosmogony that Miranda interjects himself, in a manner that is at once both rude and masterful—rude, in that it reconceptualizes our most sacred of cosmogonies, but masterful, in that the result is spectacular (both in terms of box office success and in terms of critical acclaim). Miranda's central conceit is novel: he taps into the modern, humanized methodology of the costumed superhero narrative in order to retell the cosmogonical myth. Long-time comic book readers instinctively recognize that humanization and superhero narratives are not mutually exclusive concepts when it comes to comic book cosmogonies. *Hamilton* is not a 1940s, Golden Age of Comics-style superhero story.[31] *Hamilton* is not a *Superman* story. In the *Superman* mythos, Clark Kent is *good*; all of the time, without fail. He is always on the side of truth and right and justice. He is, in the quite useful taxonomy of "alignments" from the roleplaying game *Dungeons & Dragons*, "lawful good."[32] Superman is a crusader who is honorable and humane, does the right thing all of the time, and follows all appropriate laws.[33] Miranda posits Alexander Hamilton as "lawful neutral" at best; Miranda's Hamilton is honorable but realistic, willing to do whatever it takes for his cause and to adhere to his own strict moral code (the most "lawful neutral" moment of the production comes during the second act number, "We Know," as Hamilton simultaneously admits to long having cheated on his wife while taking umbrage at the accusation he embezzled federal money; he will accept the label of scoundrel, but not the label of criminal).[34] *Hamilton* is not a *Superman* story but a Bronze Age (1970s–1980s) *Spider-Man* story: our hero has flaws, lots of flaws. He has personal problems and financial problems and gets in his own way and steps on toes and is full of rough edges. He makes mistakes, both small and enormous.

Nearly every Bronze Age superhero narrative is presented in the same way: Iron Man is a brilliant inventor and also a raging alcoholic; Captain America is a powerful symbol of American greatness and also continually unintentionally racist.[35] Note that here we are not discussing the "alter ego": Peter Parker doesn't stop being Peter Parker when he pulls on the Spider-Man mask. He still has to figure out how to take photographs of himself fighting crime as Spider-Man to sell to the *Daily Bugle*, because he has to pay his rent. Tony Stark suits up as Iron Man stone cold drunk on multiple occasions. Luke Cage once had the Fantastic Four fly him all the way from New York to the fictional Baltic country of Latveria to pummel Dr. Doom because the villain owed him $200.[36] In Bronze Age stories, the concept of the "alter ego" is changed dramatically; there is an implicit understanding that the hero is still the same person inside and outside of the costume. This is what Miranda does in the way he presents the characters in *Hamilton*.

Alexander Hamilton is humanized in a way that brings him closer to the audience and allows for a better understanding of the motivations behind his mythical actions. This does not remove Hamilton (the character or the musical) from the realm of cosmogony—it simply gives the character more nuance and makes him more realistic and believable, much like most modern comic books aspire to achieve.

Myth, conceptually, is also reflective of a society's social order. That is to say, myth reflects the beliefs, attitudes, and values of a society's people. This is why it matters so much that *Hamilton* is traditionally cast nearly exclusively with people of color. This conscious choice in casting allows for a discursive entry point into one of the most sacred of cosmogonies for American culture to those of us who have traditionally and historically been excluded from the centralizing mythos of the country. As a Black man born, raised, and living in the United States, I can anecdotally attest to feeling as though the origin story of this country has always been presented as specifically and categorically white. With rhetorical brilliance, what *Hamilton* does for Black and Brown people who have never been able to be a part of the story is to answer the question of why we have always had trouble connecting to this country's origin story. Black and Brown communities do not celebrate the "Founding Fathers" in the same way that white communities do. We have been locked out of the centralizing cosmogony of American culture.

While there is legitimate criticism that *Hamilton* intentionally avoids the true contributions of Black and Brown people in the founding of the country (largely through slavery[37]), there is a different rhetorical choice at work here: the choice to see the "Founders" not as real historical figures but as characters in a myth. Because the characters are characters, they are then unbound from historicity. If one then changes the way the characters look, so that the characters now look like Black and Brown people, it allows Black and Brown audiences to get past what the historical figures looked like to focus on the story itself. *Hamilton* redefines the social order by using the cosmogony—the centralizing mythos of our culture—intentionally and purposefully to include Black and Brown people in a way that has rarely happened before. It is a reminder, not just to Black and Brown people, but to white people as well, that we are America, *too*. And if we are, due to the nature of media ownership and media production, going to continue to be systematically locked out of telling our stories, and others will not tell our stories for us, then we will tell the cosmogonical stories and fill them with people who look like us until we're allowed to tell the stories about the people who actually looked like us. The real, historical figures who have been mythologized through cosmogony are, essentially, fair game for telling a different centralizing story—one in which we are reminded that Brown-skinned immigrants "get the job done."[38] As Kajikawa reminds:

> ... bringing Alexander Hamilton, George Washington, and Thomas Jefferson back to life with hip hop and R&B is a gesture that speaks powerfully to the humanity so long denied

to [B]lack and [B]rown people, as well as to the exploitative relationship between 'civilized' white Founders and their racial others.[39]

There is enormous rhetorical power in claiming the founding characters and filling their presence with people of color; yes, the show chooses not to present the contribution of actual, real Black revolutionaries (Hercules Mulligan's slave Cato, for instance, which Huell and Jenkins discuss in greater depth in their chapter in this volume). Instead, the show explicitly says, "This country would not exist if not for Black and Brown-skinned people, and if we have to use this society's most sacred characters to remind everyone of that fact, then that is precisely what we will do." We will, quite literally, "put [ourselves] back in the narrative."[40] After all, "you have no control[:] who lives, who dies, who tells your story."[41]

Myth is reflective of epistemology: ways of knowing and understanding the natural world. Myths "direct attention toward what can be known ... As such, frameworks of knowledge such as paradigms or ideologies signify an intertextuality of myths along a mythographical sign-chain. Myths, therefore, act as the silent conditions for our logocentric reality, enabling the potential expansion of myth analysis to all forms of knowledge."[42] Myths help us to understand the world around us; they are epistemic by nature. Cosmogonies are particularly epistemic, as they attempt to explain the origins of our society, tell us who we are, who we are supposed to be, and what our place within our society is. The particular cosmogonic myth of a shared "American" national identity[43] works because we all want the same things, regardless of skin color, because we are all human beings first, regardless of political ideology. We are able to understand Alexander Hamilton because we know what it is like to want something so badly we will do anything to get it. We understand Aaron Burr because we know what it is like to watch someone we consider to be unsavory continue to succeed, over and over. We understand their goals, their dreams, their desires, and we connect to them. It, quite literally, does not matter what they look like or what their politics are—we understand them as people. This is why this Bronze Age superhero story works in a way that it absolutely would not had it been told as a Golden Age superhero story. And, because of this, we are able to shift the rhetorical discourse into Black and Brown skin, because the core of that humanistic epistemology does not change. If this is the centralizing myth of our culture, and that myth reflects the social order, and that social order forms our epistemology, then it is vital that Black and Brown people be included in that cosmogony. This is the ultimate triumph of Lin-Manuel Miranda; he has reframed the epistemic cosmogony of America to focus on historically marginalized people in a way to which all types of audiences can connect.

Myth uses heroic characters, either godly or human, to reconcile or establish the patterns of real life. If we accept this as true, then it allows us (and Miranda) to tap into the superhuman "powers" of Alexander Hamilton to talk about how important it is to celebrate an immigrant kid who writes his way out of poverty. That seems like a superhuman feat, but contemporary Black and Brown kids perform that feat all the time through the rap game, which Miranda accesses to tell the story of Alexander Hamilton. McAllister points out that "hip hop is not only the *right* form; this culture also shares a core conceit with the birth of our nation ... hip hop emcees or lyricists often write themselves into existence by crafting originary myths or histories, and even writing themselves into and sometimes out of 'beef' with other emcees, aspiring or established."[44] This is the particular brilliance of Lin-Manuel Miranda, and of *Hamilton* as a show. If one enters into the theater with little or no knowledge of rap, hip-hop, or R&B, the show still resonates on story alone; the music is catchy and the beats are infectious. However, if one enters into the encounter more invested and knowledgeable, the show is a veritable "Who's Who" of rap pioneers and hip-hop legends. We, as an audience, may not have a wealth of knowledge about Hamilton, but we know the immigrant story of Wyclef Jean. We can parallel to other immigrant rappers, such as Slick Rick or 21 Savage, in order to solidify meaning. Miranda's conscious callbacks to established rap legends bring street-level heroes onto the Broadway stage; Miranda himself states, "I wrote Hamilton with very polysyllabic rhymes, like [rappers] Big Pun or Rakim, which showed that he was literally in a different dimension than everyone else. I had to prove that his intellect was to be feared in the room."[45] Miranda summons DMX's *Party Up* with, "Meet him inside. Meet him, meet him inside";[46] he calls forth Mobb Deep's *Shook Ones, Pt. 2* with, "only 19, but my mind is older."[47] We hear one of the cosmogonic "Founding Fathers" of East Coast rap, The Notorious B.I.G., in the cadence of Hamilton spelling out his name in "My Shot": "Spell my name one more time, check it. It's the N-O, T-O, R-I, O U-S."[48] There are crystal clear shades of Busta Rhymes every time Lafayette spits bars; we hear the old-school timing of pioneer rappers like Whodini and The Furious Five in John Laurens' measured structures. Miranda taps into the superheroes of rap in the telling of his tale, again giving urban, Black, and Brown audiences in particular access to the inner workings of the story that many mainstream audiences may not have. These are our own mythic heroes, blended into the cosmogony of the country's founding.

As earlier explained, Miranda then goes so far as to invoke the true Superman of American history—the primogenitor of the American superhero mythos—George Washington. Jeremy McCarter points out, "when he makes that brisk, bold entrance—a black man striding straight downstage, slamming his sword into a scabbard—the thought crosses your mind: Is Chris [Jackson] somehow getting all of these people to cheer for George Washington himself?"[49] As America's first president, a war hero and a statesman, Washington has come to embody the best qualities of American culture; filling that vessel with the body of a Black man and then demanding the audience remain on his side is masterful.

The number "Your Obedient Servant," in which Miranda juxtaposes Aaron Burr's smooth bars with Alexander Hamilton's staccato elucidation, draws upon decades of rap beefs to which the audience has ready cultural access. In order to create a worthy supervillain to Hamilton's superhero (a Green Goblin to Hamilton's Spider-Man), Miranda utilizes another of America's cosmogonic superheroes, Thomas Jefferson. Jefferson has to be a supervillain to adequately match up, and Miranda exacerbates his worst qualities: *Hamilton*'s Jefferson is an arrogant, preening, self-congratulatory jerk. We are not meant to side with him at all, even while we enjoy his musical numbers. This mortal struggle between Jefferson and Hamilton (expressly *not* between Burr and Hamilton; Aaron Burr is cast, in this tale, as another victim, not the villain. In film terms, he is Eric Killmonger to Hamilton's Black Panther; he is not Ulysses Klaw[50]) is used to remind us that in real life, the "Founding Fathers" were not a monolith, but existed on opposite sides of very real political divides. Yes, the musical uses rhetorical shorthands to discuss those divides (much to the consternation of history buffs), but the point is well made, nonetheless.

Myth involves events that bend or break the natural laws in order to explain the unknown. Ra rides his chariot across the sky, bringing light to the world, until he disappears behind the mountains; we know chariots cannot fly, but gods get to break the natural rules, like gravity. We do not know precisely how the "Founders" interacted with each other, so it makes epistemic sense to break the natural laws by telling a story in which, for example, rap battles stand in for cabinet meeting discussions. Is it precisely historical that the Schuyler sisters' father "ha[d] no sons?"[51] No; their brother, John, was seven years younger than Peggy, and Phillip was ten years younger than Peggy—John was 15 and Phillip was 12 when Hamilton married Eliza Schuyler. Was Samuel Seabury shouted down in the town square by Hamilton, surrounded by his cadre of encouraging friends? No; this particular exchange happened in print, via pamphlets. Did Hamilton really stop time itself in order to elucidate every feeling flashing before his eyes in the moments before Aaron Burr's pistol slug hit his abdomen? Of course not. But bending the natural laws of time and occurrence in order to better get at the motivations of the characters trumps the historical record in this particular case. We are dealing in myth, after all.

CONCLUSION

The most lasting impact that *Hamilton* may have is that Miranda introduces a retcon[52] into the cosmogony—much like George Lucas in the *Star Wars* saga. In *Return of the Jedi* (1983), Leia Organa tells Luke Skywalker that she remembers her mother as "... very beautiful. Kind, but sad."[53] Twenty-two years later, in

Revenge of the Sith (2005), it is revealed that Padme Amidala, Leia's mother, dies in childbirth, meaning there is no way Leia "remembers" one single thing about her.[54] This is only one example of a cinematic retcon; there are literally thousands of examples across film, television, and comic books. *Hamilton* represents a significant retcon of Alexander Hamilton's cosmogonic origin story—one which is likely to become, at least at some level, a new canon for those not intimately familiar with American history. *Hamilton* already stands as a sort of "close enough" historical tale for many viewers; Chernow's book is a densely packed, tough slog that most *Hamilton* audience members will not undertake. The account presented by Miranda is "close enough." The retcons he introduces into the cosmogony are likely to fundamentally alter (or, in some cases, literally construct out of whole cloth) American understanding of Alexander Hamilton's role as "Founding Father."

Myth answers the very questions of ontology: Who are we? What is our purpose?[55] The ontology of American cosmogony invokes our most basic structures: good and evil. Hamilton and Jefferson. In the end, we, as a culture, love *Hamilton* because we have been socially engineered specifically to love it. It taps into our most cosmogonic of myths, and invokes our culture's most central heroic figures. It takes our origin story and widens the point of entry, through music, staging, and casting, removing the previously essential barrier to millions of new believers. *Hamilton* creates a new superhero out of a very old one. It reaches back to another time, in another world, and summons the superhumanity of the most unknown of the "Founding Fathers," pairs him with America's Superman, turns Thomas Jefferson into a worthy supervillain, gives us a fatally flawed Aaron Burr to pity, and retells our culture's most sacred story to a new generation. In doing so, it both restructures and reifies this culture's cosmogonic myth—the origin story of America.

NOTES

1 Christopher Bell, Associate Professor, University of Colorado Colorado Springs, cbell3@uccs.edu. Express thanks to Megan and Olivia Bell for their research support, and to Marissa Lammon for her proofreading and editing assistance.
2 Elie Wiesel, *The Gates of the Forest: (A Novel)* (New York: Holt, Rinehart, and Winston, 1966).
3 Jeffrey S. Lang and Patrick Trimble, "Whatever Happened to the Man of Tomorrow? An Examination of the American Monomyth and the Comic Book Superhero," *The Journal of Popular Culture* 22 (1988): 159.
4 John Shelton Lawrence and Robert Jewett. *The American Monomyth* (Garden City, NY: Anchor Press, 1977), xx. It would take an entire chapter just to delineate the permutations of the American Monomyth; it is one of the most central and widely covered topics in the study of popular culture. Lawrence and Jewett's *The American Monomyth* is an excellent place to start an exploration of the subject.

5 Lang and Trimble, "Whatever Happened to the Man of Tomorrow?," 159.
6 James W. Loewen, *Lies My Teacher Told Me: Everything Your American History Textbook Got Wrong* (New York: New Press 1995).
7 Here, at the outset, it may be important to understand the nature of the landscape upon which we are about to embark, so to speak. The field of rhetorical analysis is wide, and no doubt the chapters of this volume cover a variety of differing approaches. This essay interrogates *Hamilton* largely (but not entirely) from the perspective of comic studies; that is, *Hamilton* will be engaged as a superhero text. That said, I recognize that not everyone is steeped in comic book lore and possesses intimate knowledge of comic book tropes and conventions. It is entirely likely that members of the reading audience may have never even opened a comic book, or at least, have not read one in years. I will endeavor in this essay not to get lost in the comic book weeds, and to offer terminological explanations to the non-comic-studies audience where appropriate.
8 Thomas E. Porter, "Drama as Text: Mythos and Praxis," *WORD* 37 (1986): 97, https://doi.org/10.1080/00437956.1986.11435769.
9 Andrea Capra, "Seeing through Plato's Looking Glass. Mythos and Mimesis from Republic to Poetics," *Aisthesis* 10 (July 11, 2017): 84.
10 Richard Howells, *The Myth of the Titanic* (London, UK: Palgrave McMillan, 1999), 37.
11 Howells, *The Myth of the Titanic*, 37.
12 Bruce Lincoln, "The Indo-European Myth of Creation," *History of Religions* 15 (1975): 121.
13 Lincoln, "The Indo-European Myth of Creation." See also: Franciscus Bernardus Jacobus Kuiper, "Cosmogony and Conception: A Query," *History of Religions* 10 (1970): 91–138; Norman J. Girardot, "The Problem of Creation Mythology in the Study of Chinese Religion," *History of Religions* 15 (1976): 289–318.
14 Mircea Eliade and Elaine P. Halperin, "The Prestige of the Cosmogonic Myth," *Diogenes* 6 (1958): 9.
15 Leroy G. Dorsey and Rachel M. Harlow. "'We Want Americans Pure and Simple': Theodore Roosevelt and the Myth of Americanism," *Rhetoric & Public Affairs* 6 (2003): 55–78.
16 Charles Hatfield, Jeet Heer, and Kent Worcester, eds., *The Superhero Reader* (Jackson: University Press of Mississippi, 2013), 3.
17 One thing to take note of when thinking about superhero origin stories: by design, new writers are brought in from time to time to take over and refresh comic titles. When a new writer takes over a character, that writer often first re-presents the origin story in a new way. The purpose of this is to signal to the reader the writer's position on the character is, what the writer will be focusing on, and what values will be emphasized in the text. There is never just *one* origin story in comics; the function of telling and retelling the origin story is, in addition to reminding readers of the cosmogony, also about establishing expectations and values.
18 In the 2017 film version, Wonder Woman is from Themyscira.
19 "No John Trumbull (Intro)," featuring The Roots, track 1 on *The Hamilton Mixtape*, Atlantic, 2016.
20 Peter Coogan, "The Hero Defines the Genre, the Genre Defines the Hero," in *What Is a Superhero?* eds. Robin Rosenberg and Peter Coogan (New York: Oxford University Press, 2013), 3.
21 Ross Murray, "The Feminine Mystique: Feminism, Sexuality, Motherhood," *Journal of Graphic Novels and Comics* 2 (2011): 55–66.
22 Federico Pagello, "The 'Origin Story' Is the Only Story: Seriality and Temporality in Superhero Fiction from Comics to Post-Television," *Quarterly Review of Film and Video* 34 (2017): 729.
23 Pagello, "The 'Origin Story' Is the Only Story," 729.

24 Jeffrey A. Brown, "The Superhero Film Parody and Hegemonic Masculinity," *Quarterly Review of Film and Video* 33 (2016): 133.

25 Owen R. Horton, "Rebooting Masculinity after 9/11" (PhD diss., University of Kentucky, 2018), doi:10.13023/ETD.2018.187.

26 Nick Couldry, "Media Rituals: Beyond Functionalism," in *Media Anthropology*, eds. Eric W. Rothenbuhler and Mihai Coman (Thousand Oaks, CA: SAGE Publications, Inc., 2005), 3.

27 Simon Cottle, "Mediatized Rituals: Beyond Manufacturing Consent," *Media, Culture & Society* 28 (2006): 415.

28 S. Elizabeth Bird, "From Fan Practice to Mediated Moments: The Value of Practice Theory in the Understanding of Media Audiences," *Theorising Media and Practice* 4 (2010): 85.

29 James Curran and Tamar Liebes, "The Intellectual Legacy of Elihu Katz," in *Media, Ritual and Identity*, eds. Tamar Liebes and James Curran (New York: Routledge, 2002), 4.

30 Elissa Harbert, "Hamilton and History Musicals," *American Music* 36 (2018): 412–28.

31 The Golden Age of Comics is generally understood to run from the 1930s until the mid-1950s, and is characterized by ultra-good, urban superheroes fighting against crooked businessmen, gangsters, and other street-level criminal elements. The Silver Age of Comics ran from the mid-1950s until the mid-1970s, and introduced more supervillains, as well as focusing more on the hero outside of the costume. The Bronze Age of Comics ran from the mid-1970s through the late 1980s, and comics focused mostly on social issues, humanizing the superhero with real-world problems, and introducing more female and minority superheroes into the genre.

32 While there are endless academic sources for the discussion of ethics and morality, I still find the decidedly non-academic "alignment" chart from *Dungeons & Dragons* the most immediately discursively useful because it is easily and quickly understood. There are two axes of moral behavior: one deals with orientation toward rules (Lawful, Neutral, and Chaotic) and the other deals with orientation toward self-interest (Good, Neutral, and Evil). Combine the two axes, and there are nine possible "alignments" a person can fall into. Spider-Man can be viewed as "Neutral Good" (he does the morally just thing to make life better for other people, even if it means ignoring a law here or there to do so), while someone like Lord Voldemort can be seen as "Lawful Evil (he has a complete respect for laws and institutions, and seeks to use those mechanisms to gain and keep personal power). Again, not the most academic, social scientific, or rigorous of taxonomies, but definitely one of the more tacitly useful.

33 Christopher E. Bell, "Riddle Me This: The Moral Disengagement of Lord Voldemort," in *Legilimens!: Perspectives in Harry Potter Studies*, ed. Christopher E. Bell (Newcastle upon Tyne, UK: Cambridge Scholars Publishers, 2014), 57.

34 Bell, "Riddle Me This," 57.

35 One of the major hallmarks of Captain America's Bronze-Age storyline is his relationship to his Black partner, The Falcon. Captain America's narrative arc is an exploration of how he comes to learn about race relations in the late 1970s through his partnership with The Falcon.

36 Steve Englehart and George Tuska, *Luke Cage, Hero for Hire*, no. 9 (New York: Marvel Comics, 1972).

37 This is well documented in Heather S. Nathans, "Crooked Histories: Re-Presenting Race, Slavery, and Alexander Hamilton Onstage," *Journal of the Early Republic* 37 (2017): 271–78. See also: Leslie M. Harris, "The Greatest City in the World? Slavery in New York in the Age of Hamilton," in *Historians on Hamilton: How a Blockbuster Musical Is Restaging America's Past*, eds. Renee C. Romano and Claire Bond Potter (New Brunswick, NJ: Rutgers University Press, 2018), 71–93; Lyra D. Montiero, "Race-Conscious Casting and the Erasure of the Black Past in Lin-Manuel Miranda's Hamilton," *The Public Historian* 38, no. 1 (2016): 89–98.

38 Lin-Manuel Miranda and Jeremy McCarter, *Hamilton: The Revolution* (New York, NY: Grand Central Publishing, 2016), 121.
39 Loren Kajikawa, "'Young, Scrappy, and Hungry': Hamilton, Hip Hop, and Race." *American Music* 36 (2018): 471.
40 Miranda and McCarter, *Hamilton: The Revolution*, 280.
41 Miranda and McCarter, *Hamilton: The Revolution*, 120.
42 Robert Cooke, "The Precipice of Myth: Mythology/Epistemology," in *Myth and Narrative in International Politics: Interpretive Approaches to the Study of IR*, ed. Berit Bliesemann de Guevara (London, UK: Palgrave Macmillan, 2016), 74–75.
43 Benedict Anderson refers to this shared "American" identity as an "imagined" community: "It is imagined because the members of even the smallest nation will never know most of their fellow-members, yet in the minds of each lives the image of their communion." Benedict Anderson, *Imagined Communities: Reflections on the Origin and Spread of Nationalism* (London: Verso Books, 2006), 6.
44 Marvin McAllister, "Toward a More Perfect Hamilton," *Journal of the Early Republic* 37, no. 2 (2017): 280.
45 Lin-Manuel Miranda, quoted in Kajikawa, "'Young, Scrappy, and Hungry.'" 473.
46 Miranda and McCarter, *Hamilton: The Revolution*, 104.
47 Miranda and McCarter, *Hamilton: The Revolution*, 169.
48 "Going Back to Cali," track 4 on Notorious B.I.G., *Life After Death*, disc 2, Bad Boy Records, 1997.
49 Miranda and McCarter, *Hamilton: The Revolution*, 59.
50 "In film terms" is used deliberately here; in Bronze Age comics, both Killmonger and Klaw are traditional villains. The *Black Panther* film treats Eric Killmonger much more gently.
51 Miranda and McCarter, *Hamilton: The Revolution*, 83.
52 Retcon: "Retroactive continuity." *Comic Vine* defines a retcon thusly: "Retcon or retroactive continuity is a term that is used when writers reveal something new to a previous story already told which usually changes the original back story to something new ... At its simplest, it can be a piece of information that alters a character's background, shedding some light on their reasoning and, at worst, a contradiction of a fundamental aspect or plot point of a characters previous established story arcs. The nature of comics [is] to be the amalgam of many artists, writers and even publishers, [which] has the obvious flaw of, over time, their story becoming convoluted ... errors and omission are bound to occur and means that retcon can be as much of a plot device as it can be [a] tool to correct previous errors." "Retcon," *Comic Vine*, https://comicvine.gamespot.com/retcon/4015-43566.
53 *Star Wars, Episode VI: Return of the Jedi*, directed by Richard Marquand, 1983.
54 *Star Wars, Episode III: Revenge of the Sith*, directed by George Lucas, 2005.
55 By extension, comic book origin stories (particularly origin story retellings) also ask, "What do we emphasize? What are our values?"

CHAPTER SIX

Hamilton and Public Memory of the Founding Era: Myth, Humanization, and Comforting Whiteness in "Post-Racial" America

JOHN CLYDE RUSSELL[1]

Because, no matter how "fictional" the account of these writers, or how much it was a product of invention, the act of imagination is bound up with memory.
—Toni Morrison, "The Site of Memory"[2]

People love *Hamilton: An American Musical*. Blacks and Whites,[3] liberals and conservatives, Broadway experts and those who have never been to Broadway extol the musical and all things associated with it.[4] *Hamilton* thrives outside the Broadway production in an unprecedented way. It lives in streaming playlists, YouTube views, and history classes. Its circulation within popular culture is so wide that "Weird Al" Yankovic's "The Hamilton Polka" debuted on the Billboard charts at number one, which preceded the popular track reprise, "One Last Time," featuring former president Barack Obama.[5] *Hamilton* has become part of the American lexicon as it permeates popular culture, politics, and academia.

A *New York Times* review calls *Hamilton* "the rarest of theatrical phenomena" because it is "not only a hit, but a turning point for the art form and a cultural conversation piece."[6] What makes it a "cultural conversation piece" is that Black and Brown people are portraying White historical figures.[7] Thus, *Hamilton* has the ability to positively raise issues about race because its multiracial cast reframes and retells the founding of the United States in new ways. Instead of being separate from the founding, as most popular culture narratives have traditionally treated them, Black, Indigenous, People of Color (BIPOC) are driving the American narrative. This has been part of its success, but it has also been a focal point for criticism. The critical view of *Hamilton* is that despite its casting the musical celebrates wealthy, White, slave-owning men. Although BIPOC actors portray all the main characters, the musical is devoid of characters who were enslaved, Native Americans, Black abolitionists, or free African Americans.[8] *Hamilton* is groundbreaking, in large part because of its casting and musical style, because its inclusivity and image of what the "Founders" looked like. This, however, cannot dissuade legitimate criticism that *Hamilton* whitewashes its retelling of history—and, thereby, is a form of public memory that comforts whiteness.[9]

David Glassberg explains how "audiences actively reinterpret what they see and hear by placing it in alternative contexts derived from their diverse social backgrounds."[10] If we associate race with "diverse social backgrounds," it becomes easier to understand why both BIPOC and White audiences both praise and criticize the musical's casting. *Hamilton* is a polysemic text that renders more than one interpretation—that is, as Leah Ceccarelli argues, "distinct meanings exist" within the text, which are "identifiable by the critic, the rhetor, or the audience."[11] One reading, as Michael Paulson writes, is that the casting allows "the creators to comment," on America's fractured present through its past, and vice versa,"[12] and another reading, according to historian Lyra D. Monteiro, is that the casting is "misleading and actively erases the presence and role of [B]lack and [B]rown people in Revolutionary America."[13]

One reading, as the musical itself declares, recognizes that *who* tells the story matters. Those who create the narrative shape the narrative. For *Hamilton*, it is a powerful endeavor to feature Black and Latino people in the founding of a nation that has historically denied their humanity and citizenship. In a sense, they are taking ownership of the American identity. Another reading, however, recognizes that presence alone does not mean equality or diversity. Patricia Herrera succinctly writes, "these historical erasures in *Hamilton* put into question how we can practice diversity without actually being inclusive."[14] Simply putting Black and Brown bodies in a space is not what racializes or diversifies a space. It is incorrect to think spaces only become raced when a non-White body is present. All spaces are already raced. Any act of public memory that is all White is still "racial" for two reasons: one, White is a racial category and, two, it represents or signals choice. The dialectical irony to this is that narratives do not simply become unraced (diverse) just because there are White and Black people occupying the same space. As Kenneth Burke explains, there is a difference between bodies moving in a space and bodies acting in a space.[15] Joseph R. Gusfield summarizes it this way: action "implies reflection upon one's interests, sentiments, purposes, and those of others."[16] Agency matters. To examine the rhetorical nature of *Hamilton*'s casting, we must investigate what actions the bodies—both as performers and characters—are taking and to what end. We should examine the choices that are made about race. Black bodies moving rather than acting while White characters act has just as detrimental an effect on equality as no Black bodies present at all.

A retelling of the founding without BIPOC acting rather than absent or moving is incomplete and centers whiteness. So what does it mean to include BIPOC, to have BIPOC drive the narrative, yet still center on whiteness? Since the diverse casting is central to the retelling, it is helpful to examine its treatment of racism—particularly what it communicates about slavery. To do this is to go beyond presence and examine agency within that space, which I argue creates comfort or discomfort for whiteness that can reveal aspects of its ideology.

This chapter examines what the presence of Black and Brown bodies in *Hamilton* communicates rhetorically with regard to whiteness and public memory of the Founding Fathers and founding era. My analysis is an inquiry into the criticism of *Hamilton*'s casting and attention to slavery to locate and examine the (dis)comfort of whiteness and its relationship to public memory. Nearly five years after its debut, the musical grossed over $4 million in one week, setting another record, and Disney purchased the rights to release a film version of the staged musical for a record $75 million, so its popularity and acclaim may have never been higher.[17] Yet, poignant criticisms of erasing BIPOC characters and whitewashing history remain. In a time when slavery is finally being recognized in museums and tours of Monticello, Mount Vernon, and Montpelier, it seems unlikely—and rightfully so—that an all-White production of a musical such as *Hamilton* that glosses over slavery would become a cultural phenomenon and suffice the contemporary movement toward honoring those who were enslaved. But if *Hamilton* is another whitewashed retelling of history that erases BIPOC, how does the casting and music genre promote that whitewashing rather than hinder it? And if the musical connects Americans to their history in extraordinary ways, how does the casting and music stymie that whitewashing rather than help it?

To answer these questions, I briefly explain what the (dis)comfort of whiteness is and its relevance to U.S. historical narrative. Then I describe the founding era as it relates to whiteness, public memory, and the mythic absence of slavery in popular narrative. This bolsters our understanding of *Hamilton*'s distinct, yet traditional, mythic storytelling that exists inside and outside the casting and music. Next, I offer a textual analysis of the musical and the ways visceral whiteness is addressed through humanization, a key aspect of whiteness ideology. I argue that whiteness is so calcified in America's storytelling tropes that the casting—while seemingly controversial or requiring a suspension of disbelief—actually is welcomed by a White audience and is symptomatic of the "post-racial era" misnomer that many advocated after the election of Barack Obama. I conclude by illuminating the rhetorical implications for public memory and the ideological aspects of whiteness that become visible when examining the (dis)comfort of whiteness in American narratives—especially narratives of its founding.

WHITENESS AND (DIS)COMFORT

A prominent aspect of whiteness has always been and continues to be a matter of comfort or discomfort. Whiteness' supposed centralized role within and feelings about U.S. history is ingrained and is a powerful force in how White people maneuver within racial discourse or remember racism of the United States. More than thinking their way through racial discourse, White Americans tend to feel their way, and we can see how this has borne out historically.

Consider Frederick Douglass' open letter to his former enslaver, which put White comfort on notice by "concentrating public attention on the system, and deepening their horror of trafficking in the souls and bodies of men."[18] Also consider that two watershed moments of the civil rights era address White (dis)comfort: Rosa Parks' refusal to give up her seat—to sacrifice her comfort for that of a White person—was inspired by Emmett Till's open casket, which invited the White world to see, to experience, to face the uncomfortable reality of racism.[19] Underscoring why these tactics were necessary, Martin Luther King, Jr. writes in "Letter From Birmingham Jail" about the "white moderate, who prefers a negative peace which is the absence of tension to a positive peace which is the presence of justice."[20] In this instance King, as he often did elsewhere, correlates comfort and inaction. He places them in direct opposition to progress' requirement of discomfort and action. Furthermore, King identifies the "white moderate" as the primary agent whose comfort is at stake. Whereas whiteness is obvious at the extreme ends of anti-Black racists, disrupting the comfort at the moderate level does more to promote change because it locates whiteness at the level where it can hide. This is significant because whiteness maintains its advantage when it is invisible and therefore deniable.

From abolitionists to civil rights leaders, challenging White comfort has carried over into the contemporary discourse about race. Inspired by Colin Kaepernick's protest of police brutality, Michael Bennett, who plays professional football, wrote a book titled, *Things That Make White People Uncomfortable*.[21] It is a personal account of the ways racism is present in all areas of American life, and the title reflects how engaging in that discussion alone makes whiteness uncomfortable.

However effective challenging White comfort as a measure for legal and social change may have been or however persistent it may still be, the feelings of deserved comfort ingrained in whiteness remain. Recently, a Fox News commentator, on the verge of tears, said she was uncomfortable with the conversation about race and the White supremacist events in Charlottesville.[22] Discussing and labeling White people as racist produced a feeling of discomfort too great for her to continue the segment. This is an example of what Robin DiAngelo terms "white fragility," which describes how "the smallest amount of racial stress is intolerable" for White people.[23]

This visceral nature of whiteness is rhetorical because it has consequences for memory and identity, particularly in the historical narratives we celebrate about race. Greg Dickinson, Carole Blair, and Brian L. Ott's examination of memory centers on six "consensual" assumptions.[24] One assumption is particularly relevant here, which is that memory is "animated by affect."[25] People are emotionally tied to their histories and, thus, the narratives that preserve or create them. This is where (dis)comfort factors as a feeling that sustains or challenges whiteness because narratives about U.S. history and race can either comfort or discomfort whiteness' memory of that history and its particular role within the narrative. This is not to put whiteness on a pedestal or mark it as the judge of racial narratives; however, I argue that when a racial narrative comforts whiteness, it is because whiteness itself benefits as the center of that particular narrative. In other words, racial narratives either comfort or discomfort whiteness and determining which is happening is a useful way of decentering and illuminating whiteness.

The visceral nature of whiteness needs addressing because it reinforces attitudes or creates identities and shapes ideas about people and their material and discursive interactions. In short, the rhetorical aspects of whiteness create, sustain, and sometimes challenge ideologies of race. But before discussing some of those ideological aspects, and to put into context whether *Hamilton*'s casting (dis)comforts whiteness, it is important to recognize the mythical nature of the founding narrative.

THE FOUNDING ERA: MYTH, SLAVERY, AND WHITENESS

The founding and the Founders of the United States are mythic. Americans celebrate and deify the people (almost exclusively men) and the events of the Revolution in popular culture and politics. Tales of the war and of its revolutionaries are revered in films, whether it is Nicholas Cage following a hidden map on the back of the Declaration of Independence or Mel Gibson portraying the "caring" slaveholder who avenges his son's death by leading a colonial militia in South Carolina.[26] Both of these films suggest a particular responsibility of sorts for the (White, male) protagonists. They are bound to uphold or defend their country's ideals, which in turn, has a positive outcome for the country and the main characters. Reinhold Niebuhr writes in *The Irony of American History* that Americans perceive their beginning not only as divine but also as just and innocent.[27] Outside popular culture, these characteristics endure in the collective imagination as rhetorical devices in the succeeding eras. Lincoln's first words at Gettysburg call back to the founding; Martin Luther King, Jr. makes use of metaphor and the founding at the March on Washington; and President Barack Obama often refers to the United States as on a perpetual quest toward "a more perfect union."[28] These are effective storytelling devices and rhetorical maneuvers, in part, because public memory of the founding is associated with freedom, fairness, newness, and righteousness. Such ideals are not, however, associated with slavery, which contrary to popular narratives, was prevalent in and critical to the revolution.

Niebuhr prompts us to consider how such misperceptions of innocence inform what we think about the Founding Fathers and the time period, particularly in regard to slavery. Depictions of slavery in founding narratives are often limited to debates about the "peculiar institution" and do not feature or realistically consider the humanity of those enslaved.[29] This places slavery outside the American narrative rather than fully immersed in it. Such retellings of the founding place slavery—the institution that produced prosperity for *all* of the colonies—as an aside or as some curious problem for a few White people some day in the future to figure out.[30] They frame slavery as an enigma or conundrum that escapes their capacity to eradicate. One prominent example is in the popular 2008 mini-series about John Adams. When Adams, Jefferson, and Benjamin Franklin discuss slavery and the wording of the Declaration of Independence, Franklin wonders why Jefferson wrote about slavery and King George III but "nothing of slavery itself" in the colonies. Jefferson replies, "slavery is an abomination and must be loudly proclaimed as such, but I own that neither I nor any man has any, uh, immediate solution to the problem."[31] The discussion ends there, in a typical treatment of slavery that comforts whiteness—a treatment that leaves slavery as a "problem" without a solution. This, too, is a myth.

Thomas Jefferson's *Notes on the State of Virginia* was among the first prominently published writings to offer race theory to excuse slavery in a country that espoused equality and inalienable rights.[32] Jefferson was a prolific writer who we prefer to remember for "all men are created equal" rather than his musings on White supremacy because those specific racist ideas do not conform to the present memories of revolution for the sake of freedom. Also, we tend to associate slavery and the Founders as personal failings rather than in political or structural terms. For example, consider the redeeming stories about the Founders and their struggle with a necessary evil of slavery that would supposedly die out on its own; or the romanticization of Jefferson and Sally Hemings portrayed by Nick Nolte and Thandie Newton in *Jefferson in Paris*; or the comforting stories about clauses in Founders' wills for freeing their slaves.[33]

These selected memories allow Jefferson and other presidents who enslaved people to be revered in government and the Bill of Rights, but shamed in certain aspects of their personal lives. Slavery as a personal flaw of the Founders reinforces the myth of slavery as outside the founding and revolution—outside the fabric of American infrastructure—and solely as part of a particular moral failure of particular Founders. Narratives that frame the Founders and slavery as a puzzle of contradiction allow us to forget slavery's institutional role; however, if we look to Jefferson's *Notes* or Madison's *Federalist Paper* #54 and the Three-Fifths Compromise, we see how they explained and built into the structural aspects of the United States. Public memory of slavery predominantly reflects the personal failings of some Founders and less so as practical problems for the new government that the Founders negotiated amongst themselves. This allows the present to place slavery as unfortunate failings indicative of the era rather than essential to it.

The irony of such founding narratives is that the Founders defeated, against all odds, the world's greatest empire to gain their independence—that they conceived and realized a truly revolutionary government. Yet, they could not muster an idea about how *not* to enslave others. Of course they could, but the reality lies with motivation rather than conception. Slavery emerges later as an evil and existential threat to the United States that is ultimately eradicated by White people. Both of these treatments of slavery in the American narrative are mythic, but remain powerful for reconstituting whiteness and national identity. They endure in public memory because they neatly conceive of slavery as outside the American founding and resolved through American tragedy.[34]

Public memory of slavery in the founding era does not exist outside the mythic realm. *Hamilton*'s storyline regarding slavery reinforces the mythical characteristics of innocence, justice, and desired-but-delayed abolition. It reassures and comforts whiteness, and so the deeply ingrained (mis)understandings of the U.S. founding and its relation to slavery endure. The myth helps sustain whiteness ideology and whiteness helps sustain the myth. The question here is, if *Hamilton* sustains the founding era's traditional narrative, how does the nontraditional casting factor in the public memory and myths of the founding?

HUMANIZATION THROUGH BLACK BODIES

In what has become a landmark text for critical whiteness studies, Toni Morrison argues in *Playing in the Dark: Whiteness and the Literary Imagination* that Black characters, named the "Africanist presence," function as a metaphor in early American literature used to define whiteness and create a White American identity.[35] Morrison explains how the imaginary writings of White authors such as Herman Melville, Edgar Allen Poe, Mark Twain, and Ernest Hemingway use what she terms "American Africanism" to conceptualize the United States as White by defining it through a negation of blackness.[36] For example, Morrison asks us to consider Africanism as:

> the vehicle by which the American self knows itself as not enslaved, but free; not repulsive, but desirable; not helpless, but licensed and powerful; not history-less, but historical; not damned, but innocent; not a blind accident of evolution, but a progressive fulfillment of destiny.[37]

In short, an influential way White Americans came to know themselves was through the American African characters or tropes in popular literature as written by White people. Many declare these works to be classics and they remain influential, especially in high schools and higher education classes, for generations of students conceptualizing American identity.[38]

Morrison suggests four areas for literary critics to investigate the ways the Africanist presence or blackness influences the American narrative and the effects those understandings render. Each is relevant to my argument about *Hamilton*'s casting comforting whiteness. The four areas are as follows: one, "Africanist character as surrogate and enabler" for White characters; two, "the way an Africanist idiom is used to establish difference ... or to signal modernity"; three, "the technical ways in which an Africanist character is used to limn out and enforce the invention and implications of whiteness"; and finally, "the manipulation of the Africanist narrative ... as a means of meditation—both safe and risky—on one's own humanity."[39] These areas provide an effective means for locating whiteness and its contrived influence in the American identity and imagination—sometimes literal and other times allegoric. Morrison's suggestions are useful to this analysis, as they provide historical context and help explain how *Hamilton* comforts whiteness—not just despite its casting but because of it.

Hamilton's casting immediately speaks to Miranda's goal to tell the story of America then by America now. By separating from the traditional visual portrayals of the Founders, the bodies on stage make the story relatable. Using contemporary vernacular and music creates a sense of realness to the story because the past becomes accessible. But that accessibility can keep us from recognizing how the Black and Brown bodies on stage reconstitute whiteness by telling a story that humanizes White historical characters. And this is an important distinction to make between historical character and bodies on stage. Carla L. Peterson explains:

> When invoking the term "body," we tend to think first of its materiality—its composition as flesh and bone, its outline and contours, its outgrowth of nail and hair. But the body, as we well know, is never simply matter, for it is never divorced from perception and interpretation.[40]

The body is rhetorical because it invites interpretation, so also consider the implications for choice and include Alan Gross' examination of presence as argument.

He writes that presence, as defined by Chaïm Perelman, is a rhetorical effect in which speakers and writers focus the attention of their audiences on certain aspects of their subjects that they think are most likely to promote the case they want to make.[41] In other words, we can consider the casting as bodies for interpretation and their presence as a major contributor to the musical's narrative.

Hamilton's brilliance as a narrative of the Founding Fathers is to tell personal and relatable stories. Up to this point, depictions of the Founders might as well have been walking oil paintings if not caricatures of how those in the paintings might act. They were formal and stiff, with perfect posture, and had jaws that lifted forward as if they always knew how things were going and would proceed. They spoke with muddied accents that suggest either brilliance or arrogance. These types of portrayals do little to make the Founders relatable. The mini-series *John Adams* breaks this mold somewhat with the lead character showing doubt, emotion, a physique, and body language that do not lend itself to a portrait. I would argue, however, that Adams is the only Founding Father portrayed this way in the mini-series, and it speaks to Paul Giamatti's acting and to the series' plot. Adams is the main character.[42] Audiences are meant to connect with him and his story. What is different about *Hamilton* is that it celebrates and exposes each character in their humanity, their faults as well as their strengths.

The musical depicts Hamilton favorably in his rise from a penniless orphan to the first Treasury Secretary, his importance to the revolution as Washington's "right hand man,"[43] and as the main Constitutional proponent because of his writing domination in the *Federalist Papers*. But the musical also depicts his arrogance, rush to judgment, infidelity, and combativeness. Thomas Jefferson wins a rap battle and is introduced in a celebrity fashion in his opening number, "What'd I Miss?" He is a fun and likeable character, but in a "lovable jerk" kind of way. He is also exposed in his hypocrisy regarding slavery and his absence in the war. George Washington is perhaps the closest to the mythical conception we get of the Founders, but even he is depicted as "despondent" and "in dire need of assistance" from Hamilton.[44]

Hamilton's portrayal of the Founders as admirable *and* flawed humanizes them for audiences. They no longer stand stiff in statues or are the stoic faces on money. They are relatable in their interpersonal relationships, their mistakes, and their choices. There are a number of songs that humanize them in specific ways. For example, "My Shot" illustrates Hamilton's ambition, but does so in a new way. Often in traditional founding narratives, the Founders appear to be already within the thralls of revolution with clear resolve. In this song, Hamilton and Burr exhibit and debate their strategic differences and paths for their futures—particularly how they can use the revolution to benefit themselves rather than their participation as some selfless act for America.

"Dear Theodosia"—a mix between a lullaby and a dedication—shows Hamilton and Burr in their insecurity and selfless affection as new fathers. It represents the complexity and happiness and worry that parenthood brings. "Say No To This" is Hamilton's conscience wrestling with his desires and loneliness as he begins his affair with Maria Reynolds. "Hurricane" reveals Hamilton's faulty logic and selfish motive to explain the affair, while "Burn" is Eliza's painful, heart-wrenching response and notice that she is taking control of the narrative. And "It's Quiet Uptown" is heartbreaking empathy for the reconciliation of their relationship and the mourning of their deceased child. The song opens with "There are moments that the words don't reach; There is suffering too terrible to name."[45] These two lines brilliantly describe the silence and incomprehension that accompany personal tragedy.

All of these songs draw the audience into a human narrative with relatable, personal experiences. The Founding Fathers and their families become people we know; they become like us. Our memories of the Founders transform from names of rigid figures in history lessons into people with relatable intimacy. But because slavery is mythical and largely absent in the narrative, it is easy to forget that some of the personal experiences we see dramatized on stage were only privileged to whiteness. For example, the song "One Last Time" is at once beautiful, inspiring, ironic, and awful. It tells the story of George Washington explaining that he will not seek a third term as president, and by doing so he hopes the country appreciates his service that he affirms "outlives me when I'm gone."[46] Arguably the most eloquent and influential act as first president, to encourage and exemplify a peaceful transfer of power, is captured in the song. The song also captures Washington's desire to go home and rest. "Everyone should sit under his own vine and fig tree," he sings. This humanizes him; it shows us that he is tired and wants to "rest in the nation we've made."[47] Washington is no longer the vigorous general heading a boat across the Delaware. He has given his best to his new country, and he wants to retire to enjoy it.

While conveying all these humanizing and relatable aspects, the song is also expressing something by what it is not saying. Going home to Mount Vernon and looking out over the rolling hills means that on those hills are people Washington has enslaved who will never get to rest—never get to enjoy the freedom of the new country they have built. As *Hamilton* emotionally describes Washington's retirement, his deserved rest, and opportunity to reflect on his choices, I am reminded of Frederick Douglass' autobiography in which he describes what happens to women who are slaves and become too old to work or care for the children. Douglass explains how they are unceremoniously taken to a shack in the woods and left to die. So Washington quoting the Bible, "everyone should sit under his own vine and fig tree,"[48] is only relatable to whiteness in this context. Washington gets to realize the fruits of his labor while those he and others have enslaved do not. "One Last Time" could communicate something different if the enslaved persons who served Washington were represented on stage. The presence of an enslaved Black body would be discomforting in its acknowledgement of the difference between bodies who act and bodies that move. The musical humanizes the White characters, and the corresponding lack of representation of historical BIPOC on stage allows audiences to forget *their* humanity. The Founders are relatable as humans; those enslaved and slavery as an integral part of the founding era remain abstract. The casting choices may obscure this as whiteness takes comfort and mistakes the Black and Brown bodies on stage as representing the humanity of the historical BIPOC that the narrative erases.

Another example of the Black and Brown bodies on stage humanizing White historical characters that would communicate something different had BIPOC characters been included is a scene in the musical that does not appear on the soundtrack. Titled "Tomorrow There'll Be More of Us," it takes place between "Dear Theodosia" and "Non-Stop." Still sitting, Hamilton is smiling and in amazement of his son as Eliza slowly approaches with a letter. Hamilton brushes it off, saying it is from John Laurens and he will read it later. Eliza replies that the letter is actually from Laurens' father. She then reads the letter aloud, which reveals Laurens has been killed in battle. Eliza goes on to read that John's dream of "emancipating and recruiting 3,000 men for the first all-[B]lack military regiment … dies with him." In the scene, Laurens' character is positioned stage right to Hamilton and Eliza and sings a reprise of "The Story of Tonight," ending in an elevated volume: "Tomorrow they'll be more of us!"[49] The first two renditions of "Story of Tonight" are hopeful and then playful. This final reprise is declarative—almost defiant. It is a powerful moment that suggests a budding abolitionist movement and the Black soldiers in the Civil War and both World Wars that are to come. The scene focuses attention on the failures to "solve" slavery. But again, without Black soldiers acting on stage, there is not a chance for the scene to humanize them. Hamilton's shock and grief at the loss of his friend and Laurens' admirable abolitionism are the humanized aspects acting on stage. The immediate concern seems to be more about Hamilton and Laurens than it does about abolition of slavery. And this reluctantly but effectively defers freedom to the future.

Erasing BIPOC from the narrative invites an audience to reside in the comforting myth that suggests slavery was not critical to the founding and that the Founders were reluctant purveyors of the necessary evil. This is not to say that the musical altogether ignores slavery. Miranda and other original cast members point to the lines referencing the need to end slavery or mocking Jefferson for "who's really doing the planting."[50] But the limited efforts to acknowledge slavery do not challenge whiteness. In fact, it is consistent with whiteness ideology in that slavery is dealt with on a surface level that does not propel or suppress the story. Although Black and Brown people dominate the stage and connect with audiences in telling—effectively participating in—American history, whiteness is front and center rhetorically. It is a comforting inclusion that reminds whiteness that it is still essential and the center of American identity.

As Morrison exhibits, whiteness is accustomed to using Black people to define itself. The trope in American literature to define whiteness (and, thus, America) through the use of Black bodies, the "Africanist presence," relates to what Manning Marable argues when he explains that the invention of blackness generated the construction of whiteness.[51] Whiteness becomes the negation of blackness: whiteness is civilized because blackness is not, whiteness controls because blackness needs controlling, et cetera. One significant ramification of this is that whiteness humanizes and individualizes White people while de-humanizing and grouping Black people. *Hamilton* represents an evolved way of doing so that comforts contemporary whiteness.

The White American writers Morrison investigates defined White characters with possessed agency and attained autonomy by describing the negation of those attributes in the Black characters. As racism has morphed over time in America, and as White America appropriates other cultures, *Hamilton* represents whiteness defining itself through blackness as if whiteness is *with* blackness. Hip-hop and the presence of people of color help humanize and make cool the Founding Fathers. It allows instances in the musical for the Founders to dance or respond to affairs with "oh shit."[52] Moreover, it allows the genre of music to sound and appear authentic. Cabinet meetings become entertaining as rap battles. Whiteness is able to use blackness.

Taking into consideration the explanation above about the humanization of White characters through Black bodies, it is worth asking if the opposite is also happening. Are mythic memories of White historical people humanizing Black bodies? In other words, does a Black or Brown body on stage representing a Founding Father humanize the Black or Brown body? George Yancy writes, "As the transcendental norm, the Black body is framed through white ontological assumptions about Black bodies."[53] How might portraying White people, who are framed through ontological assumptions that include American identity and mythic characteristics of the founding, frame Black bodies? The question here flips what assumptions are being transferred from the Black actors onto their historical counterparts into what assumptions are transferred from their historical counterparts onto the Black actors.

The collective memory of Washington, for example, includes the general fearlessly heading a boat that is crossing the Delaware.[54] When Washington is introduced in *Hamilton*, he is no less brave or prominent—an embodiment of the American spirit. In fact, he appears center stage in a commanding posture that resembles the Delaware painting. The question for whiteness is whether the memory of Washington changes the relationship whiteness has with Black or Brown bodies. In other words, does the image of Washington as a Black man decenter whiteness? Might the presence of a Black body that is suddenly associated with all that Washington exemplifies in the collective imagination change the relationship whiteness has with Black bodies? The question for *Hamilton* is whether it suggests BIPOC as American or if BIPOC are American as they become associated with White historical figures such as the Founding Fathers.

IMPLICATIONS AND IDEOLOGICAL ASPECTS OF WHITENESS

Hamilton is the story of America's beginning. That is important because just as every act "sets a precedent,"[55] the stories we tell about our origin reflect how we see ourselves now and in the future. How one remembers the founding and Founders affects the imaginative possibilities for the contemporary moment, and it also allows for what *could* be. Acts of public memory are as much about the present and future as they are about the past. *Hamilton* tells a compelling story with nuanced and well-written lyrics and songs that incorporate both the hip-hop and musical worlds. The "America now" that is telling the story helps make the people of "America then" relatable and real. But it is worth examining the elements in *Hamilton* as an origin story that could be sustaining myths that are contradictory to its inclusive casting. *Hamilton: The Revolution* declares, "American history can be told and retold, claimed and reclaimed, even by people who don't look like George Washington and Betsy Ross."[56] While inspiring and true, my goal in this chapter has been to show how the casting and the myths the narrative upholds create a tension, a space where we can identify, as Alessandra Raengo puts it, "the process whereby whiteness draws a line around itself."[57] Furthermore, it prompts us to challenge the myths that dominate the founding era that work as stabilizers for the contemporary racial ideologies that not only inform imagination and public memory but also affect contemporary political and social inequalities.

Contemporary narratives about America's racial history can illuminate some of the ways acts of public memory rhetorically protect or challenge whiteness. *Hamilton* is unique in its use of race within the narrative. Films about slavery or civil rights present obvious racial aspects. The structures within the story are not new; we expect certain things to happen and certain characters to act in explicit, familiar ways. *Hamilton* both adheres to this familiarity and disrupts it. Although the musical barely scratches the surface on any racial plot or subplot, race is there. I argue that race is there because that is, in part, how Miranda bills the show "America then, told by America now";[58] it is a dominating discourse around the show and its popularity. *Hamilton*, in some ways, is changing the Founders' narrative, and yet still centers and comforts whiteness. When rhetorical choices such as casting and narrative tropes are comforting whiteness, that is the place for White people to begin a critical analysis of why such narratives are satisfying. I argue this is necessary if American society is to take up Morrison's goal to "peck away at the powerful normative structure of whiteness."[59] The ideology of whiteness is exposed, and therefore susceptible, in its discomfort.

Elsewhere in this volume it was noted that President Obama was in attendance for the first public performance from *Hamilton* at the White House in 2009. The irony of *Hamilton*, the musical with Black and Brown actors portraying presidents, being greeted with laughter by the first Black president is thick, but it is also poetic. *Hamilton* represents the beginning of the United States, but in many ways it also represents the beginning of the Obama era in which new racial possibilities and realities were affecting the way America thought about its racial past, present, and future. Eduardo Bonilla-Silva defines racial ideology as "the racially based frameworks used by actors to explain and justify (dominant race) or challenge (subordinate race or races) the racial status quo."[60] Understanding the rhetorical choices and tropes in racial narratives is important if White people are to dismantle the former and embrace the latter. Whiteness and ideology are paired in this chapter but are not meant to reflect individual beliefs or feelings. Bonilla-Silva describes ideology as "a political instrument, not an exercise in personal logic."[61] Ideologies of whiteness can transcend personal cognition, but when that happens, I argue, there are visceral elements or reactions to racial narratives that can expose those ideologies. My argument here has been that the dialectical relationship—the tension—between praise and critique, comfort and discomfort, bodies who act and bodies that move, is extended to the significance and adaptability of the racial status quo.

NOTES

1 John Clyde Russell, faculty member, Kennesaw State University, jruss105@kennesaw.edu or john-clyderussell@gmail.com. Special thanks to Dr. Patricia Davis for the first revisions and edits of this chapter.
2 Toni Morrison, "The Site of Memory," in *Inventing the Truth: The Art and Craft of Memoir*, ed. William Zinsser, 2nd ed. (New York: Houghton Mifflin, 1995), 98.
3 I have chosen to use the capital "W" when referring to White people. It is important, I think, to do this because it signifies "White" as a race. Whereas whiteness has so often tried to separate itself from racial categorization by being the "norm" or place from which others become raced, making White a proper noun indicates a racial identity. This also signifies an ideology that relies on skin color. Black is often capitalized for the same reason: to signify a racial identity and history as people of the African diaspora. Also, I am specific in this chapter to signal Latino, Asian, Native American, or Black, Indigenous, Person of Color (BIPOC).

4 For example, see Jordan Fabian, "Obama: 'Hamilton' Is the Only Thing Dick Cheney and I Agree On," *The Hill*, March 14, 2016, https://thehill.com/blogs/in-the-know/in-the-know/272964-obama-hamilton-is-the-only-thing-dick-cheney-and-i-agree-on.
5 Ed Mazza, "'Weird Al' Yankovic Just Made History in the Weirdest Way Possible," March 16, 2018, *Huffington Post*, https://www.huffingtonpost.com/entry/weird-al-hamilton-polka-billboard_us_5aab475ee4b05b2217fd8f62.
6 Michael Paulson, "'Hamilton' Heads to Broadway in a Hip-Hop Retelling," *New York Times*, July 12, 2015, http://www.nytimes.com/2015/07/13/theater/hamilton-heads-to-broadway-in-a-hip-hop-retelling.html.
7 I use "(dis)comfort" hereafter when referring to the comfort/discomfort dynamic.
8 To read about such stories see Ray Raphael, *A People's History of the American Revolution: How Common People Shaped the Fight for Independence* (New York: The New Press, 2001).
9 Lyra D. Monteiro, "Race-Conscious Casting and the Erasure of the Black Past in Lin-Manuel Miranda's Hamilton," *The Public Historian* 38, no. 1 (2016): 89–98.
10 David Glassberg, "Public History and the Study of Memory," *The Public Historian* 18, no. 2 (1996): 10.
11 Leah Ceccarelli, "Polysemy: Multiple Meanings in Rhetorical Criticism," *Quarterly Journal of Speech* 84, no. 4 (1998): 398.
12 Paulson, "'Hamilton' Heads to Broadway."
13 Monteiro, "Race-Conscious Casting," 93.
14 Patricia Herrera, "Reckoning with America's Racial Past, Present, and Future in *Hamilton*," in *Historians on Hamilton: How a Blockbuster Musical Is Restaging America's Past*, eds. Renee C. Romano and Claire Bond Potter (New Brunswick, NJ: Rutgers University Press, 2018), 272.
15 Kenneth Burke, *A Grammar of Motives* (Berkeley: University of California Press, 1945).
16 Joseph R. Gusfield, *Kenneth Burke: On Symbols and Society* (Chicago, IL: University of Chicago Press, 1989), 9.
17 Nina Zipkin, "'Hamilton' Makes History with More Than $4 Million Holiday Week," *Entrepreneur*, January 3, 2019, https://www.entrepreneur.com/article/325682; Chaim Gartenberg, "Hamilton Is Getting Released a Year Early as a Disney Plus Exclusive," *The Verge*, May 12, 2020, https://www.theverge.com/2020/5/12/21255693/hamilton-musical-disney-plus-early-release-date-streaming-broadway-miranda.
18 Frederick Douglass, "Letter to Thomas Auld, September 3, 1848," in *Frederick Douglass: Selected Speeches and Writings*, ed. Philip S. Foner (Chicago, IL: Lawrence Hill Books, 1999), 111.
19 Timothy B. Tyson, *The Blood of Emmett Till* (New York: Simon & Schuster, 2017); Devery S. Anderson, *Emmett Till: The Murder that Shocked the World and Propelled the Civil Rights Movement* (Jackson: University Press of Mississippi, 2015).
20 Martin Luther King, Jr., "Letter from a Birmingham Jail," April 16, 1963, 9–10, http://okra.stanford.edu/transcription/document_images/undecided/630416-019.pdf.
21 Michael Bennett and Dave Zirin, *Things That Make White People Uncomfortable* (Chicago, IL: Haymarket Books, 2018).
22 Carla Herreria, "Fox News Host Cries Because Conversation on Race Makes Her 'Uncomfortable,'" *Huffington Post*, August 16, 2017, https://www.huffingtonpost.com/entry/fox-news-melissa-francis-race_us_5994d26ce4b0d0d2cc841dbf.
23 Robin DiAngelo, *White Fragility: Why It's So Hard for White People to Talk about Racism* (Boston, MA: Beacon Press, 2018), 2.

24 Greg Dickinson, Carole Blair, and Brian L. Ott, eds., *Places of Public Memory: The Rhetoric of Museums and Memorials* (Tuscaloosa: The University of Alabama Press, 2010).
25 Dickinson, Blair, and Ott, *Places of Public Memory: The Rhetoric of Museums and Memorials*, 6.
26 *National Treasure*, directed by Jon Turteltaub (Walt Disney Home Video: 2004); *The Patriot*, directed by Roland Emmerich (Columbia Tristar Home Video, 2000).
27 Reinhold Niebuhr, *The Irony of American History* (Chicago, IL: The University of Chicago Press, 1952).
28 Although Obama would use this phrasing throughout his presidency, its most noted usage can be found in the speech he gave during the 2008 campaign to address the Rev. Jeremiah Wright controversy. See "Transcript: Barack Obama's Speech on Race," *NPR*, March 18, 2008, https://www.npr.org/templates/story/story.php?storyId=88478467.
29 For a demonstration of slavery and American popular memory see George Lipsitz, *Time Passages: Collective Memory and American Popular Culture* (Minneapolis: University of Minnesota Press, 1990); Alison Landsberg, *Prosthetic Memory: The Transformation of American Remembrance in the Age of Mass Culture* (New York: Columbia University Press, 2004); William L. Van Deburg, *Slavery & Race in American Popular Culture* (Madison: University of Wisconsin Press, 1984).
30 For a detailed explanation of slavery's importance to the U.S. economy and rise of capitalism see Edward E. Baptist, *The Half Has Never Been Told: Slavery and the Making of American Capitalism* (New York: Basic Books, 2014).
31 *John Adams*, directed by Tom Hooper (Home Box Office, 2008).
32 Thomas Jefferson, *Notes on the State of Virginia* (London: Stockdale, 1787); Merrill D. Peterson, "Thomas Jefferson's *Notes on the State of Virginia*," in *Studies in Eighteenth-Century Culture*, vol. 7, ed. Roseann Runte (Madison: University of Wisconsin Press, 1978).
33 *Jefferson in Paris*, directed by James Ivory (1995; Burbank: Merchant Ivory Productions, 2004), DVD.
34 For example, an investigation into how K-12 U.S. History content standards is an excellent reflection of how slavery is taught and often portrayed in popular culture. See Carl B. Anderson and Scott Alan Metzger, "Slavery, the Civil War Era, and African American Representation in U.S. History: An Analysis of Four States' Academic Standards," *Theory & Research in Social Education* 39, no. 3 (2011): 393–415.
35 Toni Morrison, *Playing in the Dark: Whiteness and the Literary Imagination* (Cambridge: Harvard University Press, 1992).
36 Here I use Manning Marable's phrasing, "negation," to describe the way whiteness gets defined by what it is not. Manning Marable, *Living Black History: How Reimagining the African-American Past Can Remake America's Racial Future* (New York: Basic Books, 2006).
37 Morrison, *Playing in the Dark*, 52.
38 For example, see David Handlin, "One Hundred Best American Novels, 1770–1985 (a Draft)," *The American Scholar*, July 16, 2014, https://theamericanscholar.org/one-hundred-best-american-novels-1770-to-1985-a-draft/#.Xul3CWpKhm_.
39 Morrison, *Playing in the Dark*, 51–53.
40 Carla L. Peterson, "Forward: Eccentric Bodies," in *Recovering the Black Female Body: Self-Representations by African American Women*, eds. Michael Bennett and Vanessa D. Dickerson (New Brunswick, NJ: Rutgers University Press, 2001), ix.
41 Alan G. Gross, "Presence as Argument in the Public Sphere," *Rhetoric Society Quarterly* 35, no. 2 (2005): 5–21.

42 For more on public memory of John Adams—especially as it pertains to the conventional memory of his persona and perceived position on race—see Trevor Parry-Giles, "Fame, Celebrity, and the Legacy of John Adams," *Western Journal of Communication* 71, no. 1 (2008): 83–101; Arthur Scherr, *John Adams, Slavery, and Race: Ideas, Politics, and Diplomacy in Crisis* (Santa Barbara, CA: Praeger, 2018).
43 Lin-Manuel Miranda and Jeremy McCarter, *Hamilton: The Revolution* (New York: Grand Central Publishing, 2016), 60.
44 Miranda and McCarter, *Hamilton: The Revolution*, 61.
45 Miranda and McCarter, *Hamilton: The Revolution*, 253.
46 Miranda and McCarter, *Hamilton: The Revolution*, 210.
47 Miranda and McCarter, *Hamilton: The Revolution*, 210.
48 Miranda and McCarter, *Hamilton: The Revolution*, 210.
49 Miranda and McCarter, *Hamilton: The Revolution*, 133.
50 Miranda and McCarter, *Hamilton: The Revolution*, 161.
51 Manning Marable, *Living Black History*.
52 Miranda and McCarter, *Hamilton: The Revolution*, 87.
53 George Yancy, *Black Bodies, White Gazes: The Continuing Significance of Race in America*, 2nd ed. (New York: Rowman & Littlefield, 2017), 3.
54 Emanuel Leutze, *Washington Crossing the Deleware*, 1851, oil on canvas, 149 × 255 in., https://www.metmuseum.org/art/collection/search/11417.
55 Miranda and McCarter, *Hamilton: The Revolution*, 152.
56 Miranda and McCarter, *Hamilton: The Revolution*, 95.
57 Alessandra Raengo, *Critical Race Theory and Bamboozled* (New York: Bloomsbury Academic, 2016), 175.
58 Tommy Kail, quoted in Miranda and McCarter, *Hamilton: The Revolution*, 33. The quotation has also been attributed to Lin-Manuel Miranda, see Edward Delman, "How Lin-Manual Miranda Shapes History," *The Atlantic*, September 29, 2015, https://www.theatlantic.com/entertainment/archive/2015/09/lin-manuel-miranda-hamilton/408019.
59 Yancy, *Black Bodies, White Gazes*, 172.
60 Eduardo Bonilla-Silva, *Racism without Racists: Color-Blind Racism and the Persistence of Racial Inequality in the United States* (New York: Rowman & Littlefield, 2003), 9.
61 Bonilla-Sliva, *Racism without Racists*, 10.

CHAPTER SEVEN

Patriarchy and Power: A Feminist Critique of *Hamilton*

EMILY BERG PAUP[1]

At its core, the Broadway musical *Hamilton* is a work of rhetorical history—one that engages in acts of recovery, analysis, and interpretation. Lin-Manuel Miranda's words and music both maintain and create the public memory of the figures featured in the story. Miranda highlights this mission when multiple characters sing the lyrics, "who lives, who dies, who tells your story" at key points throughout the show, including in its concluding moments.[2] He ultimately attributes this public memory project to Alexander Hamilton's wife, Elizabeth "Eliza" Schuyler Hamilton. Miranda writes a narrative in which it is Eliza who becomes the voice for Alexander's legacy. "I put myself back in the narrative," she sings. "I stop wasting time on tears. I live another 50 years. It's not enough."[3] In an initial reading, this move feels meaningful and progressive. It seems to finally give Eliza the agency and power that the audience craves on her behalf. A feminist critique of the show as a whole, though, reveals a text that reifies gender norms and perpetuates the ever-present notion that women have a voice only because of, in service to, and for men.

While perhaps accurately reflecting the realities of history, the patriarchal maintenance of gender and power of *Hamilton*'s plot sequence, characters, and lyrics misses an opportunity to push the boundaries of gender as the show does with notions of race and identity. A feminist critique of *Hamilton* implores us to think about the historical injustices that women have faced. It also forces us to grapple with how rhetorical history can tell us as much about the past as it does about our present. While there are a few references to the constraints that women faced at the time, the musical as a whole perpetuates traditional patriarchal notions of gender. As a result, audiences are not encouraged to critique the system that dictates many of the limitations that women still face today.

While *Hamilton* radically revises our notions of the American founding through hip-hop and diverse voices, the show fails to question the creation of the patriarchal system that has and continues to limit women's agency and power. This chapter will begin by explicating just what that system looked like through a discussion of coverture, the gendered expectations of separate spheres, and republican motherhood. It will then use feminist criticism to show how the characters in *Hamilton*, and most especially the character of Eliza, embody the outmoded "ideals" of eighteenth/nineteenth century womanhood. These patriarchal ideologies are not just a part of the historical narrative of the story but embedded in the musical text and performance itself. Even when the systemic injustices that women faced at the time are dramatized, they are done so only in service to furthering the plot of Alexander's story and without a critique of those systems. I will conclude with a deliberation about the obligations of rhetorical history. Ultimately, *Hamilton* sustains the constraints of eighteenth- and nineteenth-century gender laws and ideologies in an otherwise radical and innovative piece of theater.

PATRIARCHAL SYSTEMS AND SUBVERSIVE AGENCY

Gender has always dictated power. Legal limitations and socially dictated behavioral barriers dominated society in the Early Republic, despite the founding generation's revolutionary approach to representative government. The system of coverture, the ideology of separate spheres, and the expectations of republican motherhood all limited what women could do in all facets of life. Despite these barriers, some women, including Elizabeth Schuyler Hamilton, found agency in subversive ways. *Hamilton* alludes to these historic realities but also normalizes them in a way that prevents the audience from critically questioning their influence on gender expectations today.

Coverture and Separate Spheres

As the nation began to consider how it would set up its government and define the rights of its citizens, the authors of the Constitution proclaimed an outright commitment to the ideals of a Republic while ostensibly breaking from British traditions. However, while the Revolutionary generation tried to redefine the structure of government, they "did not have the heart or the energy to reconstruct the entire legal system."[4] As a result, the Early Republic operated under the British legal system that dictated the rights of men and women called "coverture."[5] This was "the principle that at marriage the husband controlled the physical body of the wife ... By treating married women as 'covered' by their husbands' civic identity."[6] This prevented women from having control over their bodies, their own property, their labor, their finances, and the lives of their children. Coverture also limited women's political identities. As Francis Cutting, a Democrat from New York said in 1855, "by the act of marriage itself the political character of the wife shall at once conform to the political character of the husband."[7] This, in turn, seemingly made women's enfranchisement "unnecessary" because they were thought to be politically represented by their husbands.

This system also helped to sustain gendered behavioral expectations for the demographic group to which the Hamiltons and others in the founding generation belonged. Upper-class, able-bodied white men and women operated in two separate and distinct spheres. Men occupied the "public" sphere of business, law, and politics. Women were meant to stay in the "private sphere" and were expected to be pious, pure, submissive, and domestic.[8] It was considered improper for women to speak in public, be present at polling places, and even to be present for political debate. Women were considered delicate and in need of protection; men in contrast were resilient, strong, and perfectly suited for the raucous nature of public life. The United States was built around the idea that gendered and raced political and social hierarchies were necessary to maintain society's class and social structure. The ideology of separate spheres mandated that "no 'true woman' could be a public persuader."[9]

Republican Motherhood and Subversive Agency

Most women and men in the Early Republic did not combat the prescribed place of women in the home. Historical evidence shows that some white women found subversive agency within the patriarchal system itself.[10] "Republican motherhood" was "a privatized feminine ideal ... that essentially linked women's citizenship to their role as care givers in the home."[11] Women were thought to embody civic virtue. Through their nurturance and patriotism, it was believed that women could best serve the nation in cultivating civically minded husbands and sons. This idea stems from the myth of the classical Spartan Mother, "who raised sons prepared to sacrifice themselves to the good of the *polis*."[12] Women, and specifically mothers, had the duty of educating their sons to be patriotic and virtuous.[13] Women could not participate in politics in public, but could cultivate political minds in their homes. In fact, the behavioral expectations of women in politics to this day are rooted in republican motherhood.

The home was transformed into political space as early as the American Revolution. Women enacted political agency by boycotting imported goods, petitioning, and running their husband's farms and businesses while they were away at war—all activities typically reserved for men, but still consistent with a woman's role in the home and the community.[14] The Revolutionary War also provided women with the opportunity to create political identities and assist their government through writing.[15] In fact, the Revolutionary period gave the country a few women who are now revered in history for their political thought, like Judith Sargent Murray, Susannah Rowson, Mercy Otis Warren, and Hannah Webster Foster.[16]

In addition, women's goals and ambitions were considered "purer and nobler than men's, untainted by self-interest or the pursuit of personal gain."[17] Whereas some of the "virtues" of true womanhood such as piety and sentimentality were conditions that excluded women from political life,[18] "her emotional and guileless nature provided strengths in pursuing the important tasks of binding community divisions and upholding moral norms."[19] Existence in a "separate sphere" allowed upper-class white women to congregate and foster group identity.[20] Moral reform organizations gave women the opportunity to participate in public life while maintaining their role as moral protector. Women took on "moral" issues like prostitution, temperance, public health, slavery, poverty, education, and childcare. Women's groups argued that their work "served 'the interests of civil society' by improving the moral character of the poor and promoting social order."[21]

There is also extensive evidence that women in Washington D.C. participated in partisan politics in the Early Republic. They served as hostesses for political functions, networked with other political wives, held political discussions with other women, and played a role in "shaping the national discourse" by connecting their political husbands and driving policy debates.[22] The role of political wife became an especially important aspect of women's political participation.[23] Abigail Adams is an example of one of these first political partnerships. John Adams frequently discussed political issues with his wife, leading her to comment in a letter in 1780, "What a politician you have made me."[24]

The Agency of Elizabeth Schuyler Hamilton

In historical narratives, Elizabeth Schuyler Hamilton embodied republican motherhood and seemed to be the ideal domestic wife. Hamilton biographer Ron Chernow describes her as, "short and pretty, she was utterly devoid of conceit and was to prove an ideal companion for Hamilton, lending a strong home foundation to his turbulent life."[25] Chernow emphasizes her domesticity again when he writes, "In many respects, Eliza, who loved to sew and garden, was typical of the young Dutch women of her generation who were domestic and self-effacing, thrifty in managing households, and eager to raise large broods of children."[26] Later, he writes "Eliza would gladly have devoted herself to private life alone, but she submitted good-naturedly to the demands of her husband's career."[27] Eliza was apparently, "the most self-effacing 'founding mother,' doing everything in her power to focus the spotlight exclusively on her husband."[28]

Eliza had quite a bit of political power in this role, though, as evidenced by the fact that she helped Alexander as he wrote the *Federalist Papers* and secured his legacy as the author of Washington's "Farewell Address"—now considered to be one of the most significant pieces of political rhetoric in history.[29] In addition, Eliza's social activism increased once Alexander died. Miranda does acknowledge some of this work when Eliza sings about founding the "first private orphanage in New York City."[30] Despite the fact that Eliza sings only that she "established" the orphanage, she served as the first directress of the New York Orphan Asylum Society for 27 years. In fact, Chernow claims that she ran it in full—involving herself in development, fundraising, public relations, and handling finances.[31] This sort of work gave women of the time the political agency and voice that the patriarchal system prevented them from having.

Although she never became the First Lady, Eliza was treated like one during the latter part of her life. The Monument Society appointed her, Dolley Madison, and Louisa Catherine Johnson Adams directors of a "committee of ladies," to raise money around the country for what would become the Washington Monument (which is mentioned in a lyric at the end of the show[32]). She and Madison were honored guests at the cornerstone-laying of the monument on July 4, 1848.[33] Once she moved in with her daughter in 1848 at the age of 91, politicians, dignitaries, and community leaders would often visit. Eliza was powerful and someone whose blessing was sought by many U.S. presidents. She was considered a "last living link to the Revolutionary era."[34] Unfortunately, a feminist reading reveals that *Hamilton* undersells these achievements in a way that is damaging to both Eliza's legacy and to audiences' abilities to question the patriarchal value systems so dominant still today.

A FEMINIST CRITIQUE OF THE WOMEN OF *HAMILTON*

A feminist analysis of *Hamilton* demonstrates that popular culture can be innovative and progressive while simultaneously buttressing certain systems of oppression. A feminist critic's principal interest is in rhetoric's ability to "disrupt" (or in the case of this study, neglect to disrupt) "hegemonic structures."[35] This chapter engages in a close textual reading aimed at one of feminist criticism's most fundamental objectives, which is to analyze "artifacts that oppressed, subordinated, or silenced individuals in order to identify the ways in which oppressive conditions are created."[36] *Hamilton* nods to gender inequities but does so in a patriarchal way that "is male dominated, male identified, and male centered."[37] A feminist reading of *Hamilton* helps to highlight just how subtle and pervasive patriarchal ideations can be.

Because the past can influence the way people view the present, those textually re-creating history can tailor its memory to influence audiences. Retelling the past can build "symbolic bridges between today and yesterday."[38] The past can become a symbol for interpreting the meaning of social practices and current events.[39] In other words, "the present develops from a past still inherent in it."[40] History itself can be strategically reproduced by its authors to influence present social conditions.[41] As a result, the past can be used "to mediate competing interpretations and privilege some explanations over others."[42] The past is collectively experienced, and as such, its retelling provides an opportunity for thoughtful critique. This is the space in which a feminist textual critique can shed light on how patriarchal systems permeate "our socio-political, economic, and cultural life" and "are communicated in the language we use."[43] *Hamilton*'s audiences are seeing the dramatization of a patriarchal system designed to keep women as second-class citizens without much acknowledgement of why that system is problematic. Women's agency is downplayed, and the story is structured around the male experience. As a result, audiences watch as gendered tropes are performed without question and thus perpetuated.

The women in *Hamilton* are controlled by a narrative that centers on their love for Alexander and their dedication to family life, whereas the male characters are driven by ambition and politics. This is perhaps no more obvious than when after a series of emotional scenes about the relationship between Eliza and Alexander and the death of their son, Thomas Jefferson sings, "Can we get back to politics? Please?"[44] Here, they implore the audience "to return to the *real* story" and "its masculine concerns about power" in the public sphere at the exclusion of the women in the story.[45] Coverture, separate spheres ideology, and the domestic expectations of republican motherhood are not just represented through the historical narrative that Miranda tells, but are enacted and performed through the lyrics, staging, and character choices. A feminist rhetorical reading offers an in depth look at just how pervasive gender ideology is and how engrained it is today.

Coverture in *Hamilton*

Hamilton often points out the ironies and contradictions of the American founding, like through its cabinet "battles" about freedom and slavery. Yet, while the entire first act of the musical is a celebration of the heroes of the Revolutionary War and the principles of liberty that drove the effort, systems like coverture took hold as a legal tradition unchallenged in the creation of the new nation and unquestioned in Miranda's retelling. There is an obvious contradiction in the idea that the Revolutionary generation engaged in a war against the patriarchal domination of

King George III and then instituted continued patriarchal control over women.[46] As historian Catherine Allgor argues, *Hamilton* "rarely conveys the centrality of gender as a system that ordered and organized society" and thus "misses one of the most important stories of the American Revolution: the failure of the revolution to challenge 'coverture'" as the central organizing system for power and access in the Early Republic."[47] The men do almost all of the debating, thinking, and philosophizing. The men dominate all scenes that are about decision-making, law, and politics. The women are part of the story only when acting in ways consistent with the limiting domestic expectations of womanhood.

There are a few moments during which coverture is referenced in a veiled way. When we first meet the Schuyler sisters, Peggy sings of needing their father's permission to go downtown New York City.[48] Angelica Schuyler sings that her only job is to "marry rich"[49] and of finding a "wealthy husband,"[50] demonstrating that it would have been common for a woman to weigh her future husband's financial and political prospects in her decision to marry.[51] Eliza also references the power that her father would have in her choice of husband.[52] Later in the show, Maria Reynolds sings of her desperation for money and seeks protection from an abusive husband. This demonstrates just how dependent women were on men for support, especially when she asks Alexander for it pleading, "please don't leave me with him helpless."[53] Finally, because divorce and/or any legal recourse for Alexander's affair was impossible for women under this system, Eliza's only punitive response to her husband's infidelity was to make him "sleep in his office instead."[54] For the most part, though, the notion that women's lives and rights were at the mercy of their male keepers is mostly ignored in what is otherwise a celebration of the pride that the founders had in their newfound liberty and independence.

Coverture demanded that women adhere to their husband's political identity and be fully represented in the public sphere by their husbands. This was apparently of primary importance to Alexander Hamilton. In a letter that he wrote in April of 1779 to John Laurens, he writes of his ideal wife: "In politics, I am indifferent what side she may be of." He then boasts, "I think I have arguments that will easily convert her to mine."[55] Chernow describes Eliza as having "never deviated from his beliefs, identified implicitly with his causes, and came to regard his political enemies as her own."[56] The character of Eliza demonstrates this too, as she willingly supports both her husband's and her father's political pursuits. A republican mother like Eliza would not outwardly participate in politics, but she might understand political strategy so as to be able to explain it to her son, just as she explains her father losing his seat in the Senate by singing "sometimes that's how it goes."[57] Similarly, Alexander discusses political strategy with Angelica via private letter in "Take a Break." Eliza actually has more political agency in an earlier workshop version of the song "Schuyler Defeated." In this version, Eliza closely follows politics, knowing her father was initially running for senate "unopposed" before being challenged by Aaron Burr.[58] She then sings, "I gotta go, I gotta find Alexander ... he'll consider this a personal slander, I've got to stop a homicide."[59] Here, she not only keeps track of political strategy but also seemingly takes an active part in controlling her husband's public messaging. In the final version of the show, though, the system of coverture is performed and spoken of as if par for the course, without the clever asides that Miranda infuses in the rest of the musical.

Separate Spheres in *Hamilton*

Just as coverture seemingly erased female civic identity, it reinforced male participation in the public. The female characters in *Hamilton* venture out of "domestic" spaces only once during the entirety of the musical—when the Schuyler sisters venture downtown New York as young single women. Even this act is portrayed as transgressive, though, as if they are disobeying their father.[60] All of the other scenes featuring women take place either in homes or close to them. Even the side reference to a woman of color that comes when Thomas Jefferson sings "Sally be a lamb, darlin', won'tcha open it" in a "shout-out" to Sally Hemings is in keeping with the women acting as domestic helpmates.[61] In contrast, Miranda emphasizes how important the public sphere is to Alexander when he frames going home as a punishment given to him by General George Washington in "Meet Me Inside."[62] Men and women are assigned their separate spheres again when only the women first sing "Thomas Jefferson's coming home!" when Thomas Jefferson appears at the top of the second act, as if welcoming him back to their sphere.[63] This same pattern emerges during George Washington's final number when only the women sing, "George Washington's going home!" before the rest of the ensemble joins in.[64]

The political freedom that was celebrated by the founding generation was reliant upon the dominance of masculine power and keeping women in their place. "The presentation and primacy of masculine values," Allgor writes, "is one of the most historically accurate aspects of *Hamilton*."[65] Public power has and continues to be predicated on a hierarchical relationship between masculinity and femininity, the former being superior to the latter.[66] Politics has long operated as "symbolic contests over competing definitions of 'real manhood' and thus over what kind of man can, and should, be in charge."[67] Moreover, many believed that a woman's physical "feebleness" and "meekness" were further justification of her inability to participate in the world of public affairs.[68] The "last thing the male revolutionaries would do would be to call their masculine authority into question by freeing their wives."[69] This control is dramatized in the song "Let it Go," cut from the final Broadway musical. In it, Alexander yells at his wife, "What in the hell are you doing downtown?" in an aggressive and angry way.[70] In this light, Eliza's "let me be a part of the narrative" sounds more like she is asking for permission.[71]

Miranda does not just nod to this weak/tough dichotomy but uses it as the basis for his dramatization of the power struggle between the revolutionaries and the British crown. Alexander often uses physical toughness as a source of power. After the show's first duel scene, Alexander sings to Washington that "John should have shot him in the mouth; That would've shut him up." He goes on to beg Washington to "give him command of a battalion."[72] It is clear in this scene and others that Alexander believes that his most important task is to show physical strength in battle. Later in the show during "Cabinet Battle #1," Hamilton sings "turn around, bend over, I'll show you wear my shoe fits," while on the verge of a physical confrontation.[73] Finally, the most obvious and ironic portrayal of masculinity is dramatized in the final duel. In his final letter to his wife (which he directed not to be given to her "unless I shall first have terminated my earthly career"), Alexander wrote that had he been able to avoid the duel he would have done so. But he continued that, "it was not possible, without sacrifices which would have rendered me unworthy of your esteem." He continued, "I need not tell you of the pangs I feel, from the idea of quitting you and exposing you to the anguish which I know you would feel. Nor could I dwell on the topic lest it should unman me."[74] It is clear in both history and in Miranda's retelling that Hamilton's masculine honor was at stake—a masculinity that both necessitated a response to a physical challenge and required an avoidance of any discussion of emotion. This ideology of public masculinity is what ultimately led to his demise.

While Hamilton and his compatriots are frequently fueled by their "tough masculinity," the two primary foil characters that represent loyalty to the crown—the characters of Samuel Seabury and King George III—are both stereotypically feminized. In "Farmer Refuted," Alexander mocks Seabury for his physical toughness in a reference to his "mange" being the same as a domesticated dog. Miranda comments on the intentionality of physical/vocal dominance in his margin notes about this song, commenting that it was written because Hamilton "using the same vowels and cadences and talking over him . . . felt like the kind of superpower Hamilton could deploy to impress his friends."[75] Those who have seen the musical performed will recognize a similar pattern in the way that actors play King George III as an effeminate, whiny, and emotionally unstable ruler.

Miranda doesn't just portray masculinity as strong and femininity as weak. The musical goes further, showing femininity as manipulative and threatening. Alexander jokes during his proposal to Eliza that her sister Angelica, arguably the most out-spoken woman in the show, "tried to take a bite of me."[76] King George III's effeminate yet tyrannical portrayal comes with a threat as he sings "I will kill your friends and family to remind you of my love."[77] In Miranda and McCarter's book about the show, they describe Jonathan Groff's original performance as George III as "seductive" and "haughty"—two adjectives rarely used to describe men in our current culture.

In the second act, it is also female manipulation and seduction that leads to the downfall of Alexander's political career. Alexander's mistress, Maria Reynolds, appears on stage dressed in a low-cut red dress and sings in a low, tantalizing alto tone as Alexander sings that she "led me to her bed, let her legs spread."[78] She is portrayed as the aggressor and he as passive, as he sings repeatedly "I don't know how to say no to this," and she directs him, "don't say no to this."[79] To further drive home this framing, Alexander explains the affair later in the show to Madison, Jefferson, and Burr by saying, "She courted me; Escorted me to bed and when she had me in a corner; That's when Reynolds extorted me."[80] In history, Hamilton describes her similarly when in the "Reynolds Pamphlet" he writes: "The intercourse with Mrs. Reynolds, in the mean time, continued; and, though various reflections ... induced me to wish a cessation of it; yet her conduct, made it extremely difficult to disentangle myself."[81] Maria Reynolds was portrayed by both Hamilton himself and Miranda as manipulative and Alexander just a victim. Although much of *Hamilton* reimagines history, the women in the show are still presented in stereotypical ways and without the critical eye that Miranda employs in his other creative choices.

Republican Motherhood in *Hamilton*

Republican mothers like Eliza, "attempted to meet the obligations of the ideal female patriot" by accentuating their "other-centric nature and muted their own political and public ambitions."[82] As a result, "they sacrificed their own physical and intellectual development and suppressed their own public interest in order to support the active citizenship of their husbands and sons."[83] This seems to be Eliza's purpose in the entire musical. The character of Eliza Hamilton is a reflection of women in the Early Republic—a domestic, private woman who is wholly dedicated to the life of her husband. The paradox of republican motherhood was that while women had some agency and influence within the home, their voice was still not accepted in public. Their work was "generally considered in terms of their service roles to others."[84] Republican motherhood "emphasized women's labor on behalf of others as their primary and preferred means of participating in the country's development."[85] Eliza's actions to preserve Alexander's legacy were most likely in service to this obligation.

We are first introduced to Eliza fully in the song "Helpless," where she sings about being helplessly in love with Alexander and justifies her life choices because there is "nothing that" *his* "mind can't do."[86] She provides solace and calm for Alexander during the Revolutionary War, she teaches her children piano, French, and about politics, and she works for decades to solidify her husband's place in American history. Even the song "Burn," when we hear Eliza grappling with the moral failure of her husband, is centered around Alexander as she sings the words "you" and "your" 38 times in a song that is only about six stanzas long.[87] In the finale, Eliza justifies her work in the public sphere as a continuation of Alexander's work when she sings, "I ask myself what would you do if you had more time?"[88] After this, there is a gesture to Eliza's own agency when she sings "will they tell my story?" but the voices of the chorus drown out that lyric as they sing simultaneously "will they tell your story" in reference to Alexander.[89] We say goodbye to Eliza still in deference to Alexander when she sings, "Oh I can't wait to see you again."[90] Eliza's character begins and ends as solely dedicated to her husband's life. Because "political accomplishments for women were earned vicariously through the valor and achievements of their husbands and sons,"[91] it is likely that Elizabeth Hamilton did in fact view her work through this lens. But still, the only time Eliza finds her voice in public during the musical is in her attempt to preserve Alexander's legacy. This overlooks the fact that Eliza became one of the most honored voices of the founding generation. When Miranda frames her work as only in memory of and service to Alexander's legacy, he downplays her accomplishments.

Women were expected to uphold the moral fabric of both their home and society at large. Gendered behavioral expectations in the early nineteenth century assumed that men had a "greater capacity for immoral behavior."[92] Women, on the other hand, had a "special moral nature" that "suited her to ensure the moral and social order."[93] As explained earlier in this chapter, women did this from the confines of the private sphere. In fact, one of a patriotic woman's central tasks was to instill morality in her children and enforce it in her husband.[94] Miranda acknowledges this as a hallmark of Eliza when he writes, "Eliza's warmth and vibrancy made her a remarkable woman, but they also make her a challenging character."[95] This is dramatized through songs like "That Would Be Enough," during which she seemingly knows Alexander's mind better than he does.[96] It is enacted again every time she sings "look around, look around, at how lucky we are to be alive right now."[97] Later in the show, Eliza encourages Alexander to "take a break" at home and Angelica advises him to "sit down" and "compromise."[98] Even if not intentional, this reinforces the public/private split that dictated gendered behavior at the time. It is perhaps telling that when Miranda and McCarter reflect on Eliza's character, they begin and end with the assumption that she was "pure goodness."[99] Eliza's moral goodness is explicitly performed by the actors who play her, the music, and the script. Her songs all exhibit delicate tones, calm melodies, and pretty harmonies.

This "goodness" is then contrasted in the narrative with Alexander's lack of it during his affair with Maria Reynolds. It is important to note that Alexander seems to associate his affair with embarrassment but not a lack of morality when he sings "Yes, I have reason for shame, but I have not committed treason and sullied my good name."[100] His "good name" could seemingly remain intact as long as his moral misstep was not in relation to politics. Eliza, on the other hand, would become, "one of the first in a long line of political wives who made enormous, humiliating sacrifices to save their husband's careers."[101] The lyrics in the song "Burn" suggest that Eliza's choice to remove her reaction from the historical record was about privacy, because "the world has no right to my heart."[102] Understanding gender roles at the time though suggests a different reason. Eliza chose to erase "herself from the narrative" by burning letters that included her reaction to the affair after Alexander's death.[103] Because the ideal republican mother was responsible for maintaining her husband's virtue, Eliza was most likely embarrassed by her husband's behavior. In burning letters that involved her reaction to the affair after Alexander's death, she might have been attempting to control what historians would know about her. In this way, she could, in theory, remain unassociated with his transgressions and thus preserve her own moral reputation.

As republican mothers and under the system of coverture, women's voices always came second to men's. In an overarching way, a similar pattern emerges in the musical. *Hamilton*'s plot is driven by a few male voices—those most well-known to us as the Founding Fathers. The experience of the women in Alexander Hamilton's life are part of a secondary storyline that centers around his romantic relationships with them. Unfortunately this is a common pattern in history as, "the lives and words of women and other 'others' are relegated to the periphery of the narrative."[104] Theater critic James McMaster notices this when he writes, "The female characters simply do not get enough stage time and, when they do appear onstage, their desires, fears, hopes, plans, and narratives exist only in relation to Alexander, the man at the center of Miranda's musical."[105] This is in keeping with the way that Ron Chernow describes Eliza in the biography on which the musical is based. He writes, "Both Alexander and Eliza attended the first inaugural ball on May 7. Eliza was well placed to be a social ornament of the new regime and later looked back fondly on those days."[106] An "ornament," not a key character. Ultimately, *Hamilton* enacts a historically accurate and traditional narrative of nineteenth century womanhood that fails to highlight the injustices that women faced and instead just reinforces these gendered patterns.

IMPLICATIONS

If one were to analyze Miranda's *Hamilton* for its allegiance to history, his portrayal of women of the time is, in some ways, accurate. As this essay details, the character of Eliza Hamilton in particular embodies gendered expectations in the Early Republic. It should also be noted that the audience's introduction and farewell to female characters gives a nod to gender agency. Angelica Schuyler's intellectualism is on display in the beginning (with an implied recognition of gender limitations) as she sings, "I've been reading 'Common Sense' by Thomas Paine; So men say that

I'm intense or I'm insane; You want a revolution?; I want a revelation; So listen to my declaration." She then delivers one of the show's early applause lines singing she would "meet" and "compel" Thomas Jefferson to "include women in the sequel" to the Declaration of Independence.[107] The line is delivered with enough punch that the audience comes to expect this same sort of agency to be bolstered throughout the show. One could argue that placing the narrative in Eliza's hands at the end of the musical is similar. The fact that the musical ends with Eliza is both poignant and meaningful for many women in the audience, including myself. By giving Eliza the last word, Miranda might be "reinforcing his over-all project, which is in part to displace the founding story as the province of white men."[108] Elizabeth Schuyler Hamilton did embark on a massive biographical project in partnership with her son, John Church Hamilton, and her efforts are part of the reason that we know what we do about the Hamiltons today.[109] Perhaps, "by implicitly equating Eliza's acts of narration with his own," Miranda is "acknowledging the women who built the country alongside the men."[110] Yet, bookending the show by giving women agency and voice is not enough.

The issue is not necessarily in *Hamilton*'s historical "accuracy," but it lies rather with the larger rhetorical project to which the musical contributes. *Hamilton*'s ambitious casting of people of color and a gender-neutral ensemble suggests that Miranda wants to "reclaim American history from the white men who created it on behalf of a multicultural generation whom he seeks to represent."[111] *Hamilton* demonstrates that "the past is not completely knowable, that we must extrapolate from what we know, that we can remake the world of the past in our own image, represented by two dozen actors of color in costume as the founding fathers."[112] Due to its inclusive casting, historian Joseph Adelman further claims that "the past comes alive," in *Hamilton*, "in new and fresh ways in the bodies and sounds of the present."[113] While this may be true in terms of race, this progressive project does not extend to a re-imagining of the role of women.

I began this chapter by arguing that Miranda is engaged primarily in a project of rhetorical history. The genius of this show is that it takes an oft-forgotten Founding Father and turns him into someone with whom young audiences might connect. While audience members "understand that having a largely minority cast peopling a story of great white men is a comment of sorts about historical truth," they "still seem to think that the play *is* history."[114] *Hamilton* does, in fact, contain "a remarkable amount of history for a piece of musical theater."[115] Educators are using it across the country in their lessons for this reason. Being able to teach American history through hip-hop music and nontraditional voices is a wonderful resource and way to connect students to the past. Because of this, the portrayal of women in *Hamilton* is that much more important.

Those who write these sorts of histories have the power to not only shape how we collectively remember the past, but also how we use that past to make sense of today. In many ways, *Hamilton* is "about interpreting the past through the lens of the present, which reverses the interest of most historians to understand the past on its own terms."[116] Rhetorical history "aides in understanding the present by placing it in the context of the past."[117] Individual pasts are often reproduced under the influence of present social conditions and are thus "usable."[118] The ability to "render the present familiar" is important for both recovery and interpretation of the past.[119] Many of Miranda's choices in music, lyrics, character development, and staging seem to be explicitly in pursuit of this idea. The characters "consciously refer to the shaping of historical memory through the play"[120] with interpretive lyrics meant to help the audience understand Hamilton's decisions and motivations. Lines like "what is a legacy?" "some notes at the beginning of a song someone will sing for me," "look around at how lucky you are to be alive right now," and "history has its eyes on you"[121] repeating throughout the show all point to this overall rhetorical purpose. Hamilton's story, as told by Miranda, is painted as timeless and resonant no matter the historical age.

This is where the potential of *Hamilton* falls short in terms of gender roles. As this analysis demonstrates, not only are we not encouraged to think of women in a different way, but the art itself bolsters these gender limitations. To those in the Early Republic, "the celebration of the wife and mother roles filled by most female citizens was encouraging to many women because it openly acknowledged their value."[122] But that was in the early 1800s. *Hamilton* was first performed in 2015, some 200 years later and it still does the same thing. The musical "still offers a traditional story of the founding" for women, just as it "largely marginalizes and ignores the actual experiences of people of color."[123] This idea led theater critic Caryn Robbins to ask: "Is this 'progressive' musical, which makes us think so differently about our founding fathers, doing the same for the women who lived alongside them?"[124] *Hamilton* places women in traditional positions and assigns them stereotypical tropes, all without question. This not only hurts the progress of women in the public sphere today, but it also places enormous and often impossible expectations on their behavior. Furthermore, it is only wealthier white women who have ever been in the position to fulfill these expectations in the first place. Because the only female characters we see embody these tropes, it implies that these are the only roles available to women even today.

Feminist criticism is "oriented toward the achievement of gender justice," which often seeks to understand "the concept of gender itself as politically constructed."[125] This analysis demonstrates that *Hamilton* plays a role in maintaining this gendered hierarchy. The women of *Hamilton* have limited agency. Their stories, their scenes, and their rhetorical worlds exist either within or adjacent to Alexander's life and space. This is yet another piece of evidence that popular culture can contribute "to our understanding of why feminism remains marginalized and why power imbalances between men and women remain intractable."[126] *Hamilton*'s portrayal of women suggests "that Americans do not fully understand, or have not come to terms with, the idea that our founding happened with an instrument of gender domination like coverture in place."[127] The worry is that while audiences are experiencing the American founding through new and fresh voices, they are also seeing traditional gender roles left unquestioned. Consider the idea that, "the best art challenges what we think we know, even as it relies upon implicit and explicit assumptions shared by the audience."[128] Gender role expectations are assumptions shared by the audience and are left undisputed and largely ignored in what is otherwise a groundbreaking musical. Overall, *Hamilton* largely demonstrates just how the silencing of women in history and society continues.

NOTES

1. Emily Berg Paup, Assistant Professor, College of Saint Benedict and St. John's University, epaup@csbsju.edu.
2. Lin-Manuel Miranda and Jeremy McCarter, *Hamilton: The Revolution* (New York, NY: Grand Central Publishing, 2016), 120.
3. Miranda and McCarter, *Hamilton: The Revolution*, 280.
4. Linda Kerber, *No Constitutional Right to Be Ladies: Women and the Obligations of Citizenship* (New York, NY: Hill and Wang, 1998), xxiii.
5. Kerber, *No Constitutional Right to Be Ladies*, xxiii. "Coverture" stems from William Blackstone's *Commentaries on the Laws of England*, a series of legal writings that were influential for many areas of American law.
6. Kerber, *No Constitutional Right to Be Ladies*, xxiii.
7. Nancy Cott, "Marriage and Women's Citizenship in the United States, 1830–1934," *American Historical Review* 103, no. 5 (1998): 1456.
8. Barbara Welter, "The Cult of True Womanhood: 1820–1860," *American Quarterly* 18 (1966): 152.
9. Karlyn Kohrs Campbell, *Man Cannot Speak for Her: A Critical Study of Early Feminist Rhetoric* I (New York, NY: Praeger, 1989), 9–10.
10. See Paula Baker, "The Domestication of Politics: Women and American Political Society, 1780–1920," *American Historical Review* 89 (June 1984): 620–47; Nancy Cott, *The Bonds of Womanhood: 'Woman's Sphere' in New England, 1780–1835* (New Haven, CT: Yale University Press, 1977).
11. Wendy Gunther-Canada, "Jean-Jacques Rousseau and Mary Wollstonecraft on the Sexual Politics of Republican Motherhood," *Southeastern Political Review* 27, no. 3 (1999): 470.
12. Linda Kerber, "The Republican Mother: Women and the Enlightenment—An American Perspective," *American Quarterly* 28, no. 2 (1976): 188.
13. Gunther-Canada, "Jean-Jacques Rousseau and Mary Wollstonecraft," 475; Kerber, "The Republican Mother," 203.
14. Baker, "The Domestication of Politics," 624.
15. Linda Kerber, *Women of the Republic: Intellect & Ideology in Revolutionary America* (New York, NY: W.W. Norton & Co., 1986), 269.
16. Kerber, *Women of the Republic*, 11.
17. Rosemarie Zagarri, *Revolutionary Backlash: Women and Politics in the Early American Republic* (Philadelphia: University of Pennsylvania Press, 2007), 86.

18 Baker, "The Domestication of Politics," 629.
19 Baker, "The Domestication of Politics," 630.
20 Welke, *Law and the Borders of Belonging*, 101.
21 Anne Boylan, "Women and Politics in the Era Before Seneca Falls," *Journal of the Early Republic* 10 (Fall 1990): 373–74.
22 Catherine Allgor, *Parlor Politics: In Which the Ladies of Washington Help Build a City and a Government* (Charlottesville: University Press of Virginia, 2001), 119; Robert J. Dinkin, *Before Equal Suffrage: Women in Partisan Politics from Colonial Times to 1920* (Westport, CT: Greenwood Press, 1995), 21–22.
23 Louise Young, "Women's Place in American Politics: The Historical Perspective," *Journal of Politics* 38 (August 1976): 304–7.
24 Dinkin, *Before Equal Suffrage*, 15.
25 Ron Chernow, *Alexander Hamilton* (New York, NY: Penguin Press, 2004), 130.
26 Chernow, *Alexander Hamilton*, 147.
27 Chernow, *Alexander Hamilton*, 335.
28 Chernow, *Alexander Hamilton*, 130.
29 Chernow, *Alexander Hamilton*, 247–48, 508.
30 Miranda and McCarter, *Hamilton: The Revolution*, 281.
31 Chernow, *Alexander Hamilton*, 728–29.
32 Miranda and McCarter, *Hamilton: The Revolution*, 281.
33 Kat Long, "Why Elizabeth Hamilton Is Deserving of a Musical of Her Own," *Smithsonian Magazine*, February 25, 2016, https://www.smithsonianmag.com/history/why-elizabeth-hamilton-deserving-musical-her-own-180958214; Catherine Allgor, "The Politics of Love," *Humanities: The Magazine of the National Endowment for the Humanities* 31, no. 1 (January/February 2010), https://www.neh.gov/humanities/2010/januaryfebruary/feature/the-politics-love.
34 Long, "Why Elizabeth Hamilton Is Deserving of a Musical of Her Own."
35 Sonja Foss, *Rhetorical Criticism: Exploration and Practice*, 5th ed. (Long Grove, IL: Waveland Press, Inc., 2018), 154.
36 Foss, *Rhetorical Criticism*, 143.
37 Allan Johnson, *The Gender Knot: Unraveling Our Patriarchal Legacy* (Philadelphia, PA: Temple University Press, 2005), 5.
38 Bruce E. Gronbeck, "The Rhetorics of the Past: History, Argument, and Collective Memory," in *Doing Rhetorical History: Concepts and Cases*, ed. Kathleen Turner (Tuscaloosa: The University of Alabama Press, 1998), 56.
39 Maurice Halbwachs, *On Collective Memory*, ed. and trans. Lewis Coser (Chicago, IL: The University of Chicago Press, 1992), 188.
40 David Lowenthal, *The Past Is a Foreign Country* (New York: Cambridge University Press, 2003), 61.
41 Halbwachs, *On Collective Memory*, 49.
42 John Bodnar, *Remaking America: Public Memory, Commemoration, and Patriotism in the Twentieth Century* (Princeton, NJ: Princeton University Press, 1992), 14.
43 Lisa Gring-Pemble and Cher Weixia Chen, "Patriarchy Prevails: A Feminist Rhetorical Analysis of Equal Pay Discourses," *Women & Language* 41, no. 2 (2018): 83.
44 Miranda and McCarter, *Hamilton: The Revolution*, 258.
45 Catherine Allgor, "'Remember . . . I'm Your Man': Masculinity, Marriage, and Gender in Hamilton," in *Historians on Hamilton: How a Blockbuster Musical Is Restaging America's Past*, eds. Renee C. Romano and Claire Bond Potter (New Brunswick, NJ: Rutgers University Press, 2018), 101.

46 Kerber, *No Constitutional Right to Be Ladies*, 13; see also Welke, *Law and the Borders of Belonging*, 29.
47 Allgor, "'Remember . . . I'm Your Man,'" 95.
48 Miranda and McCarter, *Hamilton: The Revolution*, 42.
49 Miranda and McCarter, *Hamilton: The Revolution*, 82.
50 Miranda and McCarter, *Hamilton: The Revolution*, 142.
51 Miranda and McCarter, *Hamilton: The Revolution*, 82–83.
52 Miranda and McCarter, *Hamilton: The Revolution*, 72.
53 Miranda and McCarter, *Hamilton: The Revolution*, 176.
54 Miranda and McCarter, *Hamilton: The Revolution*, 238.
55 Chernow, *Alexander Hamilton*, 126–27.
56 Chernow, *Alexander Hamilton*, 205.
57 Miranda and McCarter, *Hamilton: The Revolution*, 191.
58 Lin-Manuel Miranda, "Workshop Cast: Schuyler Defeated," Hamilton Workshop, published April 12, 2017, https://archive.org/details/Hamilton_Workshop/Workshop_Cast_-_Schuyler_Defeated_(mp3.pm).mp3.
59 Miranda, "Workshop Cast: Schuyler Defeated."
60 Peggy sings "Daddy said to be home by sundown" and Angelica respond, "Daddy doesn't need to know." See Miranda and McCarter, *Hamilton: The Revolution*, 42.
61 Miranda and McCarter, *Hamilton: The Revolution*, 152. The wholesale erasure of the experience of women of color in *Hamilton* presents an entirely different issue that could be the subject of another project.
62 Miranda and McCarter, *Hamilton: The Revolution*, 104–5.
63 Miranda and McCarter, *Hamilton: The Revolution*, 152.
64 Miranda and McCarter, *Hamilton: The Revolution*, 210.
65 Allgor, "'Remember . . . I'm Your Man,'" 112.
66 Kathleen Hall Jamieson, *Beyond the Double Bind: Women and Leadership* (New York, NY: Oxford University Press, 1995), 121.
67 Jackson Katz, *Man Enough? Donald Trump, Hillary Clinton, and the Politics of Presidential Masculinity* (Northampton, MA: Interlink Books, 2016), 1.
68 See Welke, *Law and the Borders of Belonging*, 8; Baker, "The Domestication of Politics," 629.
69 Allgor, "'Remember . . . I'm Your Man,'" 112.
70 Lin-Manuel Miranda, "Workshop Cast: Let It Go," Hamilton Workshop, published April 12, 2017, https://archive.org/details/Hamilton_Workshop/Hamilton_Workshop_Cast_-_Let_It_Go_(mp3.pm).mp3; Lindsey Sullivan, "Guess Which Hamilton Song Lin-Manuel Miranda Had to 'Let Go' After Frozen Became a Smash Hit?" *Broadway World*, September 16, 2016, https://www.broadway.com/buzz/186007/guess-which-hamilton-song-lin-manuel-miranda-had-to-let-go-after-frozen-became-a-smash-hit.
71 Miranda and McCarter, *Hamilton: The Revolution*, 110.
72 Miranda and McCarter, *Hamilton: The Revolution*, 104.
73 Miranda and McCarter, *Hamilton: The Revolution*, 162.
74 Alexander Hamilton, "Letter to Elizabeth Hamilton, July 4, 1904," *Founders Online*, accessed July 6, 2020, https://founders.archives.gov/documents/Hamilton/01-26-02-0001-0248.
75 Miranda and McCarter, *Hamilton: The Revolution*, 49.
76 Miranda and McCarter, *Hamilton: The Revolution*, 76.
77 Miranda and McCarter, *Hamilton: The Revolution*, 57.

78 Miranda and McCarter, *Hamilton: The Revolution*, 176.
79 Miranda and McCarter, *Hamilton: The Revolution*, 178–79.
80 Miranda and McCarter, *Hamilton: The Revolution*, 230.
81 Alexander Hamilton, "Printed Version of the 'Reynolds Pamphlet,'" *Founders Online*, accessed July 6, 2020, https://founders.archives.gov/documents/Hamilton/01-21-02-0138-0002.
82 Tammy R. Vigil, *Moms in Chief: The Rhetoric of Republican Motherhood and the Spouses of Presidential Nominees, 1992-2016* (Lawrence: University Press of Kansas, 2019), 29.
83 Vigil, *Moms in Chief*, 29.
84 Vigil, *Moms in Chief*, 19.
85 Vigil, *Moms in Chief*, 26.
86 Miranda and McCarter, *Hamilton: The Revolution*, 71–72.
87 Miranda and McCarter, *Hamilton: The Revolution*, 138.
88 Miranda and McCarter, *Hamilton: The Revolution*, 280.
89 Miranda and McCarter, *Hamilton: The Revolution*, 280.
90 Miranda and McCarter, *Hamilton: The Revolution*, 281.
91 Vigil, *Moms in Chief*, 26.
92 Baker, "The Domestication of Politics," 633.
93 Baker, "The Domestication of Politics," 633.
94 Vigil, *Moms in Chief*, 26.
95 Miranda and McCarter, *Hamilton: The Revolution*, 107.
96 Miranda and McCarter, *Hamilton: The Revolution*, 110.
97 Miranda and McCarter, *Hamilton: The Revolution*, 170, 110, 44–45.
98 Miranda and McCarter, *Hamilton: The Revolution*, 168–69.
99 Miranda and McCarter, *Hamilton: The Revolution*, 107.
100 Miranda and McCarter, *Hamilton: The Revolution*, 230.
101 Carrington O'Brien, "Helpless: Why Aren't We Talking about Gender in *Hamilton*?" *The Female Gaze*, June 16, 2016, https://thefemalegaze.org/2016/06/16/helpless-why-arent-we-talking-about-gender-in-hamilton.
102 Miranda and McCarter, *Hamilton: The Revolution*, 238.
103 Miranda and McCarter, *Hamilton: The Revolution*, 238.
104 Allgor, "'Remember . . . I'm Your Man,'" 97–98.
105 James McMaster, "Why Hamilton Is Not the Revolution You Think It Is," *HowlRound Theatre Commons*, February 23, 2016, https://howlround.com/why-hamilton-not-revolution-you-think-it.
106 Chernow, *Alexander Hamilton*, 277.
107 Miranda and McCarter, *Hamilton: The Revolution*, 45, 44.
108 Michael Schulman, "The Women of 'Hamilton,'" *The New Yorker*, August 6, 2015, https://www.newyorker.com/culture/cultural-comment/the-women-of-hamilton.
109 Chernow, *Alexander Hamilton*, 727.
110 Michael Schulman, "The Women of 'Hamilton.'"
111 Adelman, "Who Tells Your Story," 292.
112 Adelman, "Who Tells Your Story," 292.
113 Adelman, "Who Tells Your Story," 278.
114 Allgor, "'Remember . . . I'm Your Man,'" 97.
115 Joanne B. Freeman, "'Can We Get Back to Politics? Please?': Hamilton's Missing Politics in *Hamilton*," in *Historians on Hamilton: How a Blockbuster Musical Is Restaging America's Past*, eds.

Renee C. Romano and Claire Bond Potter (New Brunswick, NJ: Rutgers University Press, 2018), 43.

116 Joseph Adelman, "Who Tells Your Story?: *Hamilton* as a People's History," in *Historians on Hamilton: How a Blockbuster Musical Is Restaging America's Past*, eds. Renee C. Romano and Claire Bond Potter (New Brunswick, NJ: Rutgers University Press, 2018), 292.

117 David Zarefsky, "Four Senses of Rhetorical History," in *Doing Rhetorical History: Concepts and Cases*, ed. Kathleen J. Turner (Tuscaloosa: The University of Alabama Press, 1998), 31.

118 Halbwachs, *On Collective Memory*, 49.

119 Lowenthal, *The Past Is a Foreign Country*, 39.

120 Lyra Monteiro, "Race-Conscious Casting and the Erasure of the Black Past in *Hamilton*," in *Historians on Hamilton: How a Blockbuster Musical Is Restaging America's Past*, eds. Renee C. Romano and Claire Bond Potter (New Brunswick, NJ: Rutgers University Press, 2018), 59.

121 Miranda and McCarter, *Hamilton: The Revolution*, 273, 44, 120.

122 Vigil, *Moms in Chief*, 27.

123 Renee C. Romano and Claire Bond Potter, "Introduction," in *Historians on Hamilton: How a Blockbuster Musical Is Restaging America's Past*, eds. Renee C. Romano and Claire Bond Potter (New Brunswick, NJ: Rutgers University Press, 2018), 10–11.

124 O'Brien, "Helpless."

125 Bonnie J. Dow and Celeste M. Condit, "The State of the Art in Feminist Scholarship in Communication," *Journal of Communication* 55 (September 2005): 449.

126 Dow and Condit, "The State of the Art in Feminist Scholarship in Communication," 467.

127 Allgor, "'Remember . . . I'm Your Man,'" 106.

128 Allgor, "'Remember . . . I'm Your Man,'" 94.

PART THREE

Hamilton and Rhetoric of Democracy and Social Change

CHAPTER EIGHT

Bondage and Circulation

BRANDON INABINET[1]

Thomas Jefferson's New York City lodgings at 57 Maiden Lane serve as the all-important room in Lin-Manuel Miranda's *Hamilton*. In that space, on June 20, 1790, Jefferson hoped to gain the nation's capital in his home state, rather than Northern financial headquarters. This act would cement his legacy of centering national symbols around virtuous agrarian landholding and republican value.[2] In exchange, Hamilton needed the votes on his assumption plan, which would consolidate all state debts from the American Revolution into his national treasury. The results over the coming years were the achievement of Jefferson's goal (10 square miles along the Potomac), alongside Hamilton's goal of a consolidation of the national debt in the first Bank of the United States, headquartered in northern Philadelphia. Interspersed with these iconic political compromises, Hamilton gets caught in the ultra-compromising position of his extramarital affair with Maria Reynolds. True to melodramatic form of the musical, this private vice of promiscuity and being trapped in a personal lie are made parallel to broader social changes, so the audience is forced to read binaries of virtue and vice in more complex (political) situations.

For this reason, Miranda's *Hamilton* is a gift to scholars of rhetoric and public address. In particular, Miranda depicts how circulation converts hidden and taboo acts into publicly acceptable forms—a melodrama not just in the play itself but in actual political reality, then and now. The misdeeds and sins of the Founders are transferred into vote swapping and tradeoffs. They are modified in rumor and innuendo. They are exposed in various forms that bolster news readers' *ethos*. And finally they become founding narratives and values, often hypocrisies to the political realities. In particular, Miranda usefully foregrounds Southern slavery's absolution into Northern capitalism (private exploitation and immorality became a "public good") and indebtedness into civic trust. Meanwhile Hamilton's affair created new pressrooms and democratic fervor in a supposedly "enlightened" republic.

Taboo bondage gained cover in new, democratic forms of communication. Human bondage became the basis for modern financial circulation, when slave traders and slavers could finance bank loans. Hamilton's very private bondage in sexual entrapment became a bedrock for news circulation, when ordinary citizens judged Hamilton incapable of holding office for his sins. Debt bondage became the basis for civic trust, when all Americans could be linked together in their dependency of central banking. In each pair, an unspeakable taboo became sublimated into something white elite males could use to hold power as virtue. What appears to be transparent and obvious in each of the three actually stem from a darker communicative exchange than Miranda reveals.

As Schwarze has argued, "melodrama's capacity to articulate moral concerns makes the frame an especially attractive option when scientific, technological, and bureaucratic discourses are blocking meaningful participation in public affairs and restricting discussion to technical spheres of controversy."[3] Although the hit musical's more obvious payoff is an inclusive American Dream, as Hamilton gets his shot, Miranda also offers a powerful keyhole to "The Room Where It Happens." In other words, he disrupts that broader narrative of opportunity to tell us how melodrama dictates power—by hiding something dirty under symbolic action that appears virtuous, but may be suspicious on second inspection. Whether chattel slavery, indebtedness that feeds imperial ambitions, or extramarital sex and personal sin, Hamilton's vices and compromises are American sins. The desire to restore Hamilton as an immigrant hero is certainly identifiable, but also comes with the charade of self-made prosperity (built on slavery), unity (built on capitalism's indebtedness), and civic morality (built on Othering sin).

This chapter focuses only on the first minutes of Act II of the musical, from "Cabinet Battle #1" to "The Room Where It Happens." I pair close textual analysis of lyrics with a deep dive into the original pamphlets and diaries from the 1780s and 1790s. Doing so will help move forward what Stuart Hall called a "negotiated reading" of the text—one that takes into account the dominant reading (often intended by the encoder) as well as resistive readings, and yet finds some third path.[4] For example, Ishmael Reed's "The Haunting of Lin-Manuel Miranda" and a slate of critics (including *The New Yorker*) have panned the musical for whitewashing Hamilton as an immigrant hero and recasting the other Founders as non-white liberators, rather than elites unhappy about paying taxes on the profits from non-white labor. Guided by both the dominant interpretation and these resistive reads, this analysis looks back at the act of encoding, mediating, and reading again.

In doing so, it illuminates the transposition of the world of Hamilton's dramatism to the melodrama of the stage, allowing us to better see what was always there.

The idea that the dirty deeds of the early republic, or what some theorists have called "foundational violence," spurred the American project is not new to historical scholarship.[5] Ron Chernow of course features quite a few provocations to this effect in the biography that is the narrative basis for the musical. More generally, the trend is clearer in works by historians such as Edward Baptist who focus on America's economic base in slavery, as well as works by cultural anthropologists like Donald Graeber, who now put national debt (and debt equity) at the center of civic relationships and trust. Communication scholarship lags in this area, reading founding myths not in light of systems of circulation (which include communication), but in terms of reputational ethics and resentment.[6]

This chapter seeks to remedy this lack. It first looks at "The Room" of exploitation and wealth, reviewing how rhetorics of enslavement fueled finance without being publicly communicated. The second section then takes the Reynolds Affair, exploring how the revealed indignity of Hamilton's inability to say "no" corrupts satisfaction and domestic bliss (again, elevating the moral superiority of the nation's citizens who circulate). And the third section then looks at the federally-funded debt and Bank scheme, which forced civic trust into an economic rhetoric, rather than affairs of honor. In each case—exploitation/wealth, indignity/virtue, and debt/trust—the systemic logic of communication is to elevate the public sense of self while burying the moral evil of the melodrama.

EXPLOITATION/WEALTH

The first federal census of 1790 counted 697,897 enslaved persons as "three fifths of all other Persons" for the purpose of representation and direct taxation. Miranda assumes that knowledge as Thomas Jefferson returns home from France. The second act of the musical begins with Jefferson's asking Sally Hemings to open a letter from George Washington, and James Madison's presentation of the new assault on the nation's integrity through financial schemes.[7] Miranda's focus on "the Virginians" in general, and slaveholding in particular, here is important. Hip-hop embedding of lyrics and non-white acting, discussed elsewhere in this book, serve as a strategic lens on republican discourses. As the Obamas have done in their reflections on U.S. history, Miranda most often chooses to celebrate immigrants and narratives of gritty overcoming, uplifting contributions to the fabric of America and highlighting roots outside America.[8] Yet, when the curtain is drawn on Act II, Miranda hits a "reset" on the upstart story. We learn that those stories, too, would not be possible without exploitation and a broad agenda of domination and violence.

The Hamilton of the musical plans to follow Burr's advice to "talk less, smile more."[9] Rather than resisting the practice of slavery, Hamilton plans to "hate the sin, love the sinner."[10] In order to strengthen the entire economy, Hamilton is willing to give the slaveholders a monumental win in the form of power and opportunity. The contrast is heightened in the lyrics by the continual reference to the two men as "the Virginians," opposed to all the refrains of "New York" in Act I as a place where "you can be a new man."[11] The Virginians, though amiable, polite, and easily pleased with "a smile," are in the end "merciless."[12] Hamilton's bargaining on behalf of the North *could* provoke the viewer into a more negotiated re-reading of the "you can be a new man"[13] refrain, even as it is also possible to see the South as the only evil force at work.

Despite almost no mention of slavery in the primary documents of the financial negotiations of the early Republic, Miranda skillfully drops that bomb into "Cabinet Battle #1" between Jefferson and Hamilton.[14] Jefferson begins the Act depicting his utopian vision of an agrarian republic, focused on individual work and ingenuity.[15] Hamilton cuts him off saying that he won't take "civics lessons from a slaver," mocking Jefferson for pretending to plant seeds in the soil himself. Hamilton concludes with "we know who's really doing the planting."[16]

After the reply by the chorus that Hamilton doesn't have the votes, Washington pulls him aside for this apparent below-the-belt hit to Virginian integrity and commands Hamilton to convince more House members of his plans. Washington's urging reads as a defense of Southern "politeness"—avoiding the issue of slavery.[17] In real life, of course, Hamilton was not actively provoking Southerners on issues of slavery, nor needing "counsel" from Washington that doing so was impolite. Rather than reading this as poor historiography on Miranda's part, we can see this as an opportunity for the audience to witness a first sublimation—of driving down slavery into an unspoken, behind-closed-doors negotiation.[18]

The rhetoric of white enslavement was an active part of the Revolution—as the original draft of the Declaration of Independence and nearly every cry for freedom, including Patrick Henry's "Liberty or Death," explicitly contrasted American values against the condition of servitude and subjugation. The years from 1776 to 1790 were a decade-and-a-half of economic rhetoric taking increased priority.[19] Hamilton's offer to excuse slavery for shared economic gain was the last nail in the coffin of Northern exception to a slave-based economy. After the creation of a common currency, bank, and national debt dependent on future slaveholding, those founding days of rational enlightenment yielded to amoral economics (to be increasingly interrupted by social movement abolitionism). Agricultural taxes from slavery would be the foundation stone for Northern note circulation and wealth accumulation; and the Virginians could walk away with the capital to symbolize their moral and political victory. In Washington D.C., a slaveholder's capital, no person of color presumed to be a "new man."[20]

Interestingly, the room of the negotiation was probably not as private as Miranda makes it out to be, as even Hamilton's biographer Chernow points out that there were likely political leaders other than just Madison, Jefferson, and Hamilton present at Jefferson's Maiden Lane apartment in New York.[21] Miranda is again heightening the melodramatic perversion of the ethical system. The chorus in "The Room Where It Happened" sings, "No one really knows how; The game is played; The art of the trade; How the sausage gets made; We just; Assume that it happens."[22] In real life, it is pretty clear how the sausage was made: Madison remained consistent to his anti-debt-assumption view; at the same time, he could ask four other members of Congress (in secret) to support Hamilton's side and give him the votes he needed.[23] One could maintain rap battle street cred through such consistency, even while bargaining the soul of the country. In so doing, we witness "the art of the compromise," in which to broker slavery's ascendancy, white men were to "hold your nose and close your eyes."[24] Miranda gets us very close in these lyrics to note the dirty deeds of founding being sheltered from the public eye.

INDIGNITY/VIRTUE

Miranda's weaving of the Reynolds affair and the Schuyler sisters' virtue into the musical dialogue in this specific section of the musical shifts us to also see the framing about what is fair and right, and who gets the communicative power to determine their interpretation. The viewer can then transfer that reading onto the unhealthy secrecy and moral equivocation Hamilton faces in other scenarios. The scenes lay bare power relationships in stark terms, whereas politeness and secrecy usually function to hide the ethically questionable work of political founding.

As soon as Washington commands Hamilton to pursue votes after "Cabinet Battle #1," a scene change puts us in a private domestic scene with Hamilton, his wife Elizabeth Schuyler Hamilton, and son Philip learning the piano. Angelica, Elizabeth's sister, has come home from Britain for a summer vacation in Albany with the Schuyler family. They advise Hamilton to "Take a Break" but Hamilton instead must stay to get his plan through Congress.[25] Hamilton stays in the City, but does not exclusively focus on the propaganda for his Public Credit. The melodramatic song "Say No To This" allows the audience to most palpably feel the dilemma between right and wrong, as Hamilton chooses to indulge in an affair with Maria Reynolds.[26]

Miranda's mostly family-friendly musical goes headstrong with lyrics in this moment, saying Maria enticed Hamilton with "her legs spread." The ensuing back-and-forth and "ruining" of Hamilton through the affair and hush-money payments to Reynolds' abusive husband give the audience a strong image.[27] Secrecy might again protect Hamilton from being reviled by public disgust. Just as the audience begins to empathize with Hamilton's bargain to continue his affair and maintain his street cred, we are thrust right back into the debate over the financial plan. Hamilton concludes the tragic love song, with the hope that "nobody needs to know."[28] Again here, Miranda (consciously or not) tells us to transfer our feelings of good and evil onto sublimation—forcing into private what "must be done" to get the next successful founding act accomplished outside the press. Meanwhile, national press would eventually end such founding secrecies and their questionable morality.

The first *Federalist Paper* anticipated "great national discussion" as one of the more abhorrent parts of forthcoming U.S. federalism.[29] Hamilton, as "Publius," wrote that such national discussions are full of "angry and malignant passions," with people trying to convert others by "the loudness of their declamations, and by the bitterness of their invectives." "Popularity" of a policy existed most often at the expense of the public good. Hamilton instead wanted to serve as a "disinterested and dispassionate umpire."[30] Of course the views of such dispassionate people, if they exist, rarely circulate. Instead, as Hamilton soon learned, propaganda and rumor were the fuel for political power, and his affairs (of politics, of honor, and even of intimacy) were the top headline.

Hamilton was a master propogandist. His financial reports had been printed in newspapers from Boston to Charleston.[31] John Fenno published the *Gazette of the United States* almost as soon as the federal government was established in New York. As a semiweekly paper supported by Hamilton's Treasury Department, it printed general government notices and attained a readership of a thousand subscribers within two years. The pseudonymous contributions from "Publicola," "Pacificus," "Amicus," "An American," and "Plain Facts" were used to conceal voices such as Alexander Hamilton, Rufus King, and John Adams, who supported the national finance system and bank. Hamilton paid agents of the press, Noah Webster, John Fenno, and eventually William Cobbett, to disseminate his views further.

To counter Hamilton's power in the press, State Secretary Jefferson and Representative Madison met with leading publishers and politicians around the country to solicit their press agents as well, especially acquiring the support of Benjamin Franklin Bache (the inventor's grandson) and his paper the *General Advertiser*. However, that paper was not suited for national circulation, being filled with local Philadelphia advertisements and news. Madison and Jefferson met Philip Freneau for breakfast on May 20, 1791, and lured him to move to the nation's capital to set up a new press.[32] This paper, the *National Gazette*, received letters from Madison, Edmund Randolph, and other anonymous contributors appearing as "Brutus," "Sydney," and "Centinel," vindicating Virginians from Federalist attacks and charging corruption in the funded debt. Thus, as we are watching these few minutes of the musical, we have gone from a press environment financed and run by Hamilton to one based around the public and private transgressions of the

Treasury Secretary.³³ Miranda's use of the Reynolds affair helps his audience make this pivot to morality, without having to detour into a new, didactic plotline dealing with public virtue and vice.

DEBT/TRUST

Salacious and sensational reporting of virtue and vice might have undone the nation, had it not been for the economic base and buy-in that Hamilton also created. A national debt and banking system stabilized the market, paid off foreign debt, and unified the national economy. Scottish philosophers such as David Hume and James Steuart had argued that banks with a publicly-funded debt had become "the great engine, by which domestic circulation is carried on."³⁴ The machine metaphor was picked up by supporters.³⁵ A rational structure of circulation could fuel trust, and hide the dirty work of political negotiation and taxing future citizens on today's wars. The banking system was the fulfillment of Enlightenment hopes for daily, systematic economic management of social intercourse that required fewer and fewer interventions on personal questions of honor. Banks and financial control, then, would manage civic ethos in a way that made unique rhetorical gymnastics mostly unnecessary.

To Hamilton, such a system was the only means to save shattered "confidence" and national "credit." Hamilton came to Congress for three consecutive sessions, presenting massive economic proposals: *Report Relative to the Provision of the Public Debt* (January 1790), *Report on the Further Provision Necessary for Establishing Public Credit* (December 1790), and *Report on the Subject of Manufactures* (December 1791). The states had amassed staggering debts from the Revolution that could not be paid off. Most were incapable of offering even modest financial support to the fragile U.S. government. Compounding the problem, those debts were not equally distributed nor had they been paid off evenly. Hamilton, in *Federalist #7*, called this state of affairs "double contingency," as it promoted internal conflict among states and weakened the whole confederated republic to external threat.³⁶

If all states shared a unified burden, then their fates were inextricably tied, not only at the level of states but by extension to individual citizens.³⁷ Couched in the language of necessity, Hamilton countered Madison and Jefferson's complaint regarding the Necessary and Proper Clause of the U.S. Constitution.³⁸ The plan was indeed necessary to restore trust and credibility at all levels. And yet, to set up that credibility and trust, Hamilton again appears to go private with a rap battle against Jefferson away from public scrutiny.

As Robert Hariman explains in his analysis of civic republican style, secrecy becomes "demonic" to public culture:

> As republican politics is thought to be an open process of persuasion among all citizens acting virtuously, the greatest threat to the republic is imagined to be a secret arrangement by a few conspirators to manipulate or circumvent agreement. In a political culture of oral argument, secrecy becomes the sign of subversion.[39]

And yet, neither slavery nor debt (as intergenerational burden) could become transparently objectionable or debatable if it was handled behind closed doors, as the rap battles in the musical *Hamilton* portray, and as Miranda chose to highlight in his "The Room Where It Happens" lyrics.

In real life, although Hamilton won the bank struggle behind closed doors and using lobbyists (then called gladiators) in the Senate, on February 24, 1791, the Virginia senators proposed the next day opening the doors of the Senate to the public. This provided them the rhetorical victory that indeed the entire "scheme" for a bank had been corrupt. Debate theatrics were feared among the early senators. Oral displays hinted at British theatricality rather than the enlightened science of politics they hoped to establish.[40] Yet even Bank supporter William Maclay believed the opening of the Senate was necessary, and criticized opponents: "If they waged war in words and oral combats; if they pitted themselves like cocks, or played the gladiator, for the amusement of the idle and curious, the fault was theirs."[41] Legislators would perform more ethically, thought Maclay, under conditions of transparency. The vote for transparency led to a more general change in government—toward direct, immediate accountability of representatives' actions to constituents through the press. But this circulation of political speech, too, relied on a foundation of financial violence paved by bank notes and public "credit" as debt to pay for an imperial war machine. Hamilton knew one was necessary for the other—transparency and political discussion could not happen unless the debaters were already bought out and bought into a fluid currency system that lets the state determine value.

While achieving quick financial success, the Bank of the United States leveraged citizen concern in a way that loosely mirrored the Founders' opinions.[42] Citizens throughout the nation questioned whether this new form of "credit" came at the expense of republican virtue, especially given Hamilton's lifestyle choices.[43] One "Independent Observer," as he styled himself, respected Hamilton's "ingenuity" and "ability," but he believed a large portion of his political principles were simply a repetition of the British "court party."[44] The "Independent Observer" went on to note that the Secretary's funding system had lost favor with the farmers and "other worthy citizens," and that if the Secretary thought he had public support, it must only be found in the cities' busiest ports, among merchants and financiers.

Echoing Jefferson's agrarian philosophy, and French physiocrats, a "Farmer" addressing the "yeomanry" attacked the system of public credit that formed the basis of Hamilton's *Reports* through a strategy of dissociation. Such "credit" was esteemed to be of great importance, but was actually "the most unjust and ruinous invention of modern times"; such a system precipitates nations into wars, and "peace itself does not relieve the people from oppressive taxes; but the misery of the present generation is unjustly transmitted to posterity."[45] The system of finance under development was one founded on "deception," and it "never has been pursued by any government but to the oppression of the great body of the people"; the author characterized the national mood as "indignant silence."[46]

Hamilton became the scapegoat of vice for these accumulated fears and resentments, doubling the press of the Reynolds affair and effectively channeling the spirit of the musical.[47] The Bank's establishment undermined "the great pillars of the government," and the institution was "capable, as an engine of corruption, of sapping the foundation of public virtue, and polluting all its measures."[48] The circulation machine metaphor returned, but now as a vile and hideous engine rather than one of Enlightened virtue. Unlike banknote circulation, said the authors of the era, political news circulation "will not violate public credit, but establish it in the public confidence; will not impair the energy to the constitution, but restore it to its pristine health, and proper functions; will not strain our national character, but exhibit it." By contrasting Hamilton's "credit" with that of a "genuine republic," the author invited his audience to evaluate news circulation rather than monetary circulation as the core of virtue.[49]

Democratic-Republican societies also cropped up across U.S. localities, as forums for discussion and promotion of egalitarian ideals of the French Revolution. With around forty such groups arising in the first years of the bank debates, citizens fed the anti-tyranny faction arrayed against Hamilton.[50] Writers in Freneau's Jeffersonian camp highlighted radical problems of obfuscation in the national government. One contributor explained through analogy that whereas a European newspaper might describe the finest clothing and jewels adorning the monarch alongside a news piece on the misery and wretchedness of the common people, American newspapers lauded Hamilton's virtue while the next new story explained how the market had brought ruin to the poor and the yeomanry.[51] In other words, the United States had just replaced the monarchy with Hamilton's corporate indebtedness.

As Hamilton wrote in a letter, "Men are governed by opinion; this opinion is as much influenced by appearances as realities; if a government appears to be confident of its own powers, it is the surest way to inspire confidence in others; if it is diffident, it may be certain, there will be still greater diffidence in others, and that its authority will not only be distrusted, controverted, but contemned."[52] U.S. credit rested on a rhetorical performance of confidence and urgency that benefitted both Hamilton's elites and the national system of finance. Moreover, it rested on a pattern of financial and communicative circulation that suggested both were necessary and inevitable; as the nation recovered from war, citizens literally bought into a discourse that forgot slavery and financial debt and instead focused on Hamiltonian affairs and duels.

Hamilton's privacy became American shared publicity. Jefferson could force non-consensual sex onto Sally Hemings without significant public uproar, but Hamilton helped make his extramarital affair the political centerpiece of the nation's discourse. The "great national discussion" Hamilton so despised in the first *Federalist*, with passions and interests embroiling the nation, became centered around him. Factions and parties would evolve out of his three sublimations (while not naming them directly) and determine the future of U.S. political discourse.[53] Rather than focusing only on "the room" as a site of foundational violence, Miranda uses the Reynolds affair to lead our eyes to the material circulation patterns. Hamilton made compromises and brokered deals to accept American vices, contain them in elite legitimation, and convert them into matters early Americans could discuss. Hamilton's private vice opened a sphere of melodramatic critique, in the newspapers of the early Republic and in the musicals of the twenty-first century.

Rather than imagining distinct public and private spheres, it behooves us to think about the public in temporary alliances of circulatory pathways—pathways of privilege formed on sublimations of societal harm. As is standard to a more general pattern, the U.S. public and its newspapers were chiefly founded around polite acceptance of slavery (symbolized in Hamilton's "smile" in the musical), legal legitimation of intergenerational indebtedness, and the antagonism to the private vices of over-ambitious immigrants.

CONCLUSIONS

Hamilton's schemes relied heavily on complex communication and news circulation not illustrated in Miranda's musical. Yet, through the depiction of the Reynolds affair and the characterization of "the room" as corruptly sealed-off, Miranda sets up a melodrama ripe for analysis. The circulation of vastly unequal wealth, bank notes of indebtedness, and salacious vice still govern American public life. Each has an origin story in the historical Hamilton and dramatizes the strength of a system concealing evil underneath layers of virtue display. Styled in melodramatic rap battles and burlesque lyrics, Miranda's musical gives audiences a tool to question or even radically resituate our own networks of circulation (racial/ideological, financial, and political). Within an upbeat and heroic immigrant-upstart musical, there's an undercurrent that the American Dream was borne out of dark misdeeds. Marginalized citizens can perhaps still hope to "be a new man"[54] today, while still disbelieving narratives of pure genius and generosity that paved their way.

Miranda's *Hamilton* ends with a focus on legacy building, blunting the radical potential of these moments. The audience is shifted from a focus on the key sublimation of misdeeds in the broad American story. Miranda turns to how Hamilton wanted to "build something that outlives" himself.[55] True to melodramatic form, virtue and vice throughout Hamilton's career come to a climax. Tragically, as Michaelah Reynolds and Ryan Neville-Shepard locate in their chapter on the broader American Dream, his precocious upstart character traits get the best of him, leading to sullied reputation and the duel with Burr. To close the musical, Miranda foregoes tragic form (in which we would be left with Hamilton's death and Eliza's demise) and fully embraces melodramatic form. He gives agency to the women of Hamilton's life, who get to "tell the story"[56] and re-narrate Hamilton as the founding genius and martyr. Virtue prevails over vice, through the intimate networks Hamilton had made with the Schuyler women. Because of this, his virtue lives through the ages. In the finale, Eliza recasts Hamilton's story by collecting his papers, interviewing Hamilton's fellow soldiers, fundraising for the Washington Monument, reuniting with Angelica, advocating against slavery, and establishing New York City's first orphanage—the children in whose eyes she sees Hamilton (given he was also orphaned and yet would become America's future).[57] The reading in this chapter has elevated a set of conclusions.

Citizens are "silent speakers of authority," as Joy Connolly has termed it in her work on Cicero's rhetorical theory.[58] We stand in circulatory networks of obligation and status to judge character. To see those networks as not just affairs of honor and virtue, but also as material sublimation updates the republican theorization with Marxist, Foucauldian, and psychoanalytic insights. In converting his own fame and glory, Hamilton birthed the financial system of the United States. Miranda is able to set this murky foundation of capitalism within the context of republicanism's street-cred problem. As citizens of republics feared, they indeed cannot build a good or long-lasting state secured from corruption or tyranny. And Hamilton, Miranda shows, created new forms of durable *ethos* through three bargains that renewed power within white male elites. These were the new determinants of worth, an ironic turn of events since Hamilton died a martyr of old republican affairs of honor, before his modern system of trust (paved by slaves' worth, debt solvency, and popular press opinion) could fully eradicate the old ways.

Madison's caution in *Federalist* #10 against "a rage for paper money, for an abolition of debts, for an equal division of property" met Hamilton's goal of converting debts and credits into compliance.[59] The boom and bust and rapidity of circulation created an alternative to honor-based speech of republicanism; paper credit, a "great engine," gave privacy and mystery to the irrationalities of public governance and citizen compliance.[60] Worth would come to be determined by vast and complex institutional dynamics, not the judgment of one's circle of elite peers. In this way, circulatory stability was created over large distances, in a world heretofore marked by performances of honor circulated among close friends and enemies.

Hannah Arendt's theories of founding, based on the American and French revolutions, teach about the impermanence of government.[61] She rejected as antipolitical that which is proposed for perpetuity. Arendt was particularly worried about the purity of such designs, following the example of the Nazis, that a state built on eternal ideology rather than negotiation and compromise was antithetical to civic virtue and the common good. She hailed the American revolution as, unlike the French revolution, one built on moderation and compromise, rather than the radically anti-human rationalism of the French example.

And yet, Arendt's mid-twentieth century celebration of American Revolution has been frustrated by twenty-first century race relations and historiography. Without any previous right to authority, such right is created through the force of arms, the taking of land from Indigenous people and the Crown, and the economic burdens of slavery and debt. Alongside that actual violence is what most scholars would call symbolic violence (although Arendt would want to distinguish this as "power"). As Joan Cocks specifies in her work on sovereignty, it is the erasure of "pre-existing right or, more broadly, the erasure of a way of life structured and animated by that right."[62] Claims to new statehood and sovereignty are always spurious, Cocks demonstrates with her focus on the United States and Israel, formed by rhetorics that claim to be legitimated by former victimhood and victory-through-virtue.

This chapter carries Cocks' claim into the case of *Hamilton* and further. The violence not only repeats and endures beyond the founding (as Cocks claims), but also gets sublimated into new communicative forms. The culture of honor died one of its greatest deaths with Burr's bullet, as Hamilton's death became a symbol of the unnecessary peril of this culture; but Miranda shows us in the first half of Act Two that Hamilton also sublimated honor in the creation of public funding. Corporations built on citizen debt, chartered by the state, became the basis for new trust—not the fickle world of personal debate and individual rhetorical performance. It guaranteed a long-term basis for a republic of corporations and institutions; on the other hand, it might also be said to have immediately killed off republicanism in putting trust in corporate supremacy.[63] "The Room" of commercial empire is quite different from that of elite compromise. Seeing that shift today is obvious: The Federal Reserve Bank of New York now sits across from 57 Maiden Street, "The Room" where it happened.

If not for his early death, Hamilton may have, like Robert Morris, become far more sullied by his association with the debts he placed on American citizens or by enhancing the riches of financiers of the slave trade. Or, like Morris, he might have died a pauper given his declining finances after the "tell all" of the Reynolds affair and his antagonism with and distance from the declining Federalist party. Instead, we have the martyr for empire. In the words of biographer Henry Cabot Lodge,

> There was no public credit. Hamilton created it. There was no circulating medium, no financial machinery; he supplied them. Business was languishing, and business revived under the treasury measures. There was no government, no system with life in it, only a paper constitution. Hamilton exercised the powers granted by the Constitution, pointed out those which lay hidden in its dry clauses, and gave vitality to the lifeless instrument.[64]

Contemporary writers similarly praise Hamilton as the Machiavellian prince of his era, appropriating republicanism insofar as it was necessary to build authority and national strength that went far beyond it, to develop the first truly modern national system (based on British, French, and Dutch ideas themselves based in republican models).[65]

We continue to rely on the misnomers formed by this melodramatic moment in American history. The rhetoric of economics calls on scholars to unmask intergenerational debt and its work on the affairs of argument that have constituted so much of our attention based on our models of antiquity.[66] It should be even more important to put that in the context shown by Edward Baptist—that Hamilton's capitalism was built on slavery's back at the same moment that Revolution had destabilized civic trust and created rhetorical leverage for freedom from enslavement.[67] By giving us a window into that room, Miranda opens up understanding of an anti-capitalist, anti-racist mode of circulation. Miranda reminds his audience that we create our "story"[68] as well, another very Arendtian point, and that the creative work of our time might be removing the damages that were assumed "necessary" when the republic was new and fragile.

Melodrama polarizes, and it can encourage reconsideration of allegiances that might normally lead audiences to accept a certain set of social and political arrangements. "In doing so," Schwarze says of environmental discourses similarly based on intergenerational debts, "melodrama can be part of a critical rhetoric that questions assertions of a single or universally shared public interest."[69] Against calls to dispassion about the Revolution, Miranda may provide a rallying point and source of identification for more voices in the conversation of corporate dominance and market determinations of value and worth. While so many elite Americans were happy to shell out thousands to see the happy story about immigrants getting the job done, our broken liberalism may yet produce new meanings from the musical.

As we have seen in this chapter, Miranda's replacement of written communication (in the actual cabinet debate) with oratory in closed-door rooms captured a broader anxiety of the era regarding transparency and secrecy. Without any scenes of Congress or the press, we see a vision of upstart immigrants, microphone drops, and identity politics in the truest sense of "the private made public." Melodrama in this 2010s style makes apparent the sense, very alive in the early republic, that individual *ethos* was central in the battle between good and evil. Yet the real-life versions of those were always murky and unsettled. Dislocation and marginalization, obligation and debt, and othering of perceived vice are in this case and in so many other cases the conditions by which publics are legitimated as networks of communicative trust and textual circulation. Let us take Miranda's invitation to resist the apparent naturalness of *ethos* and the circulation of credit, post-*Hamilton*.

NOTES

1. Brandon Inabinet, Associate Professor, Furman University, brandon.inabinet@furman.edu. The author wishes to thank the book editors for their valuable feedback, as well his student Katherine Valliant for her enthusiasm and valuable input, especially regarding Cabinet Battle #3.
2. Called the "Compromise of 1790" in Kenneth R. Bowling, *The Creation of Washington, D.C.: The Idea and Location of the American Capital* (Fairfax, VA: George Mason University Press, 1991).
3. Steven Schwarze, "Environmental Melodrama," *Quarterly Journal of Speech* 92, no. 3 (2006): 250, https://doi.org/10.1080/00335630600938609.
4. Stuart Hall, "Encoding and Decoding," in *Culture, Media, Knowledge*, ed. Hall et al. (New York: MacMillan, 1980).
5. Joan Cocks, *On Sovereignty and Other Political Delusions* (London: Bloomsbury, 2014), 28.
6. Jeremy Engels, *Enemyship: Democracy and Counter-Revolution in the Early Republic* (East Lansing: Michigan University Press, 2010); Jennifer R. Mercieca, *Founding Fictions* (Tuscaloosa: The University of Alabama Press, 2010).
7. Lin-Manuel Miranda and Jeremy McCarter, *Hamilton: The Revolution* (New York, NY: Grand Central Publishing, 2016), 152.
8. Adam Gopnik, "'Hamilton' and the Hip-Hop Case for Progressive Heroism," *The New Yorker*, February 5, 2016, accessed on July 17, 2020 at https://www.newyorker.com/news/daily-comment/hamilton-and-the-hip-hop-case-for-progressive-heroism.
9. Miranda and McCarter, *Hamilton: The Revolution*, 24.
10. Miranda and McCarter, *Hamilton: The Revolution*, 186. Complicity under the guise of politeness extends here from Northern labeling of Southern sin of slavery in the Christian tradition. By naming the sin one projects it onto others while removing one's own complicity. This extends from a misinterpretation of rhetorician Augustine of Hippo's *"Cum dilectione hominum et odio vitiorum"* (With love for mankind and hatred of sins). Jacques Paul Migne, ed., "St. Augustine of Hippo: Letter 211," *Patrologiae Latinae 33* (Paris, [n.p.]: 1845).
11. Miranda and McCarter, *Hamilton: The Revolution*, 17.
12. Miranda and McCarter, *Hamilton: The Revolution*, 186.
13. Miranda and McCarter, *Hamilton: The Revolution*, 17.
14. Miranda's Cabinet Battles as rap battles are based on very public texts. In a series of reports made to George Washington, ministers printed and publicized written arguments as "most strictly in the spirit of the Constitution." The first in-person "cabinet meeting" occurred on November 26, 1791 as "consideration and discussion" became "desirable." Given the cabinet only totaled four members at this point (with Knox as Secretary of War and Edmond Randolph as Attorney General), Jefferson reported that he and Hamilton became "daily pitted in the cabinet like two cocks." Despite the tension, Jefferson goes on to say that "the harmony was so cordial among us all, that we never failed, by a contribution of mutual views, of the subject, to form an opinion acceptable to the whole." The quoted words come from Jefferson's account of the Cabinet meetings in "Thomas Jefferson to Walter Jones, 5 March 1810," *Founders Online*, accessed December 10, 2019, https://founders.archives.gov/documents/Jefferson/03-02-02-0223.

15 Hamilton's system put manufacturing, shipping, and finance as the bedrock against war and crisis, with a United States able to produce its own finished products. On emerging capitalism, see Joyce Appleby, *Capitalism and a New Social Order: The Republican Vision of the 1790s* (New York: New York University Press, 1984).
16 Miranda and McCarter, *Hamilton: The Revolution*, 161.
17 This period of tamping down opinions over slavery, which leads to reputations of Southern politeness/civility, has been covered by the author in several articles including "When Pastors Go Public: Richard Furman's Public Letter on Slavery." *Southern Communication Journal* 76, no. 3 (2011); "Southern Honor and the Politics of Civility." *Charleston Law Review* 5, no. 3 (Spring 2011): 101–19.
18 Miranda's extends these melodramatic personal digs against Jefferson into the other Cabinet Battles. In material not included in the musical, "Cabinet Battle #3," Miranda concocts a Cabinet battle about the real abolitionist petition that was debated in Congress. The petition, signed February 3, 1790, asked the first Congress (in New York City) to "devise means for removing the Inconsistency from the Character of the American People," and "promote mercy and justice toward this distressed Race." Introduced to the House on February 12 and to the Senate on February 15, it was referred to select committee, which dismissed the petitions and awaited the ban on the slave trade in 1808, as compromised in Constitutional convention. See "Cabinet Battle 3 (Demo)," featuring Lin-Manuel Miranda, track 19 on *The Hamilton Mixtape*, Atlantic, 2016. The evidence on the historical Hamilton himself is that he had a personal distaste for slavery and the despicable conditions of the slave trade, expressed several times over his life, but his own ambitions to secure the favor of the slave-owning Schuylers and political leaders could be squared in practical action: he agreed with John Laurens that owners could free slaves to help fight the Revolution and he helped with legal work for manumission societies when in their interest of private property holders. In other words, Hamilton believed personal liberty of white social male elites was the primary goal, and their pity for the shocking conditions borne of slavery would often lead to solutions that followed private property laws. Jefferson and Hamilton's ideologies on slavery would have been nearly identical, only differentiated in degrees by social and geographical location.
19 This would happen again a century later as Reconstruction led to Redemption and Gilded Age rhetoric.
20 Miranda and McCarter, *Hamilton: The Revolution*, 17.
21 Chernow's report of the incident (which Miranda used as the primary source material for the musical) includes that there were "perhaps one or two" other present, as opposed to Miranda's key phrase that "no one else" was in the room where it happened. Ron Chernow, *Alexander Hamilton* (New York: Penguin Press, 2004), 305; Miranda and McCarter, *Hamilton: The Revolution*, 187.
22 Miranda and McCarter, *Hamilton: The Revolution*, 187.
23 It probably bears mention that Madison will need to reverse his view on the Bank publicly after the War of 1812, as the debts from the war require Hamilton's finance system that once appeared excessive.
24 Miranda and McCarter, *Hamilton: The Revolution*, 190.
25 Miranda and McCarter, *Hamilton: The Revolution*, 170.
26 Miranda and McCarter, *Hamilton: The Revolution*, 176.
27 Miranda and McCarter, *Hamilton: The Revolution*, 179.
28 Miranda and McCarter, *Hamilton: The Revolution*, 179.

29 Alexander Hamilton, James Madison, and John Jay, *The Federalist: With Letters of Brutus (Cambridge Texts in the History of Political Thought)* (New York: Cambridge University Press, 2003), no. 1.
30 For more on this interpretation, see Albert Furtwangler, *The Authority of Publius: A Reading of the Federalist Papers* (Ithaca: Cornell University Press, 1984).
31 The *Federal Gazette* and other newspapers published Hamilton's *Report*, December 23–25, 1790.
32 Lance Banning, *Conceived in Liberty: The Struggle to Define the New Republic, 1789–1793* (Lanham, MD: Rowman & Littlefield Publishers, 2004), 88 fn.30.
33 Newspapers multiplied around the nation. Only a hundred papers existed when the debt was funded, but by the end of the decade, the Reynolds Affair, the Bank of the United States charter, the XYZ Affair had led to the number doubling. In 1810, twenty-two million copies of 376 papers circulated annually, making the United States the highest consumer of newspapers in the world, mixing salacious gossip with now tolerable political transparency. Frank Luther Mott, *American Journalism: A History, 1690–1960*, 3rd ed. (New York: Macmillan, 1962), 3–64.
34 Throughout Volume II, "Of Banks," Steuart refers to banks in the language of a "great engine" for political economies. James Steuart, *An Inquiry into the Principles of Political Œconomy, IV, pt. 2*, ed. Andrew S. Skinner (1767; London: Pickering and Chattom, 1998).
35 "Credit and circulation produce punctuality; and punctuality is the soul of commerce." He went on, "CREDIT IS CONFIDENCE," one said, and the anonymous author continued to use "credit" in the double sense of loans and basic trust. [James Wilson], *Considerations on the Bank of North-America* (Philadelphia, PA: Hall and Sellers, 1785), 22. Early American Imprints, no. 19388. Pamphlet, 21. James Steuart's *Inquiry on Political Œconomy*, cited again and again for equating communicative trust with economic trust, read "Credit, therefore, is no more than a well-established confidence between men, in what relates to the fulfilling of their engagements. This confidence must be supported by laws, and established by manners." Steuart, *Inquiry*, IV: 1,1.
36 Hamilton, Madison, and Jay, *The Federalist*, no. 7.
37 Since the states had unequal parts in the effort of the Revolution, they had unequal shares of its consequences and burdens. South Carolina and Massachusetts were devastated by the war, and had $4 million in debt each; other states saw almost none of the fighting and suffered very little economic hardship. By consolidating debts into a federal plan, some citizens would be paying a tax burden twice.
38 United States Treasury Department. "Report. In obedience to the order of the House of Representatives of the 9th day of August last, requiring the Secretary of Treasury to Prepare and Report on this Day, such further provision as may, in his opinion, be necessary for establishing the public debt.... December 13, 1790." (Reprinted as pamphlet, Washington, DC: A. & G. Way, 1810), 62 pages.
39 Robert Hariman, *Political Style: The Artistry of Power* (Chicago, IL: University of Chicago Press, 1995), 110.
40 See Jay Fliegelman, *Declaring Independence: Jefferson, Natural Language, and the Culture of Performance* (Stanford, CA: Stanford University Press, 1993), 79–93.
41 William Maclay, *Journal of William Maclay. United States Senator from Pennsylvania 1789–1791*, ed. Edgar S. Maclay (New York: D. Appleton and Co., 1890), 374.
42 The Bank created in 1791 took the political damage in answering big questions about the nature of government and its relationship to private citizens, beyond Hamilton's death. Every stratum of society targeted the institution with their dissents, on state, regional, federal, and class-based levels. In the 1830s, Andrew Jackson and his supporters destroyed the Bank as a corrupt enterprise,

but then struggled to find viable alternatives. Every public person (i.e., white males) needed an opinion on the Bank, and differences of opinion on the issue served as a basis for the major U.S. political parties, until the Republicans no longer abided by Madison and Jefferson's compromise on power in the mid-1850s.

43 One of the most popular colonial publications that shaped such a mentality of promoting growth while limiting harmful effects was John Brown, *An Estimate of the Manners and Principles of the Times* (London: Royal Society, 1757), 217.
44 "An Independent Observer," [Untitled opinion column], *Pennsylvania Packet* v. 3430 (Philadelphia: 27 January 1790), 2.
45 "A Farmer" [George Logan], *Five Letters, Addressed to the Yeomanry* (Philadelphia, PA: Oswald, 1792). Library Company. Pamphlet, 36.
46 Logan, *Five Letters*, 23–24.
47 On the importance of ritual scapegoating in Kenneth Burke's work, see C. Allen Carter, *Kenneth Burke and the Scapegoat Process* (Norman: University of Oklahoma Press, 1996).
48 [John Taylor], *An Examination of the late Proceedings in Congress* [Richmond, 1793], 7. Early American imprint, no. 26245. Pamphlet, 27.
49 Taylor, *An Examination*, 28.
50 Eugene Perry Link, *Democratic-Republican Societies, 1790–1800* (New York: Columbia University Press, 1942); Philip S. Foner, *The Democratic-Republican Societies, 1790–1800: A Documentary Sourcebook of Constitutions, Declarations, Addresses, Resolutions, and Toasts* (Westport, CT: Greenwood, 1976); Matthew Schoenbachler, "Republicanism in the Age of Democratic Revolution: The Democratic-Republican Societies of the 1790s," *Journal of the Early Republic* 18 (Summer 1998): 237–61.
51 [Untitled], *The Gazette of the United States* 3, no. 91 (Philadelphia: 10 March 1792), 362.
52 "Alexander Hamilton to James Duane." (3 September 1780), in *The Papers of Alexander Hamilton*, vol. 2, ed. Harold C. Syrett et al. (New York: Columbia University Press, 1961–79), 414.
53 Robert V. Remini, *Andrew Jackson and the Bank War* (New York: W.W. Norton and Co., 1967), 177. Historian Robert Remini notes that the party system and the role of the Presidency in the modern United States emerged from the "Bank War."
54 Miranda and McCarter, *Hamilton: The Revolution*, 17.
55 Miranda and McCarter, *Hamilton: The Revolution*, 188.
56 Miranda and McCarter, *Hamilton: The Revolution*, 280.
57 Miranda and McCarter, *Hamilton: The Revolution*, 281.
58 Joy Connolly, *The State of Speech: Rhetoric and Political Thought in Ancient Rome* (Princeton, NJ: Princeton University Press, 2007), 56.
59 Turning private finance and dalliance into the engines of public trust removed the burden of regional tax collecting that clearly foregrounded slavery's economic gains (roughly 30% of GDP in South Carolina for example). John P. Diggins and Mark E. Kann, eds., *The Problem of Authority in America* (Philadelphia, PA: Temple University Press, 1981), 12.
60 Charles A. Willard, "The Problem of the Public Sphere: Three Diagnoses," in *Argumentation Theory and the Rhetoric of Assent*, eds. David Cratis Williams and Michael David Hazen (Tuscaloosa: University of Alabama Press, 1990), 147.
61 Hannah Arendt, *On Revolution* (New York: Penguin Classics, 2006).
62 Cocks, *On Sovereignty*, 51.
63 Jacques Ranciere, *Le Philosphe et ses pauvres* (Paris: Champs-Flammarion, 2006), 204.

64 Henry Cabot Lodge, *Alexander Hamilton* (New York: Houghton Mifflin and Company, 1898), 133.
65 John Lamberton Harper, *American Machiavelli: Alexander Hamilton and the Origins of U.S. Foreign Policy* (New York: Cambridge University Press, 2004); Karl-Friedrich Walling, *Republican Empire: Alexander Hamilton on War and Free Government* (Lawrence: University of Kansas, 1999).
66 Deirdre N. McCloskey, *The Rhetoric of Economics*, 2nd ed. (Madison: University of Wisconsin Press, 1998).
67 Edward E. Baptist, *The Half Has Never Been Told: Slavery and the Making of American Capitalism* (New York: Basic Books, 2014).
68 Miranda and McCarter, *Hamilton: The Revolution*, 280.
69 Schwarze, "Environmental Melodrama," 248.

CHAPTER NINE

Political Niceties and Rap in *Hamilton*

JEFFREY P. MEHLTRETTER DRURY[1]

Early in Act I of *Hamilton*, just after the audience has met the cast of characters, Alexander Hamilton engages in a political debate with Samuel Seabury, a British loyalist, in the song "Farmer Refuted." This song deepens the already apparent differences between Hamilton and his political rival, Aaron Burr. Whereas Hamilton cannot resist the temptation to debate Seabury, Burr cautions Hamilton to "leave him be."[2] Whereas Hamilton demolishes Seabury through rap, Burr urges Hamilton to stop. Their disagreement in this song peaks when Hamilton exclaims, "Burr, I'd rather be divisive than indecisive, drop the niceties."[3]

Hamilton's meaning might be clearer by substituting the word "civility" for "niceties." People often equate civility with politeness or manners and incivility with being rude or disrespectful.[4] Consequently, viewers might conclude that Hamilton is willfully uncivil in this debate, electing to mock Seabury rather than pursue "niceties" of civil debate. This connection to civility becomes starker if we consider communication scholar Michael Schudson's observation that people who are uncivil are often labeled "driven, ambitious, unreasonable, self-serving, rude, hot-headed, self-absorbed."[5] Audience members might use virtually all of these adjectives to describe Lin-Manual Miranda's version of Alexander Hamilton. In fact, Miranda himself used such adjectives in his 2015 casting call description of the title character: "An earnest, ambitious hothead, a man possessed. Speaks his mind, no matter the cost. Must be able to rap VERY well. Eminem meets Sweeney Todd."[6]

Miranda's choice to ascribe these qualities to Hamilton does not mean that the musical is promoting them. However, audience members must contend with Miranda's situating of Hamilton as a hero—a tragic one, but a hero nonetheless.[7] Narrator Aaron Burr tells us as much in the very first line of the musical, asking "How does [Hamilton]... grow up to be a hero and a scholar?"[8] Burr *presumes* that Hamilton is a hero and a scholar, indicating the musical purpose's to be an exposition of how Hamilton achieved such status.[9]

If the character of Hamilton is meant to be civic hero for the audience, it seems possible that *Hamilton* reinforces the civility crisis that many commentators and scholars have identified in contemporary political discourse.[10] In the preface to the 2019 book, *A Crisis of Civility?* Carolyn J. Lukensmeyer, Executive Director for the National Institute for Civil Discourse, explains that "the general civic spirit and civil demeanor ... have broken down in ways that we have not seen before, resulting in new threats to our institutions, our public servants, and the public as a whole."[11] Given rhetorical scholar Thomas W. Benson's observation that "uncivil speech is not merely rude but that it has effects,"[12] audience members ought to consider whether *Hamilton* plays a role in perpetuating incivility.

The need to consider *Hamilton*'s message about political civility is even more pressing due to the significant reach of the musical. In 2016, President Barack Obama recognized *Hamilton*'s potential for civic education, proclaiming that "in each brilliantly crafted song, we hear the debates that shaped our Nation, and we hear the debates that are still shaping our Nation."[13] Moreover, the musical's popularity among youth means that the children who repeatedly listen to *Hamilton* today may cultivate beliefs and attitudes toward political civility for adulthood, much as they learn civility from observing "others engaging in conversation in the neighborhood, at church, at school, or on the news."[14]

In this chapter, I explore the musical's message about civility explicitly. I argue that *Hamilton* challenges contemporary norms of civil argumentation by enacting political debate through the atypical form of the rap battle. This incongruity between the content (of political debate) and form (of rap music) invites the audience to reflect on the virtue and vices of uncivil argumentation, especially for individuals who lack access to political arenas of power. I base my conclusions on a textual analysis of the form and content of three songs that Miranda explicitly wrote as political debates: "Farmer Refuted," "Cabinet Battle #1," and "Cabinet Battle #2," all of which feature Hamilton rapping his arguments against a singular co-arguer. While my analysis is limited to these three songs, readers familiar with *Hamilton* can easily find additional examples throughout the musical that corroborate my thesis.

I demonstrate this argument through two main sections. I first illustrate how the songs in *Hamilton* might violate contemporary norms of civility when approached as political argumentation, particularly for the context in which they occur within the musical's narrative. In the subsequent section, I analyze the songs as rap battles and illustrate how this perspective recovers the rhetoric's value against potential allegations of incivility and emphasizes the value of incivility for social change. In the conclusion, I explore the implications of *Hamilton* for understanding the complicated layers of civility in U.S. political discourse.

HAMILTON AND UNCIVIL POLITICAL ARGUMENTATION

This section explores how audience members might perceive *Hamilton* to violate contemporary norms of civility in political argumentation. I define these norms through two different frameworks of civility that communication scholars tend to identify: individually-based behaviors tied to politeness and community-oriented attitudes tied to democratic processes. After explaining each framework, I will apply both to the title character's argumentation in *Hamilton*.

The framework of *individual behavior* is linked to the concept of civility as niceties and considers the specific actions and statements of the individual. Communication scholars have variously labeled this framework "civility as manners," "civility as politeness," and "individual-level civility," among others.[15] These labels emphasize the form and content of the performance, considering "the surface features of certain kinds of public actions and pronouncements."[16] This framework relies on norms or standards of civil communication while recognizing that norms depend crucially on context.[17] Put another way, incivility is often in the eye of the beholder and people tend to know it when they see it. Despite the individual-level basis of these norms, the norms often represent collective standards that in-group members can use as a means of conditioning an individual's conduct, sometimes to the point of silencing or excluding others (a point I will return to later in the chapter).[18]

The framework of *attitudes toward community* emphasizes political civility in relation to democratic processes. From this framework, civility refers not just to the rhetorical behaviors of those engaged in political debate but also to the attitude toward and, in some cases, consequences of such behaviors for democratic decision-making. Scholars have variously labeled this framework "civility as political friendship," "civility as responsiveness," and "public-level civility."[19] These labels connect civility to how individuals engage their fellow community members. Laden explains that this framework understands civility as "characterized by a certain kind of openness and a disposition to cooperate."[20] Political communication scholars tend to prefer this framework in defining civility as a concept. For instance, political scientist Susan Herbst defines civility "as constructive engagement with others through argument, deliberation, and discourse,"[21] while deliberation scholar John Gastil describes it as "engaging with political adversaries in a manner that is honest and respectful. It does not require politeness, but it avoids animus or contempt."[22]

As Gastil suggests, the attitudinal framework offers both a higher standard and stronger consequences for U.S. politics than the behavioral framework. Politeness might enhance our interpersonal relationships but Laden describes this emphasis "incidental" to the "well-functioning" of democracy.[23] Some scholars take the objection further, arguing that the focus on politeness behaviors obscures, diverts attention from, or even polices the political content of the speech. For example, communication scholars Mary E. Stuckey and Sean Patrick O'Rourke argue that the emphasis on politeness functions as "a distraction from real problems, a mode of silencing, and a potentially exclusionary understanding of community as the province of the privileged."[24]

Despite these scholars' concerns, my analysis incorporates the behavioral framework because the connection between civility and politeness tends to be what U.S. adults—who comprise the primary audience for *Hamilton*—think about when they hear the word "civility."[25] In one survey of U.S. adults, communication scholars found that "incivility in public discourse includes things perceived to be disrespectful, unnecessary, and rude," with "name-calling and vulgarity" receiving "the highest incivility ratings."[26] Additionally, Ashley Muddiman's survey of U.S. adults employed both frameworks of civility and identified "name-calling, profanity, and personal attacks"—all of which fall within the framework of individual behaviors—as more uncivil than factors related to the community attitudes framework.[27] Additionally, the indicators of the contemporary crisis of civility are grounded as much in behaviors relating to discourse norms as they are in democratic attitudes and outcomes, particularly evident in the allegations that contemporary political talk is too personal, too polarized, too pigheaded, and too pessimistic.[28]

Hamilton's hero violates the standards of civil conduct established in both frameworks, evident in Hamilton's rhetorical behavior—which uses *ad hominem* attacks and profanity—as well as his attitude—which is disrespectful and uncooperative. As mentioned in the introduction, I will focus my analysis on three debates in the musical. "Farmer Refuted" is an informal political debate between Hamilton and Seabury about the impending revolution. The two cabinet battles are meant to represent formal debates within President George Washington's cabinet about significant policy decisions facing the new nation. "Cabinet Battle #1," near the start of *Hamilton*'s second act, represents a debate between Thomas Jefferson and Hamilton about whether the U.S. Congress should legislate the Funding Act of 1790. The Act, advocated by Hamilton as Secretary of Treasury, proposed that the federal government assume state's debts resulting from the Revolutionary War by raising select tariffs, particularly on distilled spirits such as whiskey.[29] "Cabinet Battle #2" concerns whether the nation should assist the new French Republic during its impending war with England or remain uninvolved, given that the United States signed the 1778 Treaty of Alliance with the now-dead King Louis the Sixteenth. Jefferson, as Secretary of State, supports intervention while Hamilton prefers neutrality. My analysis addresses these songs thematically by considering the tone, content, and consequences of Hamilton's political argumentation and positioning them within the broader narrative trajectory of *Hamilton*.

From the framework of politeness behaviors, Hamilton's argumentation uses rhetorical tactics that align with political incivility: *ad hominem* appeals (which includes both name-calling and personal attacks) and profanity/vulgarity. Hamilton's *ad hominem* argumentation emerges in all three songs. In "Farmer Refuted," Hamilton begins with substantive concerns about the revolution but then turns quickly to attacking Seabury, exclaiming "My dog speaks more eloquently than thee! . . . But strangely, your mange is the same."[30] This line might get some laughs from the audience, but it also reinforces the tendency for political argumentation to devolve into personal attacks.

Similarly, in "Cabinet Battle #2," Hamilton attacks his co-arguer, Jefferson, rather than Jefferson's arguments when he begins with a profane, aggressive outburst assailing Jefferson's mental capacity: "You must be out of your goddamn mind if you think; The President is gonna bring the nation to the brink; Of meddling in the middle of a military mess; A game of chess where France is queen and kingless."[31] If the incivility of this appeal is not evident on its face, the debate's context enhances the negative judgment. This song is intended to represent a cabinet meeting among U.S. politicians; Jefferson had earned his place since he served as Secretary of State and former Ambassador to France. Hamilton's retort is uncivil for suggesting Jefferson's illegitimacy to participate in that forum.

Hamilton's behavioral incivility is perhaps most evident in "Cabinet Battle #1." In the musical's debate, Jefferson first offers a financial case against the Funding Act, citing the inequity of making Southern states accountable for Northern debts. Hamilton initially addresses this reason by promoting national economic growth but then quickly descends into *ad hominem* arguments against Jefferson and James Madison, declaring:

> Thomas Jefferson, always hesitant with the President; Reticent—there isn't a plan he doesn't jettison; Madison, you're mad as a hatter, son, take your medicine; Damn, you're in worse shape than the national debt is in; Sittin' there useless as two shits; Hey, turn around, bend over, I'll show you where my shoe fits.[32]

Here, Hamilton attacks Jefferson and Madison as people and uses profanity to boot. The uncivil nature of this appeal, for this context of a cabinet meeting, becomes strikingly clear when Washington immediately stops the debate and pulls Hamilton aside for a conversation. Washington's admonitions for Hamilton to "pull yourself together" and "watch your mouth"[33] correspond to the historical

Washington's interest in civility, begun at a young age when he copied by hand the 110 "Rules of Civility & Decent Behaviour In Company and Conversation."[34] Miranda's Hamilton, it seems, had yet to learn these civility lessons by 1789.

Beyond *ad hominem* attacks and profanity, Hamilton's attitude also implies incivility. Gastil and Herbst note the attitudinal framework of civility approaches deliberative exchanges in a constructive manner, with an openness that avoids hostility. Applying this framework, it is difficult to perceive Hamilton's arguments as civil. In fact, I will illustrate how Hamilton's arguments violate even Stuckey and O'Rourke's more expansive and "radical" concept of civility, which emphasizes values such as "truth telling, inclusion, and the determined advocacy of unpopular positions" as standards for civil political engagement.[35] Hamilton's obstructionist rhetoric and his verbal and physical performance of the argumentation demonstrate his interest in shouting down his opposition rather than being inclusive and open.

From an attitudinal perspective, Hamilton's argumentation might be most uncivil in "Farmer Refuted." Hamilton's preference for being "divisive" over "niceties" directly betrays an interest in inclusivity or constructive engagement. Hamilton strives to win the debate by overpowering Seabury, for example, when he exclaims: "Revolution is comin'; The; Have-nots are gonna win this, it's; Hard to listen to you with a straight face; Chaos and bloodshed already haunt; Us, honestly you shouldn't even; Talk and what about Boston?"[36] This quotation intimates incivility for a few reasons. First, Hamilton ridicules Seabury because he disagrees with him, a common trope in online trolling but not a constructive tactic for civil argumentation. His claims, "it's hard to listen to you with a straight face" and "you shouldn't even talk," demonstrate the opposite of openness, inclusivity, and advocacy of minority positions.

Second, Hamilton uses intimidation tactics by speaking over Seabury, preventing others from hearing Seabury's ideas. At one point, Hamilton even occupies Seabury's space, stepping next to him on the soapbox, and literally getting in his face. When audience members viewing the musical see Hamilton's friends the Marquis de Lafayette, Hercules Mulligan, and John Laurens laughing as Hamilton insults Seabury, they might envision this exchange as representing an effective attitude toward and conduct within a political debate. Ultimately, "Farmer Refuted" suggests that hostility to other's ideas and the bullying of dissent are virtues rather than vices in political debate.

"Cabinet Battle #1" offers a more complicated message about political civility as an attitude. In the musical, Washington stops the debate after Hamilton instructs Madison to "bend over." Before Washington can speak to Hamilton, Madison and Jefferson continue to provoke Hamilton by teasing, "You don't have the votes.... You're gonna need congressional approval and you don't have the votes"[37] This is not merely an amusing taunt; it also reveals how Hamilton's desire to win the battle—perhaps expecting the most aggressive argument to win in this scenario—blinds him of the need for a long-term political coalition. In fact, Hamilton expresses a feeling of victimization, observing to Washington that Jefferson and Madison are "being intransigent ... they don't have a plan, they just hate mine."[38] While audience members might commiserate with Hamilton's opposition to naysayers, Washington refuses to let him sulk. The president tells him, "you need to convince more folks.... You have to find a compromise."[39] Here, Washington contrasts civil strategy and compromise with Hamilton's uncivil emphasis on winning and feeling aggrieved when he fails.

"Cabinet Battle #2" also illustrates the unproductive nature of Hamilton's argumentation. Whereas Hamilton does promote national security, he builds up to a claim that is meant to win the debate, not help it productively flourish:

> We signed a treaty with a king whose head is now in a basket; Would you like to take it out and ask it? "Should we honor our treaty, King Louis' head?" "Uh ... do whatever you want, I'm super dead."[40]

Following this lyric, Washington declares Hamilton the winner of the debate by stating "Hamilton is right."[41]

Miranda's note about these lyrics suggests that Hamilton's ending provides a model for how to win a debate, explaining that "originally, Hamilton's argument was as long as Jefferson's, but I realized I wasn't gonna top this punchline [about King Louis' head].... Hamilton is winning without trying, because he and Washington are in lockstep on this issue."[42] Miranda's use of the word "punchline" is significant for its competitive connotations; the idea suggests that the line has such a force as to strike a serious blow on the topic or object of ridicule. Thus, Hamilton can win the debate through verbal force, regardless of whether his stance was the best choice forward. Here again Miranda's lyrics foreclose constructive engagement with differences of opinion. Ultimately, both frameworks of civility challenge Hamilton's hyperbolic claim in "My Shot" that his "power of speech" is "unimpeachable."[43]

HAMILTON AND THE PERFORMANCE OF RAP BATTLES

This section encourages readers to rewind the three songs and reconsider them not as political debates among U.S. politicians but as rap battles among MCs (a label applied to freestyle rappers who seek to move the crowd[44]). When Miranda first introduced *Hamilton* at the White House in 2009, he contended that Alexander Hamilton "embodies hip hop" because he "was born a penniless orphan in St. Croix, of illegitimate birth, became George Washington's right-hand man, became treasury secretary, caught beef with every other founding father, and all on the strength of his writing."[45] Moreover, all three songs for this analysis fall within the rap genre. Thus, a critical analysis of *Hamilton*'s political argumentation must also contend with that argumentation's reliance on hip-hop and rap music.

Rap is a mode of music integral to hip-hop culture. Cultural studies scholar Tricia Rose explains that hip-hop emerged as a broader lifestyle featuring rap alongside graffiti and breakdancing. Although rap was "the last element to emerge in hip hop," it "has become its most prominent facet."[46] Moreover, rap inherits earlier genres of Black musical expression such as the spiritual and R&B.[47] Unlike these earlier forms, however, rap is a unique expression tied to lifestyle. Rose calls it a "landmark moment" in which "an entire generation ... understands itself as defined primarily by a musical, cultural form."[48]

There had been relatively few efforts to infuse rap music into the Broadway musical prior to *Hamilton*. Two Tony Award winning musicals, *In the Heights* and *Bring in 'Da Noise, Bring in 'Da Funk*, included rap as significant yet secondary parts of the score to, respectively, Latin-American music and percussion beats including tap.[49] The 2014 musical, *Holler If Ya Hear Me*, was the first Broadway production to use rap as the primary form of music by setting the story to Tupac Shakur's songs. However, it was a critical and box office failure, closing after just 38 performances.[50]

Incorporating rap into musical theater is difficult, in part, due to rap's form. Linguist John McWhorter contends that rap is most useful for competitive and aggressive moments in musical theater because it entails "a chip-on-the-shoulder tone."[51] Similarly, musical producer Jack Viertel notes that rap in musical theater "wants to talk about life in America as it really is lived on the margins of society and chronicle the struggle to move toward the center of power."[52] For Jeremy McCarter, Miranda's co-author of *Hamilton: The Revolution*, Miranda's musicals succeed while prior hip-hop musicals had failed because he has used "hip hop to tell a story that had nothing to do with hip hop—using it as form, not content."[53] Ethnomusicologist Loren Kajikawa notes mores specifically that *Hamilton* "avoids elements of mainstream hip hop, such as abundant profanity, explicit sexuality, and conspicuous consumption, that some find objectionable."[54]

The form itself, however, has rhetorical implications. Lester Spence, Professor of Political Science and Africana Studies, demonstrates the creative and political power of rap when he observes that it "was created (like most [B]lack diasporal music forms) to affirm, to celebrate, to recognize, to journal, and to show the world that another reality is possible."[55] This envisioning of another reality positions rap as a verbal manifestation of hip-hop's mode of resistance. Theresa A. Martinez explains that rap "is a valid and strident form of oppositional cultural expression" voicing "a biting distrust, disillusionment with, and critique of major societal institutions and government."[56] This cultural resistance is not, as political scientist Lakeyta M. Bonnette observes, limited to a particular race or gender but applies to all marginalized communities.[57] In this way, while rap is a "a form of necessary speech" that provides a voice for those who have been historically excluded from the political process,[58] it has simultaneously been criticized as uncivil.[59] In the early 1990s, cultural critic William Grimes observed that "part of the appeal of rap is that it refuses to buy into the civility model."[60]

Rap music, then, exemplifies how civility functions to discipline behavior and silence undesirable speech.[61] Masquerading as politeness, invocations of civility frequently imply equal status among participants and can even "limit, silence or otherwise control the free expression of" those who falls outside the norms of the dominant culture.[62] This is because appeals to civility usually promote collective interest above individual interest and frame conflict in negative terms, as something to be prevented. Thus, rap's appeal is precisely because it resists norms of civility that have historically oppressed minority groups. Gastil explains how civility is often counterproductive insofar as it "constrains speakers who need to speak forcefully, dampens fires when passions need to be inflamed, and quells revolutionary messages. Civility favors the status quo, implicitly, because it asks enemies adhere to discourse rules they had no hand in setting."[63] In short, norms of civility might further disenfranchise individuals and groups.

Moreover, intentional violations of civility are often an effective means of gaining attention and political power. Confrontational strategies used by historical social movements have illustrated that incivility and civil disobedience can draw necessary attention to a controversy and reveal the corruption of those in power.[64] When those who demand change abide by civility norms, they tend to be ignored or pushed aside. Conversely, rhetorical scholars Robert L. Scott and Donald K. Smith identify confrontational rhetoric, such as that found in rap music, to be an effective "tactic for achieving attention and an importance not readily attainable through decorum."[65]

Approaching *Hamilton* as rap music rather than political argumentation offers a more hopeful evaluation of Hamilton's incivility. In this context, the main character's behavior is, to borrow Martinez's phrase, a "form of oppositional cultural expression."[66] Hamilton is protesting the status quo in both the form and content of all three songs. In "Farmer Refuted," Hamilton speaks for the "have-nots" and refutes those who are against change. Musically, Miranda intentionally juxtaposes Hamilton's use of rap against Seabury's old-fashioned waltz style to convey Hamilton's unbridled energy and progressive approach. Musicologist Kelsey Klotz explains that "[B]lack art is positioned as the powerhouse behind America's burgeoning democracy, directly contrasting the stodgy, inaccessible, white European music of an elitist government that refuses to represent the whole of its kingdom."[67] Hamilton's confrontational rhetoric communicates his vision and passion for change, which speaks to both the historical context of U.S. independence and the contemporary context of oppression based on race, class, immigration status, etc.

Hamilton's oppositional stance also emerges in the Cabinet Battles with Jefferson. Although both Jefferson and Hamilton rap the arguments, Klotz notes that Hamilton offers more sophisticated, polysyllabic rhymes compared to Jefferson who tends to offer monosyllabic rhymes, having just progressed from the older musical genre of jazz in "What'd I Miss?"[68] The content also reinforces the view of Jefferson as old-fashioned. In "Cabinet Battle #1," Hamilton welcomes Jefferson "to the present" and rails against his naysaying attitude and pro-slavery sentiment. In "Cabinet Battle #2," Hamilton supports the French revolution and refuses to be beholden to a bygone monarch. In these debates, Hamilton functions as a progressive hero striving to be heard and tell it like it is. After all, it was only by violating norms of civility that Washington noticed Hamilton and took his frustration seriously in "Cabinet Battle #1."

The perspective of rap music might also help defend Hamilton's *ad hominem* attacks and profanity from charges of unproductive incivility. For this, I consider freestyle rap battles as a rhetorical form designed to demonstrate identity and assert power. The rapper Common observes that "being an MC is about aura and persona," explaining that "it's a character you inhabit; it's a style; it's a mentality; it's a way you put yourself out there, the way you think and the way you act. It's about lyrics and voice, creativity and showmanship."[69] Communication scholars Alim, Lee, and Carris have argued that freestyle rap battles are "fiercely competitive verbal displays" that involve a playfulness tied to the rapper's identity and personality.[70] Miranda recognized explicitly that he is mapping political debates of the eighteenth century onto a genre naturally oriented toward competition and self-aggrandizement: "the stakes are not who's the best rapper. The stakes are what direction are we going to go in as a country? Every rap battle sets the historical precedent. That is the highest stakes you could have for a rap battle, higher even than *8 Mile*."[71]

Not only does rap fit *Hamilton*'s narrative about legacy and political ambition in the United States but approaching these songs as rap battles challenges the framework of civility in favor of a more creative understanding. For example, Miranda describes Hamilton's rap in "Cabinet Battle #1" as an impressive performance featuring verbal precision:

> I don't get angry easily (I'm really 5,000 times as mellow as Hamilton) but when I do, I run cold: Time slows down, and the exact right words click into place to destroy what's in front of me. Not proud of it, but it's how I'm wired. I gave this trait to Hamilton, and I think it suits him well: He rhymes the craziest when he is backed into a corner.[72]

Because the content is grounded in playfulness and topping, Hamilton and Jefferson infuse their identities into the argumentation and ensure that the political is personal. For instance, despite Hamilton's crazy rhymes, he loses "Cabinet Battle #1" when Washington shuts it down. This disconnect leads Hamilton to conclude in the very next song—"Take A Break"—that political failure is also a personal, perhaps moral, failure. As he explains it, "ambition is my folly."[73] Later, Hamilton frames politics as fundamentally connected to his identity—he's "got skin in the game," as he declares to rival Aaron Burr during the song "The Room Where It Happens."[74] In their chapter in this volume, Huell and Jenkins similarly celebrate *Hamilton*'s rap battles for igniting the political passions of the performers and audience members alike. This might explain why Miranda observes that Hamilton's "Cabinet Battle #1" performance "makes the student matinees worth it. *They lose their minds* [at his line about Madison]" (italics in the original).[75]

In addition to showcasing Hamilton and Jefferson's creativity, the raps engage and embody significant national values. Jefferson promotes populism and loyalty while Hamilton promotes progress and realism.[76] Both rappers also proclaim to have the nation's best interests at heart despite being critical of each other's stances and personae. This should not be an entirely novel conclusion given Spence's observation that U.S. rap MCs "both accommodate and criticize mainstream norms and values."[77] Indeed, Kajikawa notes that *Hamilton* offers a "familiar trope" for fans of rap music: "rappers and the personas they create are nothing less than a reflection of fundamental American ideals."[78]

"Farmer Refuted" similarly reflects the creative elements of rap battling, specifically the virtue of improvisation.[79] In one revealing moment, Hamilton chastises Seabury, "honestly, look at me, please don't read!... Don't modulate the key then not debate with me!"[80] The last line is some musical humor but it emphasizes how effective MCs have mental agility rather than relying on a script. The same quality of talking over Seabury that suggested incivility earlier can be reframed in a rap battle as an illustration of Hamilton's political and rhetorical dexterity. Miranda explained in his commentary about this song that his goal was for Hamilton to "dismantle Seabury using the same vowels and cadences and talking over him.... It felt like the kind of superpower Hamilton could deploy to impress his friends."[81] In sum, Hamilton's rhetoric here and throughout the three songs makes sense as a "superpower" and an "impress[ive]" way to demonstrate superior intellect if we approach it from the vantage point of a rap battle rather than political civility.

CONCLUSION: MERGING PERSPECTIVES

In this chapter, I have analyzed *Hamilton*'s debates from two different perspectives: as political argumentation beholden to norms of civility and as rap battles that challenge personae and power. More specifically, echoing the earlier observation that civility is in the eye of the beholder based on rhetorical context,[82] what some might perceive as creative skill and political engagement in a rap battle, others might perceive as uncivil behavior and obstructionism in a political debate. This tension between the two perspectives in *Hamilton* invites audiences to reflect on the qualities of productive public rhetoric.

Although Hamilton is framed as a model of political heroism, the analysis suggests that using Hamilton's tactics in political debate might further entrench the civility crisis in contemporary political discourse. This potential builds on McWhorter's observation that the cabinet battles are simultaneously one of "the high points of the show" but also shallow representations insofar as "argument, topping, and display are only one part of being human—or of being a character in a musical."[83] Hamilton's focus on winning is exciting in the moment but there are limits to its value as a framework for civic engagement given its potential to prevent collaborative problem-solving. Uncivil discourse surrounds us in our daily lives—through the press and mass media, online, and in our interpersonal and work relationships—but its prominence in *Hamilton* may be concerning precisely because the musical transcends politics and has a sizeable youth following that includes but is broader than those who closely follow political affairs.

Conversely, because incivility can engender social change, *Hamilton* urges advocates to consider when uncivil tactics may be appropriate. Despite having the confidence and support of the nation's first president and a position of power within institutional structures, Miranda portrays Hamilton as a progressive outsider by employing the musical form of rap, by reminding the audience consistently of Hamilton's immigrant status, and by using actors from historically underrepresented groups. These rhetorical elements enable *Hamilton* to push the boundaries of accepted and acceptable conduct in political argumentation and to resist an *a priori* rejection of uncivil tactics, especially when alluding to the oppression of minority races opposite "civilized" white founders.[84] Thus, it is incumbent on audience members—scholars and otherwise—to recognize how the very charge of incivility against Hamilton might fortify existing power structures that perpetuate oppression, particularly in light of recent civil unrest concerning racist policies and policing and the ongoing quest for racial justice in the United States.

Ultimately, Hamilton's productive obstructionism exhibits a prevailing tension in the concept of civility, as summarized by Daniel M. Chick: "political discourse needs civility, yet confrontation also plays an enduring and necessary role in creating equity."[85] Audience members might resolve this tension by recognizing the tactical nature of (in)civility in U.S. political discourse, that rhetors strategically use incivility to achieve specific aims and that these tactics have been present in U.S. political discourse since the founding era. The fact that civility is the norm—and also determined by norms—means that incivility is by its very nature an interruption. Incivility disturbs, it confronts, it offends, and it demands attention. Accordingly, Hamilton's *ad hominem* attacks and profanity are an interruption in the expectations of what political discourse might look and sound like as well as what it might accomplish given Hamilton's goals. As Kajikawa argues, "the combination of musical theater and hip hop can serve as a mirror and also, perhaps, as an inspiration for political struggle."[86] The many complicated storylines in *Hamilton*—for example, Hamilton's need for political compromise despite early success with incivility—prompt reflection on civility's limits and effects in political discourse. In the end, reflection on *Hamilton*'s political argumentation suggests that advocates ought to contextually utilize both "divisiveness" and "niceties" in seeking political change.

NOTES

1 Jeffrey P. Mehltretter Drury, Associate Professor, Wabash College, druryj@wabash.edu.
2 Lin-Manuel Miranda and Jeremy McCarter, *Hamilton: The Revolution* (New York, NY: Grand Central Publishing, 2016), 49.
3 Miranda and McCarter, *Hamilton: The Revolution*, 49.
4 Susan Herbst, *Rude Democracy: Civility and Incivility in American Politics* (Philadelphia, PA: Temple University Press, 2010), 3; P. M. Forni, *The Civility Solution: What to Do When People Are Rude* (New York: St. Martin's Press, 2008), xx; Kate Kenski, Kevin Coe, and Stephen A. Rains, "Perceptions of Incivility in Public Discourse," in *A Crisis of Civility? Political Discourse and Its Discontents*, eds. Robert G. Boatright, Timothy J. Shaffer, Sarah Sobieraj, and Dannagal Goldthwaite Young (New York: Routledge, 2019), 56.
5 Michael Schudson, "Why Conversation Is Not the Soul of Democracy," *Critical Studies in Mass Communication* 14 (1997): 308.
6 "HAMILTON–Richard Rodgers Theatre Auditions," *Broadway World*, March 12, 2015, https://www.broadwayworld.com/equity-audition/HAMILTON-Richard-Rodgers-Theatre-2015-10518.
7 Adam Gopnik, "'Hamilton' and the Hip Hop Case for Progressive Heroism," *The New Yorker*, February 5, 2016, https://www.newyorker.com/news/daily-comment/hamilton-and-the-hip-hop-case-for-progressive-heroism.
8 Miranda and McCarter, *Hamilton: The Revolution*, 16.
9 The driving assumption of Hamilton as hero appears in numerous other songs throughout the musical, particularly in "Non-Stop," when the song references Hamilton's "rise to the top," and in the finale of the show, "Who Lives, Who Dies, Who Tells Your Story?" when Elizabeth Schuyler Hamilton "ask[s her]self, 'What would you do if you had more time?'" Miranda and McCarter, *Hamilton: The Revolution*, 137, 281.
10 Daniel M. Chick, "#ActsOfCivility: Implicit Arguments for the Role of Civility and the Paradox of Confrontation," *Journal of Contemporary Rhetoric* 10 (2020): 38. Triggering events often prompt renewed concerns about civility. Chick identifies Trump's election in 2016 but earlier scholars have identified the 2011 mass shooting in Tucson (allegedly inspired by Sarah Palin's rhetoric) and Joe Wilson's interruption of President Barack Obama's joint session address by shouting "You lie!" as salient rhetorical situations connected to political incivility. Even still, writers have been professing a "crisis of civility" for decades. Herbst, *Rude Democracy*; Thomas A. Hollihan and Francesca Marie Smith, "Weapons and Words: Rhetorical Studies of the Gabrielle Giffords Shootings," *Rhetoric and Public Affairs* 17 (2014): 577–84; Diana C. Mutz and Byron Reeves, "The New Videomalaise: Effects of Televised Incivility on Political Trust," *American Political Science*

Review 99 (2005): 1–15; Deborah Tannen, *The Argument Culture: Moving From Debate to Dialogue* (New York: Random House, 1998); Benjamin DeMott, "Seduced by Civility," *The Nation*, December 9, 1996, 11–19.

11 Carolyn J. Lukensmeyer, "Preface," in *A Crisis of Civility? Political Discourse and Its Discontents*, eds. Robert G. Boatright, Timothy J. Shaffer, Sarah Sobieraj, and Dannagal Goldthwaite Young (New York: Routledge, 2019), xxi.

12 Thomas W. Benson, "The Rhetoric of Civility: Power, Authenticity, and Democracy," *Journal of Contemporary Rhetoric* 1 (2011): 23.

13 Barack Obama, "Remarks Prior to a Musical Performance by Members of the Cast of 'Hamilton,'" March 14, 2016, in *Daily Compilation of Presidential Documents: Administration of Barack Obama*, https://www.gpo.gov/fdsys/pkg/DCPD-201600146/pdf/DCPD-201600146.pdf.

14 Deborah S. Mower, "The Real Morality of Public Discourse: Civility as an Orienting Attitude," in *A Crisis of Civility? Political Discourse and Its Discontents*, eds. Robert G. Boatright, Timothy J. Shaffer, Sarah Sobieraj, and Dannagal Goldthwaite Young (New York: Routledge, 2019), 217.

15 Mary E. Stuckey and Sean Patrick O'Rourke, "Civility, Democracy, and National Politics," *Rhetoric and Public Affairs* 17 (2014): 713; Anthony Simon Laden, "Two Concepts of Civility," in *A Crisis of Civility? Political Discourse and Its Discontents*, eds. Robert G. Boatright, Timothy J. Shaffer, Sarah Sobieraj, and Dannagal Goldthwaite Young (New York: Routledge, 2019), 9; Ashley Muddiman, "How People Perceive Political Incivility," in *A Crisis of Civility? Political Discourse and Its Discontents*, eds. Robert G. Boatright, Timothy J. Shaffer, Sarah Sobieraj, and Dannagal Goldthwaite Young (New York: Routledge, 2019), 32.

16 Laden, "Two Concepts of Civility," 9.

17 Benson, "The Rhetoric of Civility," 29.

18 Robert L. Scott and Donald K. Smith, "The Rhetoric of Confrontation," *Quarterly Journal of Speech* 55 (1969): 8; Dana L. Cloud, "'Civility' as a Threat to Academic Freedom," *First Amendment Studies* 49 (2015): 13–17.

19 Stuckey and O'Rourke, "Civility, Democracy, and National Politics," 714; Laden, "Two Concepts of Civility," 9; Muddiman, "How People Perceive Political Incivility," 33.

20 Laden, "Two Concepts of Civility," 9.

21 Herbst, *Rude Democracy*, 19.

22 John Gastil, "Seeking a Mutuality of Tolerance: A Practical Defense of Civility in a Time of Political Warfare," in *A Crisis of Civility? Political Discourse and Its Discontents*, eds. Robert G. Boatright, Timothy J. Shaffer, Sarah Sobieraj, and Dannagal Goldthwaite Young (New York: Routledge, 2019), 161.

23 Laden, "Two Concepts of Civility," 26.

24 Stuckey and O'Rourke, "Civility, Democracy, and National Politics," 713–14.

25 Herbst, *Rude Democracy*, 3. Herbst explains that "When I told people I was writing a book on civility, they thought of opening doors for women, naughty children misbehaving in public, and suppressing the desire to give others 'the finger' in traffic."

26 Kenski, Coe, and Rains, "Perceptions of Incivility in Public Discourse," 56.

27 Muddiman, "How People Perceive Political Incivility," 34.

28 Shanto Iyengar and Kyu S. Hahn, "Red Media, Blue Media: Evidence of Ideological Selectivity in Media Use," *Journal of Communication* 59 (2009): 19–39; Hyunseo Hwang, Youngju Kim, and Catherine U. Huh, "Seeing Is Believing: Effects of Uncivil Online Debate on Political Polarization and Expectations of Deliberation," *Journal of Broadcasting and Electronic Media* 58 (2014): 621–33.

29 An Act making provision for the [payment of the] Debt of the United States, August 4, 1790, ch. 34, 1 *Stat.* 138–44; An Act to provide more effectually for the settlement of the Accounts between the United States and the individual States, August 5, 1790, ch. 38, 1 *Stat.* 178–79; An Act making further provision for the debts of the United States, August 10, 1790, ch. 39, 1 *Stat.* 180–82; An Act making Provision for the Reduction of the Public Debt, August 12, 1790, ch. 47, 1 *Stat.* 186–87.
30 Miranda and McCarter, *Hamilton: The Revolution*, 49.
31 Miranda and McCarter, *Hamilton: The Revolution*, 192.
32 Miranda and McCarter, *Hamilton: The Revolution*, 161–62.
33 Miranda and McCarter, *Hamilton: The Revolution*, 162.
34 Historian William Guthrie Sayen notes that the historical Washington's experiences ensured that by 1775 he "had acquired the self-restraint to be courteous even under pressure." William Guthrie Sayen, "George Washington's 'Unmannerly' Behavior," *The Virginia Magazine of History and Biography* 107 (1999): 36.
35 Stuckey and O'Rourke, "Civility, Democracy, and National Politics," 714.
36 Miranda and McCarter, *Hamilton: The Revolution*, 49.
37 Miranda and McCarter, *Hamilton: The Revolution*, 162.
38 Miranda and McCarter, *Hamilton: The Revolution*, 163.
39 Miranda and McCarter, *Hamilton: The Revolution*, 163.
40 Miranda and McCarter, *Hamilton: The Revolution*, 192.
41 Miranda and McCarter, *Hamilton: The Revolution*, 192.
42 Miranda and McCarter, *Hamilton: The Revolution*, 192.
43 Miranda and McCarter, *Hamilton: The Revolution*, 26.
44 Ice-T, "Ice-T Explains the Difference Between an MC and a Rapper on #SwayInTheMorning," SWAY'S UNIVERSE, June 8, 2012, YouTube video, 2:27, https://youtu.be/qrLmvqsljmU.
45 Lin-Manuel Miranda, "Lin-Manuel Miranda Performs at the White House Poetry Jam," *The Obama White House*, YouTube video, 4:26, November 2, 2009, https://youtu.be/WNFf7nMIGnE.
46 Tricia Rose, *Black Noise: Rap Music and Black Culture in Contemporary America* (Middletown, CT: Wesleyan University Press, 1994), 51.
47 Reiland Rabaka, *The Hip Hop Movement: From R&B and the Civil Rights Movement to Rap and the Hip Hop Generation* (Lanham, MD: Rowman & Littlefield Publishers, 2013).
48 Tricia Rose, *The Hip Hop Wars: What We Talk about When We Talk about Hip Hop—And Why It Matters* (New York: Basic Books, 2008), 8.
49 David Rooney, "In the Heights," *Variety*, March 9, 2008, https://variety.com/2008/film/awards/in-the-heights-4-1200535976; Charles Isherwood, "The View from Uptown: American Dreaming to a Latin Beat," *New York Times*, March 10, 2008, https://www.nytimes.com/2008/03/10/theater/reviews/10heig.html; Ben Brantley, "Story of Tap as the Story of Blacks," *New York Times*, November 16, 1995, https://www.nytimes.com/1995/11/16/theater/theater-review-story-of-tap-as-the-story-of-blacks.html.
50 "Holler if Ya Hear Me," *Internet Broadway Database*, https://www.ibdb.com/broadway-production/holler-if-ya-hear-me-496054.
51 John McWhorter, "Will 'Hamilton' Save the Musical? Don't Wait for It," *American Theatre*, March 2016, 52.
52 Jack Viertel, *The Secret Life of the American Musical: How Broadway Shows Are Built* (New York: Sarah Crichton Books, 2016), 266.
53 Miranda and McCarter, *Hamilton: The Revolution*, 10.

54 Loren Kajikawa, "'Young, Scrappy, and Hungry': *Hamilton*, Hip Hop, and Race," *American Music* 36 (2018): 469.
55 Lester K. Spence, *Stare in the Darkness: The Limits of Hip Hop and Black Politics* (Minneapolis: University of Minnesota Press, 2011), 17.
56 Theresa A. Martinez, "Political Culture as Oppositional Culture: Rap as Resistance," *Sociological Perspectives* 40 (1997): 279. See also: Rose, *Black Noise*, 35–36; Adam Bradley and Andrew DuBois, "Introduction," in *The Anthology of Rap*, eds. Adam Bradley and Andrew DuBois (New Haven, CT: Yale University Press, 2010), xxxviii.
57 Lakeyta M. Bonnette, *Pulse of the People: Political Rap Music and Black Politics* (Philadelphia: University of Pennsylvania Press, 2015), 2–3.
58 Bradley and DuBois, "Introduction," xxxviii.
59 Neil A. Lewis, "Friends of Free Speech Now Consider Its Limits," *New York Times*, June 29, 1990, B7, http://timesmachine.nytimes.com/timesmachine/1990/06/29/871890.html.
60 William Grimes, "Have A #%!&$@$! Day," *New York Times*, October 17, 1993, https://www.nytimes.com/1993/10/17/style/have-a-day.html. See also: William Raspberry, "Can't We Talk about Something More Positive?" *The Washington Post*, June 2, 1993, https://www.washingtonpost.com/archive/opinions/1993/06/02/cant-we-talk-about-something-more-positive/c2ad7512-e4ff-4c54-bc59-6b5494b7474a.
61 Jeffrey B. Kurtz, "Civility, American Style," *Relevant Rhetoric* 3 (2012): 19, http://relevantrhetoric.com/Civility%20American%20Style.pdf.
62 Andrew Calabrese, "Liberalism's Disease: Civility above Justice," *European Journal of Communication* 30 (2015): 540. See also: Linda M. G. Zerilli, "Against Civility: A Feminist Perspective," in *Civility, Legality, and Justice in America*, ed. Austin Sarat (New York: Cambridge University Press, 2014), 116–17.
63 Gastil, "Seeking a Mutuality of Tolerance," 164.
64 Zerilli, "Against Civility," 31.
65 Scott and Smith, "The Rhetoric of Confrontation," 7.
66 Martinez, "Political Culture as Oppositional Culture," 279. See also: Rose, *Black Noise*, 35–36; Bradley and DuBois, "Introduction," xxxviii.
67 Kelsey Klotz, "*Hamilton* Is Innovative, But Not Quite Revolutionary," *The Common Reader*, February 28, 2017, https://commonreader.wustl.edu/c/hamilton-innovative-not-quite-revolutionary.
68 Klotz, "*Hamilton* Is Innovative, But Not Quite Revolutionary"; Miranda and McCarter, *Hamilton: The Revolution*, 152.
69 Common, "Afterword," in *The Anthology of Rap*, eds. Adam Bradley and Andrew DuBois (New Haven CT: Yale University Press, 2010), 799.
70 H. Samy Alim, Jooyoung Lee, and Lauren Mason Carris, "'Short Fried-Rice-Eating Chinese MCs' and 'Good-Hair-Havin Uncle Tom Niggas': Performing Race and Ethnicity in Freestyle Rap Battles," *Journal of Linguistic Anthropology* 20 (2010): 116, 117.
71 Lin-Manuel Miranda, quoted in *Great Performances: Hamilton's America*, DVD, directed by Alex Horwitz (New York: Premiere Opera, Ltd., 2016).
72 Miranda and McCarter, *Hamilton: The Revolution*, 162.
73 Miranda and McCarter, *Hamilton: The Revolution*, 168.
74 Miranda and McCarter, *Hamilton: The Revolution*, 188.
75 Miranda and McCarter, *Hamilton: The Revolution*, 162.
76 See the chapter by Michaelah Reynolds and Ryan Neville-Shepard in this volume for how these value conflicts in the musical are connected to notions of the American Dream.

77 Spence, *Stare in the Darkness*, 9.
78 Kajikawa, "'Young, Scrappy, and Hungry,'" 474.
79 Andre Craddock-Willis, "Rap Music and the Black Musical Tradition," *Radical America* 23, no. 4 (1989): 37.
80 Miranda and McCarter, *Hamilton: The Revolution*, 49.
81 Miranda and McCarter, *Hamilton: The Revolution*, 49.
82 Herbst, *Rude Democracy*, 3.
83 McWhorter, "Will 'Hamilton' Save the Musical?" 52.
84 Kajikawa, "'Young, Scrappy, and Hungry,'" 471.
85 Chick, "#ActsOfCivility," 551.
86 Kajikawa, "'Young, Scrappy, and Hungry,'" 482.

CHAPTER TEN

Diverse Offerings for Understanding U.S. Politics: Analyzing the Invitational Rhetoric of *Hamilton* and President Barack Obama

MARK P. ORBE[1]

The election of Barack Obama as the forty-fourth U.S. president in 2008 provided an opportunity, in the eyes of some, for a country to absolve itself of the foundational sins of slavery, racism, and oppression. In similar ways, Lin-Manuel Miranda's *Hamilton: An American Musical* provided a historical account of the United States that reframes similar tainted origins. In compellingly parallel ways, both men—and their accomplishments—have been described as "unconventional," "ground-breaking," and "history-in-the-making."[2] The trajectories of both of these journeys joined forces on May 12, 2009, when Miranda introduced the first song of his groundbreaking musical at an "Evening of Poetry, Music, and the Spoken Word at the White House." The cutting-edge performance set in motion a synergistic symbolic partnership steeped in advancing social issues of diversity, inclusion, and equity. Over the next decade, the rhetoric of *Hamilton*, Miranda, and Obama would be intertwined in a socio-political movement of social change.

This chapter offers a textual analysis that situates *Hamilton* and co-constructed messages from Miranda and Obama as opportunities to offer and encourage multiple, diverse perspectives. Adopting such an approach is consistent with invitational rhetoric, which according to Sonja K. Foss and Cindy L. Griffin focuses on communicative meaning-making as "an invitation to understanding as a means to create a relationship rooted in equality, immanent value, and self-determination."[3] This approach does not define rhetoric as persuasive messages designed to change others; instead it conceptualizes rhetoric as an effort to gain an understanding of the perspectives of others in the context of self. Such an approach serves as an especially productive theoretical lens to analyze the synergistic rhetoric of *Hamilton*, Miranda, and Obama. In short, I suggest that the messages associated with these sources reflect a form of invitational rhetoric that contributes toward a social movement that promotes a more inclusive sense of democracy, political agency, and national identity. The chapter begins with a description of how *Hamilton* emerged within Obama's tenure as U.S. president.

HAMILTON IN THE AGE OF OBAMA

According to Nancy Isenberg, a professor of history at Louisiana State University who authored a biography of Aaron Burr, "Every generation rewrites the founders in their own image."[4] The creation, production, and promotion of *Hamilton* occurred in an auspicious time in U.S. history, one in which the first African American president took office and led the country for two consecutive terms. In the words of Isenberg, *Hamilton* provided the United States with a "new origin story," an audio-visual rhetorical representation provided by Miranda and his team whereby they offered international audiences a show where U.S. founders were created "in the image of Obama, for the age of Obama."[5]

The intricate relationship between *Hamilton*, Miranda, and Obama is undeniable. Their initial interaction involving the very first public presentation of *Hamilton* music is legendary: On May 12, 2009, Miranda was invited to perform something from his first Broadway show (*In the Heights*) at "An Evening of Poetry, Music, and the Spoken Word," one of the first cultural events of the Obama administration.[6] The event occurred four months after the inauguration of the first U.S. president of African descent, and according to one reporter, "the entire evening looked as if it were meant to signal a new White House taste in the performing arts."[7] For this exclusive event, Miranda decided to perform the song that would become the prologue of *Hamilton: An American Musical*. The initial skepticism of using rap music to capture one of the founders for the audience, including both the president and first lady, is palpable. Yet, their hesitancy quickly evaporates, and by the close of Miranda's performance the entire audience is in awe and erupts in enthusiastic applause. In fact, Obama is the first person to leap to his feet as the performance comes to a close.[8] While Miranda was encouraged by the appreciative reception, *Hamilton* was still in its beginning stages of conceptualization. It would not be offered in its final form for almost six years. However, the show, and its creator, would be forever linked to the Obama presidency.

The relationship between Obama and Miranda is rooted in politics. Miranda's father had a long history of involvement with democratic politics in New York, and Miranda was active in Obama's presidential campaigns.[9] In fact, Miranda served as the emcee for a 2012 fundraising event held at Harlem's Apollo Theater—the event where Obama famously offered an abbreviated rendition of Al Green's soulful ballad, "Let's Stay Together." Following the high-profile success of *Hamilton* in 2015, the Obamas attended multiple performances and ultimately invited the cast to the White House in March 2016 for a performance in the arts attended by local public school students. This visit included a freestyle rap session in the Rose Garden in which Obama fed Miranda spontaneous political words and phrases that must be used in an impromptu rap song. In June 2016, the president and first lady (via video) introduced *Hamilton* at the Tony Awards where the musical won multiple awards. On October 26, 2016—weeks before the 2016 presidential election of Donald Trump—BET hosted "Love & Happiness: An Obama Celebration" on the grounds of the White House. During this musical celebration, Leslie Odom, Jr. (who won a Tony Award for his portrayal of Aaron Burr in *Hamilton*) thanked the Obamas for their support of the show and then offered a newly created song of a hypothetical future show titled, *Barack Obama: The Musical*. This entertaining performance, in its most basic form, mirrors the 2009 offering by Miranda which focused on re-introducing Alexander Hamilton to a curious nation. On June 15, 2018, when Obama joined Miranda at the opening of *Hamilton* in Washington D.C., news reports described them as "good friends reunited."[10] Later in that year, Obama was featured on a re-mix of "One Last Time" with Miranda (an emotional song from the musical capturing the process of President George Washington relinquishing his presidency after two terms), and became the first U.S. president to have a song on the Billboard charts.[11]

The linkages between *Hamilton* and Obama go beyond his personal relationship with Miranda. The racially diverse composition of the cast and the White House administration embraced a contemporary representation of the United States not often seen in either context. Both also attracted a similar fan base of admirers. The same coalition of "Democrat voters: college-educated coastal liberals and mid-to-low-income minorities"[12] who facilitated Obama's election also serve as the foundation of *Hamilton*'s wide popularity. Similar to Obama's desire to make the White House a more welcoming and inclusively accessible place, *Hamilton*—despite the intense competition of tickets which had sold for thousands of dollars—provided opportunities for everyday people to enter a daily street lottery where tickets are available for $10 ("a Hamilton," if you will). Additionally, thousands of tickets were given to local students from lower-economic backgrounds to attend special performances.

The parallels of intense politics, personal relationships, human diversity, and political drama between *Hamilton* and the Obama presidency are also significant. These themes—as explicated in subsequent sections—are offered to U.S. (and ultimately global) audiences in the context of the first U.S. president of African descent. Chris Jackson, who played the role of George Washington in the original cast, acknowledges that "plenty of people in America are uncomfortable with a [B]lack president."[13] The powerful symbolism of racial representation in *Hamilton*, including three African Americans portraying U.S. presidents, is important in normalizing the cultural diversity in the United States.[14] These visual symbols are offered alongside diverse musical offerings from multiple genres that also represent the country's racial diversity. With little dialogue, music becomes the dominant venue of storytelling. Rap music, hip-hop, and R&B featured alongside songs that resemble those of legendary Broadway composers such as Gilbert and Sullivan, Stephen Sondheim, and Jonathan Larson.[15] According to Obama's biographer, David Remnick, this diversity of audio codes is symbolically important to represent the different languages of the United States. In addition, it offers another parallel to Obama's communication abilities:

> The musical, in effect, speaks all the cultural languages of America, and it echoes Obama's ability to change cadences depending on his audience: "a more straight-up delivery for a luncheon of business people in the Loop; a folksier approach at a downstate VFW [veterans' event]; echoes of the pastors of the [B]lack church when he is in one."[16]

As demonstrated throughout the remainder of this analysis, the invitational rhetoric of both *Hamilton* and Obama are important in creating opportunities for diverse voices across the United States to be heard and included in the conversations of meaning-making.

INVITATIONAL RHETORIC: COMMUNICATIVE MEANS TO RELATIONAL UNDERSTANDING

Traditional conceptualizations of rhetoric focus on explicit and intentional attempts to change others. Embedded in these persuasive efforts are desires to influence, control, and/or convince others to adopt particular viewpoints, in essence to exert control over others. According to Foss and Griffin, this approach to rhetoric ultimately devalues the lives and perspectives of others, who "are assumed to be naïve and less expert than the rhetor if their views differ from the rhetor's own."[17] Consistent with feminist ideologies, invitational rhetoric presents a counter-narrative to traditional conceptualizations of rhetoric. Instead of alienation, competition, and dehumanization, invitational rhetoric seeks to develop relationships based on mutual respect and understanding. By definition,

> Invitational rhetoric constitutes an invitation to the audience to enter the rhetor's world and to see it as the rhetor does. In presenting a particular perspective, the invitational rhetor does not judge or denigrate others' perspectives but is open to and tries to appreciate and validate those perspectives, even if they differ dramatically from the rhetor's own.[18]

The ontological orientation inherent to this framework revolves around feminist principles of equality (a desire for relationships steeped in intimacy, mutuality, and camaraderie), immanent value (an acknowledgement that all human beings have intrinsic worth), and self-determination (a commitment to allow individuals to make their own decisions).[19]

Invitational rhetoric assumes two different forms of rhetoric: offering perspectives and creating external conditions. First, offering perspectives involves "giving expression to a perspective without advocating its support or seeking its acceptance."[20] This is done to share one's vision of the world as a means to promote understanding, not persuade others to change their own ideas. As such, new perspectives are offered through a tentative commitment to that perspective—one open to revision and/or change. Second, creating external conditions focuses on a commitment to facilitate the type of "atmosphere in which audience members' perspectives also can be offered."[21] In order for this to be created and sustained, three conditions related to key feminist principles identified earlier must be present: safety (a feeling of security and freedom from danger), value (others are seen as having worth), and freedom (others have the power to choose or decide).

While invitational rhetoric may result in a shift of opinion, perspective, or understanding, its purpose is not rooted in a desire for change.[22] Within this approach, rhetors recognize that their ideas are just one perspective among many legitimate views; consequently they appreciate the ways in which alternative perspectives provide divergent contexts to think about an issue.[23] The goal, then, is to share perspectives, ideas, and positions while engaging the complexity of an issue that no one fully understands or supports. If change does occur, it does so when any or all individuals consider new insight and understanding gained through the exchange of different perspectives within a relational context. In this regard, invitational rhetoric is offered as a consistent means to communicate the ideals of democracy. Embedded in democratic values such as reciprocity and respect, it involves a willingness to engage in dialogue rather than debate[24]—something necessary to promote pluralistic understanding in a social order oftentimes plagued by systems of domination and oppression. As such it presents a "model for cooperative, non-adversarial, and ethical communication."[25]

Over the past two decades, rhetoricians have provided multiple examples of invitational rhetoric in speeches, visual texts, art, as well as private and public discussions.[26] Benjamin R. Bates, for example, provides a compelling argument that participatory graffiti in Brazil, known as O Machismo, reflects a visual form of invitational rhetoric.[27] Within his analysis, he describes art as a form of consciousness-raising through which the artist's message is offered to the audience who then actively participates with it to "collectively share in co-creating its message."[28] This form of invitational rhetoric increases in awareness and sensemaking and can then, for some, lead to efforts toward social change. A similar argument is made by Jennifer Emerling Bone, Cindy L. Griffin, and T. M. Linda Scholz who describe the AIDS Quilt, a publically shared art form inspired by gay rights activist Cleve Jones, as invitational rhetoric that "creat[es] the condition of freedom through choice."[29] Within their analysis, they argue that the Quilt:

> asks for reflection rather than a particular point of view and embodies the desire and need for individuals to speak up and to speak out. Rather than persuading the audience to view AIDS in a particular way, the Quilt invites its audience to share, reflect, feel, and to come away from the exchange with their own view of the disease.[30]

Through this application and engagement, scholars have also debated the inherent value and limitations of invitational rhetoric. The result of this scholarship has been a healthy discussion of the purpose, process, and practicality of invitational rhetoric in various contexts. For the purposes of this line of inquiry, I extend this discussion to explore the ways in which the synergistic relationships between *Hamilton* and Obama reflect forms of invitational rhetoric that work to promote greater democratic involvement, and ultimately social change. The next section highlights the ways in which *Hamilton* offered new perspectives to U.S. history, and in doing so, created the necessary external conditions toward greater understanding of the current political landscape in the United States.

HAMILTON AS INVITATIONAL RHETORICAL ART FORM

This section describes the ways in which *Hamilton*, as a multi-sensory art form, engages the public and invites them to participate in a process of enhanced understanding of diverse perspectives. As such, the show—and of all if its associated by-products: soundtrack, books, exhibit, mix tape, etc.—reflects invitational rhetoric that offers perspective(s) on U.S. national identity and creates external conditions through which a larger audience can participate in the co-creation of meaning. Four focal points of analysis related to this assertion follow: (1) *Hamilton*'s content regarding the role of immigrants in U.S. history; (2) *Hamilton*'s use of universal themes; (3) the "controversy" of the *Hamilton* cast's statement to Vice President-elect Mike Pence; and (4) Obama's invitational rhetoric regarding *Hamilton*.

Hamilton's Offering of U.S. History: A Story of Diverse Immigrants

Traditional, more "mainstream" history paints a picture that white men were primarily, if not exclusively, the biggest contributors to the creation of the United States. Yet, I would argue that *Hamilton* offers a different take on this narrative— an alternative narrative, if you will, of dominant perspectives largely informed by white privilege. Miranda, the creative genius behind the musical, discovered parallels between "Founding Father" Alexander Hamilton and his own father who came to the U.S. mainland from Puerto Rico in 1973. Both men came to build a life for themselves and, in doing so, contributed to the building of a new nation.[31] By highlighting the role that immigrants, and to a lesser degree women and African Americans, played in the country's origin, *Hamilton* invites diverse audiences to engage with a piece of art that allows them to see themselves as part of the history and future of the United States, an argument that other authors in this volume make explicitly.

According to Miranda, *Hamilton* "is a story about America then, told by America now."[32] The original cast, as well as subsequent national touring companies, featured extraordinarily talented actors of color from all over the United States. Miranda, a Puerto Rican, played Hamilton while African Americans were in the roles of Thomas Jefferson, Aaron Burr, George Washington, and Angelica Schuyler. An Asian American played the role of Eliza Hamilton. Interestingly, the only major role given to a European American actor (Jonathan Groff) was England's King George III.[33] The intentionality of assembling a cast "like America looks now" was crucially important to the creation of a rhetorical text offering diverse perspectives.[34]

> It's a way of pulling you into the story and allowing you to leave whatever cultural baggage you have about the founding fathers at the door ... We're telling the story of old, dead white men but we're using actors of color, and that makes the story more immediate and more accessible to a contemporary audience.[35]

At the forefront of *Hamilton* is a clear pro-immigration message, one that features newly immigrated Alexander Hamilton as a founding father who made his mark in U.S. politics. In this rhetorical context, Hamilton is not presented as white (nor are the other Founding Fathers). Instead, Hamilton is referenced throughout the production as an immigrant of color who makes tremendous contributions to the founding of the United States "by working a lot harder, by being a lot smarter, by being a self-starter" (as described in the show's opening musical number).[36] This positive representation of immigrants is offered in contrast to the pretentious attitudes of King George III, portrayed by the only white person in a major role. According to Renee Elise Goldsberry, the African American actor who plays Angelica Schuyler, "*Hamilton* is a story about America, and the most beautiful thing about it is ... it's told by such a diverse cast with a such diverse styles of music." In an interview with the *Huffington Post*, she added: "We have the opportunity to reclaim a history that some of us don't necessarily think is our own."[37] Highlighting the diversity of immigrants, and the role that they played in the founding of the United States, contributes to invitational rhetoric that allows audience members to see themselves (and others) in new ways. As seen within the next section, *Hamilton* also provides the general public opportunities to identify with historically-based events through several universal themes.

Inviting the Audience in: Crafting a Compelling Story Through Universal Themes

"Good history makes good drama."[38] This quote from Miranda captures the essence behind how the events of Alexander Hamilton's life, as comprised in Pulitzer award-winning historical author Ron Chernow's biography, immediately reflected everything necessary for musical theater. The biography, in no uncertain terms, featured a variety of universal themes inherent in the human experience. These included: search for identity/sense of belonging, overcoming the odds, ambition in competitive contexts, personal and professional desire, love/romance/heartbreak, imperfection/faults/regret, devastation and recovery, as well as the meanings associated with life, death, and one's legacy. By highlighting universal themes through powerful audio-visual rhetorical devices, *Hamilton* offers diverse audience members an opportunity to relate to different characters and explore the complex ways in which their life decisions have personal and sociocultural impact. Telling the complex story(ies) of Alexander Hamilton, and others, is inspiring in that it allows others to reflect on their own personal-cultural narratives within a greater historical context.

Such opportunities to develop a deeper understanding—of self and others as a collective, connected entity—can prompt a greater sense of democratic responsibility. This is especially true for individuals whose ancestral contributions to the birthing of a nation have been negated, marginalized, and/or erased completely. Understanding one's current life experiences within a larger historical context prompts a sense of agency and connectivity. In discussing his motivation as artist/creator, Miranda wrote: "That's the power of a real legacy: We tell stories of people who are gone because like any powerful stories, they have the potential to inspire, and to change the world."[39] Interestingly, *Hamilton* doesn't end at the time of his death. Instead it provides an opportunity for audience members to consider the events that occurred in his afterlife. According to Miranda, this rhetorical move facilitates an awareness as to what individuals leave behind after their death—"it *invites* us to think about our legacies" (emphasis added).[40]

Another feature of *Hamilton* as invitational audio-visual rhetoric is the way in which it offers a narrative filled with questions, not necessarily assertions. In the words of Miranda and McCarter, "*Hamilton* is riddled with question marks. The first act begins with a question, as does the second."[41] Other questions permeate the entire show: Is Hamilton's flawed character consistent with that of a hero? Do his failures as a husband, father, and national leader render him unacceptable to the audience? Is Eliza the heroine? How close were Angelica and Hamilton? Is Burr the villain? How did Hamilton (and others) negotiate George Washington's powerful leadership with a recognition of his own slave ownership? How is this close relationship to slavery similar to and/or different than that of Thomas Jefferson? In many ways, *Hamilton* "leaves its audiences in the dark about some basic and seemingly crucial facts . . . [and as such Miranda] forces us to work on a puzzle that has no definite answer."[42] The inherent ambiguity of the complex narrative, and lack of mutual understanding among characters, create opportunities for audience members to explore their own perspectives. As explained in *Hamilton: The Revolution*, this rhetorical feature is intentional in its ambiguity:

> Again and again, Lin distinguishes characters by what they wish they knew. "What'd I miss?" asks Jefferson in the song that introduces him. "Would that be enough?" asks Eliza in the song that defines her. "Why do you write like you're running out of time?" asks everybody in a song that marvels at Hamilton's drive, and all but declares that there's no way to explain it. *Hamilton* . . . gives an audience the chance to watch a bunch of conspicuously intelligent and well-spoken characters fill the stage with *words words words*, only to discover, again and again, the limits to what they can comprehend.[43]

Throughout the creation process, Miranda had a commitment to produce an art form that could be taken seriously by historians. He also recognized that in order to do so in a compelling, yet clear and concise, way required some poetic license.[44] Inaccuracies (e.g., chronological order of events) and exclusions (e.g., Hamilton's experiences as a slave trader) have come under fire by some historians and cultural critics. One critic, Ishmael Reed, has even created his own play, *The Haunting of Lin-Manuel Miranda*, that addresses many of the inaccuracies of *Hamilton*, including the ways in which the show glosses over the issue of slavery among Founding Fathers and excludes any representation of Native Americans and white indentured servants.[45] Miranda has not offered any official response (on record) to Reed's efforts. While not conclusive, one could argue that his nonresponse is also indicative of invitational rhetoric in that he welcomes diverse perspectives of understanding U.S. history. In fact, Miranda's commitment to creating external conditions that facilitate alternative offerings also is seen in the creation of Hamilton: The Exhibition. This extension of *Hamilton* provided a comprehensive behind-the-scenes view of the different considerations that went into the creation of the Broadway musical. It also offered a larger historical context to the story of Alexander Hamilton, including features that point out the inaccuracies of the show, relying on Joanne Freeman, professor of history at Yale, and Annette Gordon-Reed, professor of law and history at Harvard, as consultants for the exhibition.[46] Enacting the tenets of invitational rhetoric, as demonstrated in the next section, seemingly were present in other controversies regarding the show, its performers, and supporters.

An Offering and Invitation to Pence

The invitational rhetoric of *Hamilton* has extended beyond the musical itself. These include multiple public appearances by creators and actors, extended musical offerings (and countless covers), various publications, viral social media engagements, and outreach programs designed to increase accessibility and utility of the art form for underserved populations. These (inter)related rhetorical forms, individually and collectively, work to enhance the offerings of *Hamilton*'s messages. In addition, they also have created a larger-than-life movement that makes the musical more than simply a musical. This became apparent during the fall of 2016.

Shortly after the election of Donald Trump as the forty-fifth president of the United States, Pence attended the November 18, 2016, *Hamilton* performance at the Richard Rodgers Theatre in New York City. After enjoying the show with some of his immediate family members, Pence began to leave the theater as the actors were applauded by the audience. Interrupting the applause, Brandon Victor Dixon, who had assumed the role of Aaron Burr in this particular production, quieted the audience and then offered the following message:

> Vice President-elect Pence, we welcome you and we truly thank you for joining us here at *Hamilton: An American Musical*, we really do. We, sir—we—are the diverse America who are alarmed and anxious that your new administration will not protect us, our planet, our children, our parents, or defend us and uphold our inalienable rights, sir. But we truly hope that this show has inspired you to uphold our American values and to work on behalf of all of us. All of us. Again, we truly thank you truly for seeing this show, this wonderful American story told by a diverse group of men and women of different colors, creeds, and orientations.[47]

Helen Lewis describes Dixon's message, something that was jointly written by the cast, creator, and producer, as "a polite post-curtain speech from the cast about tolerance" and "one of the first acts of dissent against the Trump regime."[48] In response, Trump (via Twitter) rebuked the cast for "harassing" Pence and demanded an apology for the offensive behavior.[49] However, my analysis of Dixon's comments would conceptualize it less as a traditional form of rhetoric (speech or act of dissent) and more as an exemplar of invitational rhetoric.

Despite the backlash from then President-elect Trump, I would argue that Dixon's offering to Pence reflects the nature of invitational rhetoric in its truest form. The message of diversity, inclusion, and representation in politics—all of which were consistent with those represented in *Hamilton*—reflected the immanent value of all human beings. In terms of word choice, tenor, and other nonverbal cues, the message communicated a desire for relational camaraderie based in equality and self-determination. All of these characteristics are, by definition, inherent to invitational rhetoric.[50] Furthermore, as seen in online videos, Pence and his party entered the theater and took their seats to a mix of cheers and boos from other audience members. As Dixon began his post-performance comments, some in the crowd began to boo as he acknowledged Pence's presence. As soon as this occurred, Dixon quickly and assertively raised his hands and said, "There's nothing to boo here, ladies and gentlemen, there's nothing to boo here. We are all here sharing a story of love."[51] This important rhetorical insertion further communicated a commitment to invitational rhetoric, one in which feelings of safety and security are instrumental to the ability to share perspectives productively.

Invitational rhetoric, by definition, is not designed as a forceful attempt of persuasion with an intent to change others. Alternatively, it is offered as an invitation for others to "enter the rhetor's world and to see it as the rhetor does."[52] Pence's viewing of *Hamilton*, and subsequent exposure to the message shared by Dixon, provided an opportunity to see diverse perspectives of the American experience. While Trump's reaction to this example of invitational rhetoric was not embraced, Pence seemingly interpreted it differently. In a subsequent interview, the vice president-elect stated that he listened to the concerns that the cast expressed regarding the upcoming administration and was not at all offended by their method.[53] Miranda, upon hearing of Pence's remarks, responded in kind by stating: "I felt really grateful that Vice President-elect Pence got the message in the spirit in which we tried to give it to him ... he appreciated it, wasn't offended."[54] It remains to be seen if this exchange resulted in any shift in opinion, perspective, or understanding. Yet, as an exemplar of invitational rhetoric, it epitomizes the type of interaction that is steeped in equality, immanent value, safety, and self-determination. These values are characteristic of Obama's rhetoric in general as well[55] and, given his relationship with Miranda and *Hamilton*, serve as a reinforcing frame of the power of invitational rhetoric. This is the core idea of the final section of my analysis.

President Obama's Invitational Rhetoric Regarding *Hamilton*

Obama's comments regarding *Hamilton* consistently extended the invitational rhetoric communicated through the show. More specifically, his characterization of—and praise for—the art form highlighted the ways in which the show offered a new perspective that invited all Americans into understanding their role in the history of the country. In his introductory remarks at the March 14, 2016, White House cast performance, he stated, "the show reminds us that this nation was built by more than just a few great men—and that it is an inheritance that belongs to all of us." In explicit terms, he also articulated how *Hamilton* was an invitation to greater understanding of how democracy works, on an individual level:

> [W]e hope that they'll walk away with an understanding of what our founders got started—that it was just a start. It was just the beginning. That's what makes America so great. You

> finish the story... This is a constant work in progress, America. We're boisterous and we're diverse. We're full of energy and perpetually young in spirit. We are the project that never ends. We make mistakes. We have our foibles. But ultimately, when every voice is heard, we overcome them... I think it's fair to say that our founders couldn't have dreamt up the future that they set in motion. And it's only by exercising their greatest gift to us—the gift of citizenship—that we keep our democracy alive, and continue the work of creating that more perfect union.[56]

The connection that Obama felt to *Hamilton* was evident. "*Hamilton* touched me because it reflected the kind of history I'd lived myself, it told a story that allowed diversity in."[57] The show reflected the type of invitational rhetoric that was the staple of Obama's public persona, something that he publicly identified at a Democratic National Committee fundraiser in 2015, which featured a special presentation of *Hamilton*.[58] Following the performance, Obama used the show as a demonstrative illustration of how change ultimately comes to the United States. In part, he shared:

> Part of what's so powerful about this performance is it reminds us of the vital, crazy, kinetic energy that's at the heart of America—that people who have a vision and a set of ideas can transform the world... Every single step of progress that we've made has been based on this notion that people can come together, and ideas can move like electricity through them, and a world can change.[59]

Within this context, and throughout his political career, Obama emphasized the power of the narrative, regardless of personal, cultural, or political identity. More specifically, he utilized narrative sharing as a means to invite others into a greater understanding of one's perspective. He shared his own story in his first major public speech at the 2004 Democratic National Convention, a rhetorical practice that was standard throughout his tenure as president. "Stories can be an engine for empathy," according to Miranda and McCarter, and both Obama's and *Hamilton*'s narrative representations of inclusive diversity inspire others to tell their stories. And "every time they do, the newly kaleidoscopic America will understand itself a little more."[60]

Obama's embrace of invitational rhetoric, reflective of a more feminine approach to leadership,[61] has been applauded by some as a "welcome shift in politics."[62] However, others perceived his use of listening, coalition building, and passive-voice constructions as out of bounds in terms of what is considered "presidential" since it lacked the necessary aggression, power, and objectivity needed to influence change.[63] These two contrasting perceptions appear to mirror those that distinguish traditional and more contemporary conceptualizations of rhetoric (including invitational rhetoric, as discussed earlier). In addition, these competing assessments reflect a larger discussion regarding the utility of invitational rhetoric in facilitating social change, a point of inquiry I use to conclude my analysis.

CONCLUSION: THE UTILITY OF INVITATIONAL RHETORIC FOR SOCIAL CHANGE

Over the past two decades, rhetoricians have debated the value and limitations of invitational rhetoric in terms of facilitating social change in democratic societies. Some regard this alternative conceptualization of rhetoric as central to democracy for diverse societies where a group-centered vision of leadership encourages individuals to think for themselves within larger contexts that may inform the promotion of collectivistic harmony.[64] Others assert that invitational rhetoric is impractical: too cumbersome, time-consuming, and utopian to be effective in politics.[65] Furthermore, critics argue that the approach—rooted in civility—privileges the status quo and does little to promote social change for oppressed peoples.[66] Given this, has *Hamilton* facilitated social change? If so, how and in what form? If not, why not? These questions are difficult to answer definitively, as only time will tell.

I assert that this analysis, coupled with existing research on invitational rhetoric, provides some offerings regarding my perspective to the "field's ongoing conversations about rhetoric, feminism, and social change."[67] By analyzing the rhetoric of *Hamilton* and two men of color with a significant amount of sociocultural-political power, I've offered some insight as to how invitational rhetoric can be used by traditionally underrepresented group members with significant access to societal institutions. Their rhetoric can be best understood as an invitation to dialogue, something rooted in mutual respect and greater understanding of diverse perspectives. While invitational rhetoric does not privilege material social change over this lofty goal,[68] I would argue that the two are not oppositional or mutually exclusive. Instead, the sharing of new perspectives within a relational context of equality, respect, and self-determination can represent a crucial building block toward sustained social change. This seemingly was true in the case of civil rights leader, Ella Baker, who utilized invitational rhetoric to create a foundation for relational understanding and then, when certain situational contexts required, adopted more traditional forms of rhetoric.[69] The larger lesson here is that invitational rhetoric may not be suitable for all contexts; however, as an ontological orientation, it represents a valuable alternative to traditional forms of persuasion steeped in power, control, and manipulation. As the next stage of U.S. politics continues to unfold (i.e., The Age of Trump[70]), comparisons of various conceptualizations of rhetorical discourse will undoubtedly further inform our understanding of this complex phenomena.

In the end, this chapter itself represents a form of invitational rhetoric. Specifically, I suggest that the messages associated with *Hamilton*, Miranda, and Obama reflect a form of invitational rhetoric that promotes democracy, social change, and inclusive national identity. As such, the rhetoric epitomizes the type of interaction that is steeped in equality, immanent value, safety, and self-determination. Unlike traditional conceptualizations of rhetoric, the goal is not necessarily to persuade or change the reader. Instead the explicit goal is to present a perspective in such a way that creates conditions in which the reader feels welcome to offer alternative understandings of whether and how the rhetoric of *Hamilton*, Miranda, and Obama have contributed to a more diverse, democratic society where social change is understood as a shared responsibility. The specific contribution of this chapter to the overall objective of this edited volume, in this vein, is an expressed demonstration of the inherent value of invitational rhetoric in re-shaping the ways in which individuals engage personally, culturally, and politically.

NOTES

1. Mark P. Orbe, Professor, Western Michigan University, mark.orbe@wmich.edu.
2. Helen Lewis, "Hamilton: How Lin-Manuel Miranda's Musical Rewrote the Story of America," *NewStatesMan*, December 4, 2017, https://www.newstatesman.com/culture/music-theatre/2017/12/hamilton-how-lin-manuel-miranda-s-musical-rewrote-story-america.
3. Sonja K. Foss and Cindy L. Griffin, "Beyond Persuasion: A Proposal for an Invitational Rhetoric," *Communication Monographs* 62 (1995): 2.
4. Lewis, "Hamilton."
5. Lewis, "Hamilton."
6. Peter Mark, "The Reach of Lin-Manuel Miranda," *The Washington Post*, May 31, 2018, https://www.washingtonpost.com/news/style/wp/2018/05/31/feature/lin-manuel-miranda-is-both-artist-and-activist-just-dont-ask-him-to-run-for-office.
7. Meg Dowell, "Are Michelle Obama and Lin-Manuel Miranda Friends? Their Relationship and What She Thought of 'Hamilton' Before It Was Popular," *Showbiz CheatSheet*, November 22, 2018, https://www.cheatsheet.com/entertainment/are-michelle-obama-and-lin-manuel-miranda-friends-their-relationship-and-what-she-thought-of-hamilton-before-it-was-popular.html.
8. Lin-Manuel Miranda and Jeremy McCarter, *Hamilton: The Revolution* (New York: Grand Central Publishing, 2016), 14–15.
9. Mark, "The Reach of Lin-Manuel Miranda."
10. Emily Davies, "Lin-Manuel Miranda and Barack Obama: Together Again as *Hamilton* Hits D.C.!," *People*, June 15, 2018, https://people.com/politics/lin-manuel-miranda-and-barack-obama-together-again-as-hamilton-hits-d-c.
11. Lisa Respers France, "Barack Obama Hits the Billboard chart with Lin-Manuel Miranda," *CNN*, January 4, 2019, https://www.cnn.com/2019/01/03/entertainment/obama-billboard-chart-trnd/index.html.
12. Lewis, "Hamilton."
13. Miranda and McCarter, *Hamilton: The Revolution*, 208.
14. This move, however, has been criticized by some. This includes concerns about having people of African descent in the roles of slaveholders. See, for example, Ishmael Reed, "'Hamilton: The

Musical': Black Actors Dress Up like Slave Traders . . . and It's Not Halloween," *Counter Punch*, August 21, 2015, https://www.counterpunch.org/2015/08/21/hamilton-the-musical-black-actors-dress-up-like-slave-tradersand-its-not-halloween.
15 Lewis, "Hamilton."
16 Lewis, "Hamilton."
17 Foss and Griffin, "Beyond Persuasion," 3.
18 Foss and Griffin, "Beyond Persuasion," 5.
19 Jennifer Emerling Bone, Cindy L. Griffin, and T. M. Linda Scholz, "Beyond Traditional Conceptualizations of Rhetoric: Invitational Rhetoric and a Move Toward Civility," *Western Journal of Communication* 72, no. 4 (2008): 446.
20 Foss and Griffin, "Beyond Persuasion," 7.
21 Foss and Griffin, "Beyond Persuasion," 10.
22 Foss and Griffin, "Beyond Persuasion," 11.
23 Benjamin R. Bates, "Participatory Graffiti as Invitational Rhetoric: The Case of O Machismo," *Qualitative Research Reports in Communication* 18, no. 1 (2017): 64–72.
24 Bone, Griffin, and Scholz, "Beyond Traditional Conceptualizations of Rhetoric," 445.
25 Bone, Griffin, and Scholz, "Beyond Traditional Conceptualizations of Rhetoric," 15.
26 Bone, Griffin, and Scholz, "Beyond Traditional Conceptualizations of Rhetoric," 434–62.
27 Bates, "Participatory Graffiti as Invitational Rhetoric," 64–72.
28 Bates, "Participatory Graffiti as Invitational Rhetoric," 65.
29 Bone, Griffin, and Scholz, "Beyond Traditional Conceptualizations of Rhetoric," 450.
30 Bone, Griffin, and Scholz, "Beyond Traditional Conceptualizations of Rhetoric," 452.
31 Miranda and McCarter, *Hamilton: The Revolution*.
32 Miranda and McCarter, *Hamilton: The Revolution*, 259.
33 Lewis, "Hamilton."
34 Frank Scheck, "'Hamilton': Theatre Review," *Hollywood Reporter*, February 17, 2015, https://www.hollywoodreporter.com/review/lin-manuel-mirandas-hamilton-theater-813145.
35 Michael Paulsen, "'Hamilton' Heads to Broadway in a Hip-Hop Retelling," *New York Times*, July 12, 2015, https://www.nytimes.com/2015/07/13/theater/hamilton-heads-to-broadway-in-a-hip-hop-retelling.html.
36 Miranda and McCarter, *Hamilton: The Revolution*, 16.
37 Zeba Blay, "No, The 'Hamilton' Casting Call for 'Non-White' Actors Is Not Reverse Racism," *Huffington Post*, January 4, 2016, https://www.huffingtonpost.com.au/entry/no-the-hamilton-casting-call-for-non-white-actors-is-not-reverse-racism_n_56fd2c83e4b0daf53aeed9b9.
38 Miranda and McCarter, *Hamilton: The Revolution*, 124.
39 Miranda and McCarter, *Hamilton: The Revolution*, 277.
40 Miranda and McCarter, *Hamilton: The Revolution*, 276.
41 Miranda and McCarter, *Hamilton: The Revolution*, 250.
42 Miranda and McCarter, *Hamilton: The Revolution*, 250.
43 Miranda and McCarter, *Hamilton: The Revolution*, 250.
44 Miranda and McCarter, *Hamilton: The Revolution*, 32–33.
45 Sopan Deb, "Ishmael Reed's Play Challenging 'Hamilton' Will Get Reading," *New York Times*, January 4, 2019, https://www.nytimes.com/2019/01/04/theater/the-haunting-of-lin-manuel-miranda-ishmael-reed.html.
46 Deb, "Ishmael Reed's Play Challenging 'Hamilton' Will Get Reading." See also: Drury and Williams' chapter in this volume.

47 Patrick Healy, "'Hamilton' Cast's Appeal to Pence Ignites Showdown with Trump," *New York Times*, November 19, 2016, https://www.nytimes.com/2016/11/20/us/politics/hamilton-cast-mike-pence-donald-trump.html.
48 Helen Lewis, "Hamilton."
49 Sam Levin, "Donald Trump Is Really Upset Mike Pence Got Booed at 'Hamilton,'" *Huffington Post*, November 20, 2016, https://www.huffingtonpost.com.au/entry/donald-trump-hamilton_n_5830607fe4b099512f8315f7?_guc_consent_skip=1570541225.
50 Foss and Griffin, "Beyond Persuasion."
51 Brandon Victor Dixon, "'Hamilton' Cast Delivers Message to VP Pence," *Associated Press*, November 19, 2016, YouTube video, 1:21. https://www.youtube.com/watch?v=aWlwrUFiuUw.
52 Foss and Griffin, "Beyond Persuasion," 5.
53 Amy B. Wang, "Pence Says He 'Wasn't Offended' by 'Hamilton' as Trump Continues to Demand an Apology," *The Washington Post*, November 20, 2016, https://www.washingtonpost.com/news/arts-and-entertainment/wp/2016/11/20/pence-says-he-wasnt-offended-by-hamilton-as-trump-continues-to-demand-an-apology.
54 Jessica Chasmar, "Hamilton Creator Lin-Manuel Miranda Says Trump Election Gave Him 'Moral Clarity,'" *The Washington Times*, December 27, 2016, https://www.washingtontimes.com/news/2016/dec/27/lin-manuel-miranda-hamilton-creator-says-trump-ele.
55 Mark P. Orbe, *Communication Realities in a "Post-Racial" Society: What the U.S. Public Really Thinks about Barack Obama* (Lanham, MD: Lexington Books, 2011).
56 Remarks by President at "Hamilton at the White House," https://obamawhitehouse.archives.gov/the-press-office/2016/03/14/remarks-president-hamilton-white-house.
57 Dowell, "Are Michelle Obama and Lin-Manuel Miranda Friends?"
58 Miranda and McCarter, *Hamilton*, 284.
59 Miranda and McCarter, *Hamilton*, 284.
60 Miranda and McCarter, *Hamilton*, 285.
61 Kathleen Parker, "Obama: Our First Female President," *The Washington Post*, June 30, 2010, A17.
62 Orbe, *Communication Realities in a "Post-Racial" Society*, 72–76.
63 Orbe, *Communication Realities in a "Post-Racial" Society*, 74.
64 Mittie K. Carey, "The Parallel Rhetorics of Ella Baker," *Southern Communication Journal* 79, no. 1 (2014): 27–40.
65 Bone, Griffin, and Scholz, "Beyond Traditional Conceptualizations of Rhetoric," 434–62.
66 Nina M. Lozano-Reich and Dana L. Cloud, "The Uncivil Tongue: Invitational Rhetoric and the Problem of Inequality," *Western Journal of Communication* 73, no. 2 (2009): 220–26.
67 Lozano-Reich and Cloud, "The Uncivil Tongue," 221.
68 Bone, Griffin, and Scholz, "Beyond Traditional Conceptualizations of Rhetoric."
69 Carey, "The Parallel Rhetorics of Ella Baker," 27–40.
70 Kathleen Hall Jamieson and Doron Taussig, "Disruption, Demonization, Deliverance, and Norm Destruction: The Rhetorical Signature of Donald J. Trump," *Political Science Quarterly* 132, no. 4 (2017): 619–50.

CHAPTER ELEVEN

The Rhetorical Significance of *Hamilton* in Public Protests

NANCY J. LEGGE[1]

On Friday, November 18, 2016, the cast of *Hamilton: An American Musical* made history. The cast, led by Brandon Victor Dixon (who played Aaron Burr in the show), broke character and engaged the political sphere from the stage. While plays often have political messages, and there are numerous examples of actors addressing an audience at the conclusion of a performance,[2] this was a significant change in typical interactions between actors and audience. These actors broke character and spoke as citizens, using the stage as a podium to directly address a political leader and challenge the policies he articulated in the recent presidential campaign.[3] This chapter will explore some of the historical and rhetorical influences of this action. Specifically, this chapter contends that this event echoed some of the earliest connections between theater and democracy, and then argues that the cast of *Hamilton* articulated a rhetorical vision that resonated with, and helped galvanize, many who opposed the incoming Donald J. Trump presidential administration. In short, the cast enacted historical connections between art and politics, with reverberations that encouraged participatory democracy.

This chapter will unpack these claims by first providing some context about both the historical relationship between theater and democracy and details about the historic event in November 2016. Next, this chapter outlines the method used to identify and gather information about the rhetorical influences. Third, this chapter identifies and analyzes some of the ways that *Hamilton* was evoked by some participants in the early political protests against the Trump administration. Finally, this chapter concludes by considering some implications of these rhetorical influences on participatory democracy.

BACKGROUND

To understand the historical significance of the *Hamilton* cast speaking to a political leader about his policies and agenda, it is first important to describe some of the roots of the relationship between theater and politics. The interconnectedness between theater and politics can be traced to the first democracy in ancient Athens, where there was no clear distinction in public spaces. Theater and politics were intertwined. Discussions took place casually in the marketplace and formally in the assembly; most citizens attended theater performances and lectures, and they were active participants in the public life of the city.[4] As rhetorical theorist Gerard Hauser explains, "the Athenian political experience did not require a distinction between the discursive domains of the *agora* and the *ekklesia*; the men interacting on public issues in one were the same men who later came together to vote in the other."[5] To an Athenian, public life happened in all of these spaces. David Wiles, professor of theater at Royal Holloway University of London, suggests we should consider ancient Athenian theater—tragedy and comedy—as "material and embodied practices" of democracy.[6]

As Athenian democracy developed, the voices and power of citizens became "increasingly emphasized" in public rituals and displays, including dramatic festivals.[7] This connection between politics and art cannot be overstated. Josh Beer, classics professor at Carleton University, suggests that theater held a "central place in the life of Athenian democracy" and was "one manifestation of their zest for political life."[8] In their plays, poets, including Aeschylus, Aristophanes, Euripedes, and Sophocles, often expressed political perspectives on issues facing the *polis*.[9] Kurt A. Raaflaub, a professor of classics and history at Brown University, explains that the poets, unlike historians, typically addressed the audience about political issues. For example, Euripedes communicated "to a mass audience of his fellow citizens his thoughts and worries about their constitution and politics."[10] The interaction between politics and drama was mutual, and drama had a direct impact on the perspectives of citizens as well as policies of Athens.

Discussions about a play and its political implications spilled into public discourse and policymaking. These discussions influenced individuals and their actions in the assembly.[11] According to Peter Burian, classics professor at Duke, Euripedes' play *Supplicants* "reflects debates about democracy that were taking place among Athenians."[12] Jeffrey Henderson, classics professor at Boston University, provides additional examples: "Aristophanes' portrayal of Socrates in *The Clouds* was an important factor in the peoples' decision to condemn [Socrates] to death in 399" B.C.E.[13] Further, Aristophanes was awarded a crown by the city for advice he provided the *polis* in *Frogs*.[14] Edith Hall, classics and drama professor at Royal Holloway University of London, concludes Greek drama "transcended the moment of performance to become in its own right an active ideological influence on public discourse beyond the theatre."[15]

Entertainment and politics were mutually influential in ancient Athenian democracy: poets influenced politics and politics influenced poets. Many have recognized that this connection between theater and politics currently exists. Broadway plays often have political themes or spark political controversy.[16] We should not be surprised, then, about the collision between the political and dramatic spheres with *Hamilton*. The cast of *Hamilton* evoked a connection between theater and politics that has been common since the earliest democracy. The next section describes the cast speech in November 2016 and details some of the political aftermath of that speech.

The *Hamilton* Cast Speech and the Oppositional Public Sphere

November 18, 2016, was fewer than two weeks after the 2016 presidential election. Vice President-elect Mike Pence was in the New York City audience watching *Hamilton*. After the show, and after the standing ovation, actor Brandon Victor Dixon spoke to Pence from the stage. Dixon took out a piece of paper and read it, indicating that the speech was planned. Although Dixon spoke, he used language signaling that he spoke for "all of the cast," and the cast stood on stage with him as he delivered the speech. Dixon urged the audience to record his speech and spread the recording on social media. This was clearly a message intended for more than the immediate audience. This is the whole text of the cast's message:

> You know, we have a guest in the audience this evening. And Vice President-elect Pence, I see you walking out, but I hope you will hear us just a few more moments. There's nothing to boo here, ladies and gentlemen. There's nothing to boo here. We're all here sharing a story of love. We have a message for you, sir. We hope that you will hear us out.
>
> And I encourage everybody to pull out your phones and tweet and post, because this message needs to be spread far and wide, okay?
>
> Vice President-elect Pence, we welcome you and we truly thank you for joining us at *Hamilton: An American Musical*. We really do.
>
> We, sir, are the diverse America who are alarmed and anxious that your new administration will not protect us, our planet, our children, our parents—or defend us and uphold our inalienable rights, sir.
>
> But we truly hope that this show has inspired you to uphold our American values and work on behalf of *all* of us. All of us.
>
> We truly thank you for sharing this show—this wonderful American story told by a diverse group of men, women of different colors, creeds, and orientations.[17]

The audience applauded and cheered. Pence did not stay and listen to Dixon, but he stopped in the hallway outside and listened to the speech. After Dixon finished, Pence said nothing, but he left the theater smiling.[18]

Audience members posted pictures and recordings of Dixon's speech on social media. Reports of the speech spread in news outlets. This contributed to the already existent public space for discourse that opposed the incoming administration. The cast's statement participated in this "public sphere," which Hauser explains, is a "discursive space in which individuals and groups associate to discuss matters of mutual interest."[19] The issues discussed in a public sphere are ones the participants "perceive to be of consequence for them and their group. Its rhetorical exchanges are the bases for shared awareness of common issues, shared interests . . . agreement, and self-constitution as a public whose opinions bear on" society.[20] When Dixon explained that "we" are the diverse Americans who are "alarmed" and "anxious" about the incoming administration, he helped identify who might belong to or participate in this public sphere. Anyone concerned that the incoming administration was not going to protect them or their families was included in the sphere.

Framing their concerns as oppositional to the stated priorities and proposed policies of the incoming administration, especially policies against marginalized groups, the public sphere the cast identified with is best understood as a "counter-public sphere." Rhetorical scholar Phaedra Pezzullo describes a counter-public sphere as "the rhetorical invention of a discourse that challenges an already existing discourse that has been enabling the oppression of a particular group."[21] The incoming administration had been participating in a sphere where it was safe to degrade and dehumanize women, immigrants, minorities, and the LGTBQ+ community. The incoming president was well known for using Twitter to state his opinions and intentions, especially about those groups. President-elect Trump and his allies were also well known for using provocative and hostile language against these groups at campaign rallies and in media interviews.[22] Hauser notes that public spheres are "a web of discursive arenas, spread across society and even in some cases across national borders."[23] The *Hamilton* cast encouraged those in the audience to spread the message through social media, thereby expanding the oppositional public sphere. The event on November 18, 2016, functioned, then, to fortify and energize many who desired a space for oppositional discourse to challenge the sphere of the incoming administration.

This counter-public sphere was almost immediately a lightning rod for the incoming administration and its supporters. Even if one had not heard about the *Hamilton* cast speech or was not a fan of the show per se, the event became a point of clash in popular culture and in politics. The next morning, Trump responded to the *Hamilton* cast speech with two tweets. First, he wrote, "Our wonderful future V.P. Mike Pence was harassed last night at the theater by the cast of Hamilton, cameras blazing. This [*sic*] should not happen!"[24] Eight minutes later, he tweeted, "The Theater must always be a safe and special place. The [*sic*] cast of Hamilton was very rude last night to a very good man, Mike Pence. Apologize!"[25]

Things did not end there. That evening, twelve hours after his initial attack on the cast, Trump tweeted, and then deleted, this post: "Very rude and insulting of Hamilton cast member to treat our great future V.P. Mike Pence to a theater lecture. Couldn't even memorize lines!"[26] The deleted tweet would not be his last word on the subject. On Sunday, November 20, Trump's first tweet of the morning renewed his attack, "the cast and producers of Hamilton, which I hear is highly overrated, should immediately apologize to Mike Pence for their terrible behavior."[27]

Pence was interviewed about the event on *Fox News Sunday*. He acknowledged that he heard Dixon's speech and "I wasn't offended by what was said. I will leave to others whether that was the appropriate venue to say it."[28] Unlike Trump, Pence did not take issue with the speech, but he questioned the appropriateness of speaking from the (influential) stage. In principle, then, he supported voicing oppositional ideas, but objected to occupying this oppositional space from the theater stage.

The *Hamilton* cast speech sparked a fierce debate in media outlets, social media, and other popular culture venues about the proper roles of theater and politics. The Twitter account representing the musical posted a video of the speech. Immediately after that post are replies reflecting the divided views. As of July 10, 2020, the video has more than eight million views. The message has been retweeted more than one hundred sixty thousand times and liked more than two hundred thirty-six thousand times.[29] In the more than twelve thousand replies to the posted video, some argue that Dixon was "disrespectful"[30] and "inappropriate."[31] A typical tweet reads, "Classless. Not the right time or place."[32] Another tweet says the behavior was "shameful" and "truly intolerant."[33] These voices align with the president-elect, contending that there should be clear lines between "entertainment" and "politics." They urged others to join them in their objections and created a #BoycottHamilton hashtag on Twitter.[34] That hashtag was trending throughout that weekend in 2016; the topic was a point of controversy for several weeks.[35] In sum, these voices rejected the cast's use of the oppositional sphere as a space to challenge the agenda of the incoming administration. A boycott of the musical presumed that it would hurt the cast and teach them that there is a price to pay for voicing that oppositional discourse.

Others, defenders of the cast of *Hamilton* and/or their statement, applauded the speech.[36] Many expressed support for their message and voiced their concerns about potential policies of the incoming administration. Some thanked the cast for speaking "on behalf of ALL Americans."[37] Others offered congratulations for using the stage to spread messages of tolerance and "thanks" for "speaking up for us."[38] Some argued that the tradition of theater is to evoke politics, adding that great playwrights including Aeschylus and Shakespeare wrote plays blurring the line between theater and politics.[39] Others defended the event as an example of a legitimate use of the First Amendment. The American Civil Liberties Union endorsed the actors' right to free speech.[40] In sum, these supporters presumed that oppositional voices should have a space and expressed appreciation to the cast for bolstering that space.

While the #BoycottHamilton hashtag was popular for a few days, and divisive comments echoed through social media, within a short time it became clear that the musical did not suffer boycotts or lags in ticket sales. In fact, the opposite happened. *Hamilton* set records for the most money made in a single week on Broadway, grossing $3.3 million during Thanksgiving week 2016.[41] While the debate was clear in the media, and some may have opted not to use or buy tickets, the show did not suffer economically or in popularity. It continued to break attendance records and retained its popularity.

The oppositional public sphere was galvanized as the debate grew in the media and on social media sites. The cast's message echoed the concerns of many about the incoming administration. It helped connect members of a community by articulating a rhetorical vision, or a "composite drama that catches up large groups of people in a common symbolic reality."[42] Many found themselves connected to a community that shared their concerns, even connecting across cyberspace. At the same time, some in this oppositional public sphere were organizing protests to march against the incoming administration and its proposed agenda. Some protestors linked their opposition to the incoming administration with their support of the cast statement and the values articulated in it. The oppositional public sphere, embraced by the cast and its supporters, and occupied by those who opposed the incoming administration, expanded the space and the language for articulating their concerns about the Trump administration. The sphere gained noticeable visibility through large, organized protests against the incoming administration. An explicit connection between some of these protests and *Hamilton* emerged.

Public Protests and the Oppositional Public Sphere

Two of these protests happened in the early weeks of the administration.[43] On January 21, 2017, the day after the inauguration, millions of people across the globe took up signs and protested in the "Women's March," communicating their concerns about perceived threats against women's rights, civil rights, and human rights.[44] Organizers stated the purpose of the march was to send a message to the administration that "we expect elected leaders to act to protect the rights of women, their families, and their communities."[45] Marches took place in cities across the globe and communicated solidarity with the counter-public sphere. Estimates suggest between three and four million people participated, including protestors on every continent.⁴⁶ The organizers expressed surprise at the size of the opposition and hope that the protests would "provide a springboard for long-term political action" against Trump's "divisive politics."⁴⁷ These marchers shared the *Hamilton* cast's articulated concerns about intolerance and threats to human rights.

A second series of protests happened just two weeks later. Trump signed Executive Order 13769, "Protecting The Nation From Foreign Terrorist Entry Into The United States," also called the "Muslim Ban."⁴⁸ The Order would prohibit citizens from Iran, Iraq, Libya, Sudan, and Yemen from entering the United States for 90 days (including those with green cards), and indefinitely block citizens from Syria from entering the country.⁴⁹ The Order triggered protests at airports across the country (where people from the countries named in the Order were detained) and protesters marched in objection to the detentions and the Executive Order.⁵⁰ These protesters argued that "immigrants are welcome here" and urged "resistance" to the exclusionary policies of the administration. They echoed the concerns articulated in the *Hamilton* cast's statement—that the administration was not protecting people and the Executive Order was "harvesting hate and division."⁵¹ These protestors sought to oppose the Trump administration, especially policies relating to immigrants and oppressed minorities.

The protestors embraced the same space—an oppositional public sphere—that the cast of *Hamilton* occupied. Many protesters at both marches identified themselves as part of the *Hamilton* community. Protesters posted their photos on social media. Media outlets recognized and commented about that explicit identification in nearly every city.⁵² One reporter observed, the *Hamilton* lyrics are "becoming phrases of hope and justice."⁵³ In an interview with the *Huffington Post* about his reaction to his lyrics being used in the political protests, Lin-Manuel Miranda, the creator of the musical, offered, the lyrics are "yours for the protesting."⁵⁴ He added, "[w]hen you're making something, you don't control what happens [in response]. You can only control the thing you make. So to see it ripple back in that way, it's very moving and very humbling."⁵⁵

METHODOLOGY

To understand some connections between *Hamilton* and the protesters, I gathered news reports about the protests from mainstream media sources, focusing on those making explicit connections between protesters and *Hamilton*. I searched social media for posts and photos of the protests that emphasized *Hamilton*. I identified some websites dedicated to collecting these posts. I collected photos of the events posted across social media, highlighting the *Hamilton* connections in my notes. Many protesters wore hats or other merchandise from the musical.⁵⁶ Some protestors dressed like Hamilton and urged people to "Rise Up!" or as Angelica Schuyler and insisted that "women are included."[57] Many protesters carried signs using lyrics from *Hamilton*.[58] Websites popped up with lyric suggestions to help protesters with signs.[59]

Hamilton song lyrics were the most common artifact that surfaced in the protests.[60] I wrote each lyric used on an index card. Then, I examined the lyrics using the rhetorical method of analyzing topics. Rhetorical critics John Wilson and Carroll Arnold suggest that critics classify ideas using the Universal Topics.[61] This process reduces messages to "essential features" and uncovers patterns that may not be discernable without this rhetorical tool.[62] Thus, I labeled each lyric from the protest signs with the Universal Topic it reflected. For example, "History has its eyes on you" reflects the Universal Topic *time*. Then, I sorted the lyrics by Universal Topics, when a clear pattern of *topoi* (topics) emerged. Out of the sixteen Universal Topics, five topics were consistently reflected in the lyrics on the protest signs: *motion, desirability, potency, substance,* and *time*. For the final step in the method I identified patterns between the lyrics and *topoi*. I sorted the lyrics into themes about protesting, and then analyzed what each theme and *topoi* communicated. Rhetorical critics Roderick Hart, Suzanne Daughton, and Rebecca LaVally suggest that a topical analysis is "particularly useful for examining public controversies" because it helps reveal where the arguments begin.[63] Locating and analyzing the Universal Topics in these protest signs revealed assumptions embedded in the counter-public sphere's protests.

ANALYSIS: THE INFLUENCE OF *HAMILTON* IN PUBLIC PROTESTS

The topical analysis revealed three general themes of lyrics that were used in the protests. First, I present my rhetorical analysis of the themes and topics of the lyrics used in the protests. Then, I consider some ways those messages functioned to create a consistent vision for the protesters.

Rhetorical Analysis of Lyrics on Protest Signs

The number of protestors using *Hamilton* lyrics reinforced the musical's popularity, the strength of the counter-public sphere, and the shared vision of the participants. I distilled the major lyrics used in the protests into three themes: (1) lyrics arguing for equality/justice; (2) lyrics promoting the importance of speaking up/resisting; and (3) lyrics reinforcing the long-term commitment to protesting.

Table 11.1: Themes of Lyrics Used in Protests

Equality/Justice	Protest/Speak Up/Resist	Long-Term Commitment
"Immigrants, We Get the Job Done!"[a]	"Rise Up!"[b]	"When you got skin in the game, you stay in the game"[c]
"Another immigrant coming up from the bottom"[d]	"When are these Colonies Gonna Rise Up"[e]	"This is not a Moment, it's a Movement"[f]
"Include women in the sequel!"[g]	"Take a stand with pride, I don't understand how you stand to the side"[h]	"Tomorrow there will be more of us"[i]
"We hold these truths to be self-evident, but when I meet Donald Trump, I'm going to compel him to include women in the sequel."[j]	"I'd rather be divisive than indecisive"[k]	"The Plan is to Fan this Spark into a Flame."[l]
"Life, Liberty, and the Pursuit of Happiness . . . We shouldn't settle for less."[m]	"Tell Your Sister That She's Got to Rise Up!"[n]	"History has its eyes on you."[o]
	"If You Stand For Nothing, What Will You Fall For?"[p]	

Table 11.1 illustrates the categories and most popular lyrics used in the protests. Each theme and the Universal Topic(s) embedded therein will be discussed.

- a Capewell, "Protesters Are Using 'Hamilton' Lyrics to Defend Rights Across the Country."
- b Joanna Cagan, Twitter Post, January 21, 2017, 2:07 p.m., accessed July 10, 2020, https://twitter.com/JoannaCagan/status/822883402382737408.
- c "Hamilton Inspired Signs from the Women's March," Pinterest.
- d Bowman, "Let These 'Hamilton' Lyrics Help You Protest Trump."
- e Hamilton Signs, Twitter Post, February 1, 2017, accessed July 10, 2020, https://twitter.com/hamiltonsigns2.
- f "Hamilton Inspired Signs from the Women's March," Pinterest.
- g Meg Eubank, Twitter Post, January 21, 2017, 12:48 p.m., https://twitter.com/slchanmo/status/822863382814617600.
- h Capewell, "Protesters Are Using 'Hamilton' Lyrics to Defend Rights Across the Country."
- i Author observed and photographed protest sign at Women's March, Washington, D.C. January 21, 2017.
- j Hamilton Signs, Twitter Post.
- k Sofia Panzica, "21 'Hamilton' Signs Present at the Women's Marches," *The Odyssey Online*, January 22, 2017, https://www.theodysseyonline.com/hamilton-signs-women-march.
- l Bowman, "Let These 'Hamilton' Lyrics Help You Protest Trump."
- m Hamilton Signs, Twitter Post.
- n Hamilton Signs, Twitter Post.
- o Capewell, "Protesters Are Using 'Hamilton' Lyrics to Defend Rights Across the Country."
- p Hamilton Signs, Twitter Post.

Theme: Equal Rights/Justice. The rhetorical use of *Hamilton* lyrics in the theme of equal rights/justice reflects the topical patterns of *motion* (action), *desirability*, and *potency*. As Table 11.1 illustrates, these lyrics emphasize the idea that taking action for immigrants and women will yield positive outcomes. *Motion* is revealed through lyrics "moving up" (from the bottom), "fighting" for inclusion, and "compelling" some action (through talk).[64] The *desirability* of those actions is implied. The benefits of "getting the job done," "moving up from the bottom," or "fighting for life, liberty, and the pursuit of happiness" are enthymematic—the audience understands that these actions are inherently good and desirable.[65] The topic of *potency* is clear in lyrics: to "compel" the president to include women, and that "we shouldn't settle for less." Although the language in these lyrics promises power (*potency*), it is only hypothetical power: "*When* I meet Donald Trump," and "we *shouldn't* settle for less" (emphasis added).[66] These lyrics expose a hope or potential for power, but that power is unrealized. Taken together, the lyrics about equal rights/justice reveal a hope for the desirability of equal rights and justice but they do not go beyond that vision. Because of the new administration's language and actions, these topics promise a push back against actions that harm women, people of color, immigrants, and other marginalized communities. But, aside from expressing dissatisfaction or promising potency and pushback, it is unclear what actions would result.

Theme: Protest/Speak Up/Resist. The next rhetorical use of *Hamilton* lyrics reveals the need to protest, to speak up, and to resist. Not surprisingly, these lyrics reflect the topical patterns of *motion* (action) and *substance*. Several lyrics take the musical's phrase "rise up!" to encourage others to take action. Other lyrics urge people to act: "take a stand with pride" rather than "stand to the side."[67] These lyrics communicate an active audience that invites others to take action. The lyric that prefers being "divisive" over "indecisive" evokes the topic of *substance*.[68] It communicates that one's character (or substance) is more desirable if one takes a stand (is active). This lyric also contrasts the desirability of resisting with the undesirability of silence, even if speaking is uncomfortable. Silence is not an option; these protestors embrace the opportunity to speak. These lyrics privilege action over inaction. For these protesters, action involves speaking and protesting, which is both innately substantive and desirable.

Theme: Long-Term Commitment. The final rhetorical use of *Hamilton* lyrics reveals a theme that recognizes the long-term commitment to equality/justice and resistance (the other two themes). These protesters are committed. These lyrics reflect three topical patterns: *time*, *desirability*, and *potency*. The topic of *time* is not about "now," but instead "the future." References to *time* promise the administration that more people and more protests are in their future if equal rights/justice are undermined. The lyrics ensure the protestors won't go away because they'll "stay in the game," as this is "a movement," and "tomorrow there'll be more of us." The theme reveals a "plan" to "fan this spark into a flame."[69] The significance of these lyrics is their implied connection to the topics of *desirability* and *potency*. That is, the protests are a positive action with a great deal of potential power. What the protests may eventually lead to is, once again, not articulated. The promise is that there is commitment to the protest more than a promise for decisive action. The numerous references to "history is watching" communicates the reality that the administration's actions and policies will be judged with eyes that will see the larger, long-term impacts of the policies.[70] The clear implication is that history will judge this administration's actions harshly. The lyrics emphasize that time and judgment should be powerful checks on actions, especially those aimed at immigrants and marginalized communities. While the administration's policies are politically expedient, these protestors, with these lyrics, communicated that the judgments and significance of history should temper and constrain the administration's actions.

Taken together, the lyrics communicate protesters who were engaged in an oppositional public sphere, challenging the administration. They promised push back by speaking up and objecting to discriminatory policies. The results of that action (protesting, speaking up) is not clear. The very act of protesting and speaking up is, in and of itself, desirable. These protesters promised persistence in their resistance and used lyrics that communicated who they are by reinforcing their substance: "we speak up," "we resist," "we may be divisive." When one speaks for those who are treated unjustly, that divisiveness is justified. The power in speaking is, in and of itself, the action that is supported. The connection to policy change is not articulated nor promised. These protesters reflect a vision that democracy is strongest when citizens speak up against policies that harm others.

Absent Lyrics. Interestingly, many themes of the musical were conspicuously missing. Hart, Daughton, and LaVally encourage critics to also examine what is not said, that is, what topics are not depicted on signs.[71] The musical is set during the Revolutionary War, when colonists challenged the existing government, its policies, and its treatment of people. These revolutionaries occupied a counter-public sphere, voicing opposition to the status quo. And yet, protestors against the Trump administration did not use *Hamilton* lyrics about power struggles, fights for independence, battles, or duels that pervade the musical. Instead, the lyrics emphasized the importance of being heard (rising up, speaking up) and fighting for the rights of others.

The difference is that the 2017 protests occurred in a democracy, a system in which protests are encouraged (or at least tolerated), but also in which the status quo is presumed to have legitimacy. Unlike the revolutionaries, these protesters were not challenging the system itself. In the musical, George Washington laments, "we are outgunned, outmanned, outnumbered, outplanned"; he promises that to win, "we're going to fly a lot of flags half-mast." Hamilton suggests, "we'll need some spies on the inside," he steals cannons from the British, physically disrupting their space.⁷² The protesters in 2017 would be embracing a very different reality if they threatened to physically challenge the government in the same ways that Alexander Hamilton and his peers challenged King George III. The 2017 protesters' lyric choices reflect a democratic opposition rather than a literal battle to oust the democratically-elected administration. In 2017 the inherent value of speaking up and protesting is embraced.

The implicit message of the 2017 protests was that the fight would continue to serve as a vocal check on the administration; ideally the pressure from the protests may disrupt some of the agenda. But these protesters necessarily articulated no decisive action that would be taken outside of vocal opposition. These protesters' actions are constrained by democracy. The selected *Hamilton* lyrics communicated this reality by emphasizing the right to protest and promising persistence in participating in the oppositional public sphere. These lyrics helped protestors identify as a community of opposition committed to the "resistance." The lyrics did not focus on taking decisive action against the government, but instead, the themes communicated identity about "who we are" and created a "shared social identity from the traits, beliefs, or behaviors" they had in common with *Hamilton* and the lyrics.⁷³

Protests and Participatory Democracy

The actors in *Hamilton* helped draw attention to an oppositional public sphere and encouraged immediate and extended audience members to participate in that oppositional public sphere. These protesters should not take up arms, they should take to the streets and speak up. This vocal participation in the oppositional public sphere is central to democracy. Psychologists Emma Thomas and Winnifred Louis suggest that "participating in protest and other forms of collective action is the primary means (apart from voting) that ordinary people have of participating in the democratic process in Western liberalized democracies."⁷⁴ Hauser concurs that democracy "must be a public activity open to all."⁷⁵ The value of participation is a central trait of democracy.⁷⁶ Thomas and Louis explain that people are motivated to take collective action and protest as a response "to group norms about who 'we' are, and what 'we' do."⁷⁷ The vision created in *Hamilton* and the oppositional public sphere that galvanized after Trump was elected helped to create a collective identity for the oppositional public sphere about what America is and what Americans should stand for. The cast reaffirmed the values about a "diverse America," and urged the administration to uphold rights for "all Americans."⁷⁸ This articulation of "who we are" and "what we should stand for"⁷⁹ provided the impetus for a rhetorical vision that many embraced in the oppositional public sphere. Many protestors explicitly identified with this vision. These protestors used their shared identity to participate in protests and to stand for the values they embraced.

The cast evoked an oppositional public sphere to challenge the incoming administration. This was a sphere that was gaining momentum across the country after the election in November 2016. The president-elect countered the oppositional public sphere and specifically challenged the *Hamilton* cast's vision by insisting that there should be separate discursive spaces for "entertainment" and "politics." Trump argued that theater should be a "safe place," free from political conversations. Many who took issue with the cast's statement took issue with this blending between theater and politics. Those who supported the cast's statement also supported the oppositional public sphere and did not see a problem with a blurred line. Indeed, theater is often political. The debate about the relationship between entertainment and politics is not new. The argument is evoked whenever actors, musicians, or athletes speak out on a political issue. These non-political public figures are then told to "shut up and just" do your job,[80] reenacting the debate. But for as long as the connection between theater and politics has been divisive, they have continued to coexist and overlap throughout history, especially in democracies where public participation is protected. The strength of the oppositional public sphere that the *Hamilton* cast embraced was evident in the worldwide protests demonstrating for a counter vision of who we are and challenging the agenda and world view that the Trump administration was promising.

CONCLUSION

Hamilton has uniquely influenced and contributed to conversations in popular culture and politics.[81] While the storyline, the music, and the format of the musical are powerful, perhaps its most compelling contribution is in encouraging participatory democracy. The cast of *Hamilton* spoke from the stage and challenged a political leader. They embraced the oppositional public sphere to speak against the political agenda of the incoming administration. When protests were organized around the world to support a more inclusive perspective, some protesters turned to the lyrics from *Hamilton* to communicate who they were and what they stood for. There are two implications from this analysis.

First, one function of the oppositional space was to speak for marginalized populations. The cast articulated concern about the incoming administration's stance, especially as it targeted diverse and minority populations. Speaking for those who had no space or voice has often been an important function of theater. Classics professor Mary Beard contends that the connection between theater and democracy is "most clear" when there are threats to people.[82] In ancient Athens, where the interaction between policy and poets was mutually impactful, theater was often a place to represent those who were not heard. Peter Burian explains that Athenian theater gave voice to perspectives that were not allowed "including women, foreigners, and slaves that had no place in the political institutions of the *polis*" and helped those perspectives enter public discourse.[83] The cast of *Hamilton* spoke for those who were threatened or marginalized by the rhetoric of the new administration and contributed to the oppositional space for these voices.

This counter-public sphere grew with organized protests against the administration, where similar concerns were identified as important by protesters. Rather than embracing lyrics from the musical that evoked revolution, power struggles, or battles, these protesters selected lyrics that promoted the rights of others and the need to speak up. The oppositional public sphere helped generate a shared vision about the importance of these values. As Thomas and Louis recognize, "collective action is a fundamental tool in the battle of social change, equality, and justice."[84] The oppositional public sphere, then, emerged to help fight for the rights of the marginalized or underrepresented. Whether or not the protests resulted in immediate change is still debated, but the protests did function to solidify the oppositional sphere and to motivate those who occupied it.[85] These protesters embraced and enacted the value that protesting (speaking up in opposition) is, in and of itself, a valuable democratic principle. In contrast, these protesters communicated that silence or complacency was unacceptable.

Second, the rhetorical implications of this oppositional public sphere helped advance the legitimacy of speaking for others, even or especially, directly confronting political leaders. When the cast members confronted Pence and encouraged the audience to spread their message on social media, they contributed to expanding a public space for opposing administration policies. Those who supported the cast's message were encouraged to openly protest and advocate for others. This oppositional public sphere functioned rhetorically to help provide language for like-minded people to speak up and create messages that identified them with this oppositional public sphere. This identification helped to legitimize a rhetorical community and space that was largely defined by its willingness to speak for others and against particular ideologies.

The *Hamilton* cast directly confronted a member of the incoming administration who articulated an agenda and ideology to which the cast objected. This direct challenge expanded the traditional intertwined relationship between politics and theater. The long-term implications of this action remain unclear. Do the unparalleled cultural success of the show and/or the shift in politics ensure that the *Hamilton* cast actions remain unique? Or, will future events compel future actors to follow suit? Will we embrace the interconnected nature of politics and art? Or, will we continue to object whenever politics and art intersect?

NOTES

1. Nancy J. Legge, Professor, Idaho State University, nancylegge@isu.edu.
2. As just one example, Broadway Cares/Equity Fight AIDS often organizes events where actors speak to the audience after a show to ask for donations for the cause.
3. Email correspondence with Norman Schroder (Theater Professor, Idaho State University), September 9, 2019. Schroder writes, "I can't think of any instance" when an actor broke character and engaged a politician (like the cast of *Hamilton* did). Schroder offers John Wilkes Booth, who interrupted the show from backstage, but he wasn't a cast member. He explains an exchange in *The Imaginary Invalid* in which Moliere is attacked by a character, but that is all within the play itself. Finally, an inverse situation exists with plays at Dublin's Abbey Theatre that would "arouse audiences to near-riot conditions" because of their themes. None of these are similar to the cast of *Hamilton* uniquely speaking to Pence "as the cast" (not as actors playing parts).
4. "The Athenian Agora," Overview: The Archeological Site, The American School of Classical Studies at Athens, accessed September 7, 2019, http://agathe.gr/overview.
5. Gerard A. Hauser, "Civil Society and the Principle of the Public Sphere," *Philosophy and Rhetoric* 31, no. 1 (1998): 24.
6. David Wiles, *Theatre and Citizenship: The History of a Practice* (New York: Cambridge University Press, 2011), 23.
7. Simon Goldhill, "The Great Dionysia and Civic Ideology," in *Athenian Democracy and Imperialism*, ed. Loren J. Samons II (Boston, MA: Houghton Mifflin Company, 1998), 224.
8. Josh Beer, *Sophocles and the Tragedy of Athenian Democracy* (Westport, CT: Praeger Publishers, 2004), 16.
9. Mary Beard, "Democracy, According to the Greeks," *New Statesman*, October 11, 2010, 20; Christopher W. Blackwell, "Athenian Democracy: A Brief Overview," in Adriaan Lanni ed., "Athenian Law in Its Democratic Context." Republished in *Demos: Classical Athenian Democracy*, ed. C.W. Blackwell, February 28, 2003, http://www.stoa.org/demos/article_democracy_overview@page=1&greekEncoding=UnicodeC.html.
10. Kurt A. Raaflaub, "Tragedy and Democracy," in *Athenian Democracy and Imperialism*, ed. Loren J. Samons II (Boston, MA: Houghton Mifflin Company, 1998), 233.
11. Blackwell, "Athenian Democracy."
12. Peter Burian, Book Review of *Theseus, Tragedy, and the Athenian Empire* by Sophie Mills, *The American Journal of Philology* 121 (Spring 2000), 151.
13. Jeffrey Henderson, "Comic Politics," in *Athenian Democracy and Imperialism*, ed. Loren J. Samons II (Boston, MA: Houghton Mifflin Company, 1998), 238.
14. Henderson, "Comic Politics," 236.
15. Edith Hall, *The Theatrical Cast of Athens: Interactions Between Ancient Greek Drama & Society* (New York: Oxford University Press, 2006), 19.
16. Katherine Brooks, "News Flash: Broadway Has Always Been Political," *Huffington Post*, November 21, 2016, https://www.huffpost.com/entry/broadway-has-always-been-political_n_58332cf6e4b030997bc088f8.
17. Hamilton, Twitter post, November 18, 2016, 9:16 p.m., accessed October 17, 2019. https://twitter.com/i/status/799828567941120000.
18. Christopher Mele and Patrick Healy, "'*Hamilton*' Had Some Unscripted Lines for Pence. Trump Wasn't Happy," *New York Times*, November 19, 2016, https://www.nytimes.com/2016/11/19/us/mike-pence-hamilton.html.

19 Hauser, "Civil Society and the Principle of the Public Sphere," 21.
20 Gerard A. Hauser, *Vernacular Voices: The Rhetoric of Publics and Public Spheres* (Columbia: University of South Carolina, 1999), 64.
21 Phaedra C. Pezzullo, "Resisting 'National Breast Cancer Awareness Month': The Rhetoric of Counter Publics and Their Cultural Performances," *Quarterly Journal of Speech* 89, no. 4 (2003): 349.
22 German Lopez, "What if a Woman or Racial Minority Tried to Say What Donald Trump Has Said?" *Vox*, October 13, 2016, https://www.vox.com/2016/6/8/11873338/donald-trump-racism-sexism.
23 Hauser, *Vernacular Voices*, 71.
24 Donald Trump, Twitter Post, November 19, 2016, 6:48 a.m., accessed October 17, 2019, https://twitter.com/realDonaldTrump/status/799972624713420804.
25 Donald Trump, Twitter Post, November 19, 2016, 6:56 a.m., accessed October 17, 2019, https://twitter.com/realDonaldTrump/status/799974635274194947.
26 Eric Bradner, "'Hamilton': The Latest Feud Trump Won't Let Go," *CNN*, November 21, 2016, https://www.cnn.com/2016/11/20/politics/donald-trump-hamilton-feud/index.html.
27 Donald Trump, Twitter Post, November 20, 2016, 4:22 a.m., accessed October 17, 2019. https://twitter.com/realDonaldTrump/status/800298286204723200.
28 Bradner, "'Hamilton.'"
29 Hamilton, Twitter Post, November 19, 2016, 11:45 a.m., accessed June 11, 2020, https://twitter.com/hamiltonmusical/status/799828567941120000.
30 Danire212 on Hamilton, Twitter Post Responses, November 19, 2016, accessed July 10, 2020. https://twitter.com/HamiltonMusical/status/799828567941120000.
31 Hamilton, Twitter Post Responses, November 19, 2016, accessed July 10, 2020, https://twitter.com/HamiltonMusical/status/799828567941120000.
32 JamesHGale on Hamilton, Twitter Post Responses, November 19, 2016, accessed July 10, 2020, https://twitter.com/HamiltonMusical/status/799828567941120000.
33 JLPTalk, Twitter Post Responses, November 19, 2016, accessed July 10, 2020, https://twitter.com/HamiltonMusical/status/799828567941120000.
34 Brooks, "News Flash."
35 Andrew Blake, "#BoycottHamilton Tops Twitter's Trends List after Mike Pence's Eventful Broadway Outing," *The Washington Times*, November 19, 2016, https://www.washingtontimes.com/news/2016/nov/19/boycotthamilton-tops-twitters-trends-list-after-mi.
36 Hamilton, Twitter Post Responses, November 19, 2016, accessed October 17, 2019, https://twitter.com/i/status/799828567941120000.
37 Caroline Goodall, Twitter Post, November 20, 2016, 11:42 a.m., accessed October 18, 2019, https://twitter.com/HamiltonMusical/status/799828567941120000.
38 Keyasaurus, on Hamilton, Twitter Post Responses, November 19, 2016, accessed July 10, 2020, https://twitter.com/HamiltonMusical/status/799828567941120000.
39 Brooks, "News Flash," 2016.
40 Bradner. "'Hamilton.'"
41 Michael Paulson. "*Hamilton* Hits a New High: The Most Money Grossed in a Week on Broadway," *New York Times*, November 28, 2016, https://www.nytimes.com/2016/11/28/theater/hamilton-hits-a-new-high-the-most-money-grossed-in-a-week-on-broadway.html.
42 Donald C. Shields and John Cragan, *Symbolic Theories in Applied Communication Research: Bormann, Burke and Fisher* (Cresskill, NJ: Hampton, 1995), 41.

43 Tiffani DuPree, "The Year in Protests Since Donald Trump's Election," *Splinter*, November 8, 2017, https://splinternews.com/the-year-in-protests-since-donald-trumps-election-1820143751.
44 Anemona Hartocollis and Yamiche Alcindor, "Women's March Highlights as Huge Crowds Protest Trump: 'We're Not Going Away,'" *New York Times*, January 17, 2107, https://www.nytimes.com/2017/01/21/us/womens-march.html.
45 Robert Booth and Alexandra Topping, "Two Million Protest against Trump's Inauguration Worldwide," *The Guardian*, January 22, 2017, https://www.theguardian.com/lifeandstyle/2017/jan/22/two-million-protest-against-trumps-inauguration-worldwide.
46 Jenna Arnold, Kanisha Bond, Erica Chenoweth, and Jeremy Pressma,. "These Are the Four Largest Protests since Trump Was Inaugurated," *The Washington Post*, May 31, 2018, https://www.washingtonpost.com/news/monkey-cage/wp/2018/05/31/these-are-the-four-largest-protests-since-trump-was-inaugurated.
47 Booth and Topping, "Two Million Protest against Trump's Inauguration."
48 Susan Navhi. "Trump's Muslim and Refugee Ban: Where Are We Now?" *Friends Committee on National Legislation*, accessed July 10, 2020, https://www.fcnl.org/updates/trump-s-muslim-and-refugee-ban-where-are-we-now-1222.
49 "Executive Order Protecting the Nation from Foreign Terrorist Entry into the United States," The White House, United States Government, accessed September 20, 2019, https://www.whitehouse.gov/presidential-actions/executive-order-protecting-nation-foreign-terrorist-entry-united-states.
50 Alan Taylor, "A Weekend of Protest against Trump's Immigration Ban," *The Atlantic*, January 30, 2017, https://www.theatlantic.com/photo/2017/01/a-weekend-of-protest-against-trumps-immigration-ban/514953.
51 Lauren Gambino, Sabrina Siddiqui, Paul Owen, and Edward Helmore, "Thousands Protest against Trump Travel Ban in Cities and Airports Nationwide," *The Guardian*, January 29, 2017, https://www.theguardian.com/us-news/2017/jan/29/protest-trump-travel-ban-muslims-airports.
52 Jillian Capewell, "Protesters Are Using 'Hamilton' Lyrics to Defend Rights across the Country," *Huffington Post*, February 14, 2017, https://www.huffpost.com/entry/hamilton-lyrics-make-pretty-good-muslim-ban-protest-signs_n_58920abce4b02772c4ea8582; Leigh Blickley, "Lin Miranda Believes the Muslim Ban Is 'Deeply Un-American,'" *Huffington Post*, February 3, 2017, https://www.huffpost.com/entry/lin-manuel-miranda-muslim-ban-protests_n_58938f5ae4b09bd304ba4016?cc8qkcsacwyp919k9.
53 Blickley, "Lin Miranda Believes the Muslim Ban Is 'Deeply Un-American.'"
54 Blickley, "Lin Miranda Believes the Muslim Ban Is 'Deeply Un-American.'"
55 Blickley, "Lin Miranda Believes the Muslim Ban Is 'Deeply Un-American.'"
56 For example, see photos accompanying the article by Gambino, et. al, "Thousands Protest Against Trump Travel Ban."
57 Lin-Manuel Miranda and Jeremy McCarter, *Hamilton: The Revolution* (New York, NY: Grand Central Publishing, 2016), 27, 44.
58 Capewell, "Protesters Are Using '*Hamilton*' Lyrics to Defend Rights across the Country."
59 Sabienna Bowman, "Let These 'Hamilton' Lyrics Help You Protest Trump," *Bustle*, November 19, 2016, https://www.bustle.com/articles/196032-15-hamilton-lyrics-to-share-on-social-media-if-youre-protesting-donald-trumps-response-to-the.
60 For example, some of the websites consulted were Capewell. "Protesters Are Using 'Hamilton' Lyrics to Defend Rights across the Country"; Bowman, "Let These 'Hamilton' Lyrics Help You

Protest Trump"; and "Hamilton Inspired Signs from the Women's March," Pinterest, accessed June 11, 2020, https://www.pinterest.com/pin/420523683943436960/

61 John Wilson and Carroll C. Arnold, *Public Speaking as a Liberal Art*, 3rd ed. (Boston MA: Allyn and Bacon, 1974). The authors identify sixteen Universal Topics that a critic can use to classify topoi in a contemporary analysis: Existence, Degree, Spatial, Temporal, Motion, Form, Substance, Capacity to Change, Potency, Desirability, Feasibility, Causality, Correction, Genus-Species, Similarity, and Possibility.

62 Wilson and Arnold, *Public Speaking as a Liberal Art*.

63 Roderick Hart, Suzanne Daughton, and Rebecca LaVally, *Modern Rhetorical Criticism*, 4th ed. (New York: Taylor & Francis, 2018), 80.

64 Miranda and McCarter, *Hamilton: The Revolution*, 17, 44.

65 Miranda and McCarter, *Hamilton: The Revolution*, 121, 17, 161.

66 Miranda and McCarter, *Hamilton: The Revolution*, 44, 161.

67 Miranda and McCarter, *Hamilton: The Revolution*, 142.

68 Miranda and McCarter, *Hamilton: The Revolution*, 28, 142, 49.

69 Miranda and McCarter, *Hamilton: The Revolution*, 188, 29, 35, 26.

70 Miranda and McCarter, *Hamilton: The Revolution*, 187, 35.

71 Hart, Daughton, and LaVally, *Modern Rhetorical Criticism*, 73.

72 Miranda and McCarter, *Hamilton: The Revolution*, 60, 97, 64.

73 Emma Thomas and Winnifred Louis, "Doing Democracy: The Social Psychological Mobilization and Consequences of Collective Action," *Social Issues and Policy Review* 7, no. 1 (2013): 182.

74 Thomas and Louis, "Doing Democracy," 174.

75 Thomas and Louis, "Doing Democracy," 175.

76 Mark Chou, Jean-Paul Gagnon, and Lesley Pruitt, "Putting Participation on Stage: Examining Participatory Theatre as an Alternative Site for Political Participation," *Policy Studies* 36, no. 6 (2015): 607–22; Russell J. Dalton, "Citizenship Norms and the Expansion of Participation," *Political Studies* 61, no. 1 (2008): 76–98; Brendan McCaffrie and Sadiya Akram, "Crisis of Democracy? Recognizing the Democratic Potential of Alternative Forms of Public Participation," *Democratic Theory* 1, no. 2 (2014): 47–55.

77 Thomas and Louis, "Doing Democracy," 179.

78 Hamilton, Twitter post, November 18, 2016, 9:16 p.m.

79 Thomas and Louis, "Doing Democracy," 179.

80 Maeve McDermott, "Taylor Swift Is Hardly the First Female Artist to Be Told to 'Shut Up and Sing,'" *Chicago Sun Times*, October 24, 2018, https://chicago.suntimes.com/2018/10/24/18315271/taylor-swift-is-hardly-the-first-female-artist-to-be-told-to-shut-up-and-sing.

81 Edward Delman, "How Lin-Manuel Miranda Shapes History," *The Atlantic*, October 1, 2015, https://www.theatlantic.com/entertainment/archive/2015/09/lin-manuel-miranda-hamilton/408019; Rhian Daly, "'Hamilton' Just Broke Another Record," *NME*, March 6, 2018, https://www.nme.com/news/hamilton-just-broke-another-record-2255970; Kate Keller, "The Issue on the Table: Is 'Hamilton' Good for History?" *Smithsonian Magazine*, Smithsonian Institution, May 30, 2018, https://www.smithsonianmag.com/history/issue-table-hamilton-good-history-180969192.

82 Beard, "Democracy, According to the Greeks."

83 Peter Burian, "Five Questions on Theatre's Role in Democracy," *Duke University Research*, April 10, 2009, https://research.duke.edu/5-questions-theater's-role-democracy.

84 Thomas and Louis, "Doing Democracy," 194.

85 Karl Vick et al., "The Other Side," *Time*, February 6, 2017, 24–33.

Note on Contributors

Christopher Bell (Ph.D., University of Colorado Boulder) is an Associate Professor of Media Studies in the Department of Communication at the University of Colorado Colorado Springs. He specializes in the study of popular culture, focusing on the ways race, class and gender intersect in different forms of children's media. Dr. Bell is a TED speaker, a diversity and inclusiveness consultant for Pixar Animation Studios and WarnerMedia, a David Letterman Award winning media scholar, and the 2017 Denver Comic-Con Popular Culture Educator of the Year.

Jeffrey P. Mehltretter Drury (PhD, University of Wisconsin, Madison) is an Associate Professor of Rhetoric at Wabash College. He emphasizes political argumentation and questions of representation in his research and teaching. His work has appeared in journals such as the *Western Journal of Communication*, the *Journal of Contemporary Rhetoric*, and *Voices of Democracy*, and he is the author of *Speaking with the People's Voice: How Presidents Invoke Public Opinion* (Texas A&M University Press, 2014) and *Argumentation in Everyday Life* (SAGE, 2019).

Sara A. Mehltretter Drury (Ph.D., Pennsylvania State University) is an Associate Professor of Rhetoric and Director of Democracy and Public Discourse at Wabash College. Her research and teaching interests include political communication, deliberation, and the quality and character of public discourse in democracy. She has published in *Communication Quarterly*, *Argumentation and Advocacy*, and *Journal of Public Deliberation*, and is an Indiana Humanities Action Fellow.

Henry Egan is a student at Wabash College. He is majoring in English Literature and double minoring in Gender Studies and Asian Studies.

Jade C. Huell (Ph.D., Louisiana State University) is an Assistant Professor in the Department of Communication Studies at California State University, Northridge, where she serves as Director of CSUN Performance Ensemble: Creatives for Social Change. Huell's research rests at the intersections of live performance, African American Studies, and Memory Studies. She integrates her scholarly work and creative practice by employing a personal ethic of social justice living and maintaining a varied artistic practice as a storyteller, mixed media visual artist, director, and performer.

Brandon Inabinet (Ph.D., Northwestern University) is an Associate Professor of Communication Studies at Furman University. His dissertation (2010) focused on questions of contingency and authority in the early United States, specifically regarding banking and the early press. Related articles on early American history appear in Rhetoric & Public Affairs and Southern Communication Journal. His work has also considered these concepts in Greco-Roman antiquity and Southern history, leading to his more recent activism toward racial reckoning with history.

Lindsay A. Jenkins (L.J.) (M.A., California State University, Northridge) is a dramaturg, educator, and producer. L.J. holds a Master of Arts degree in Theatre. Her specific area of research is Black performance heritage, connecting past performances to contemporary experiences. Currently, L.J. is developing a project that explores Afrocentric methods for putting research into the acting body. L.J is the founder and Executive Creative Producer of Maroon Arts and Culture, a nonprofit organization dedicated to empowerment through arts education and cultural programming.

Nancy J. Legge (Ph.D., Pennsylvania State University), is a professor in the Department of Communication, Media, and Persuasion at Idaho State University, where she also serves as Basic Course Director. She teaches Rhetorical Theory, Rhetorical Criticism, Persuasion, and Rhetoric & Popular Culture. She is also the founder and editor of *Relevant Rhetoric: A New Journal of Rhetorical Studies*.

Her research interests include analysis of popular culture, crisis and image repair theory, and persuasive attack theory.

Ryan Neville-Shepard (Ph.D., University of Kansas) is an Assistant Professor of Communication at the University of Arkansas, where he teaches and researches in the areas of rhetorical criticism and political communication.

Mark P. Orbe (Ph.D., Ohio University) is a Professor of Communication & Diversity in the School of Communication at Western Michigan University where he also serves as a Faculty Fellow in the Office of Institutional Equity. His research and teaching interests explore the inextricable relationship between culture, power, and communication in diverse contexts.

Emily Berg Paup (Ph.D., University of Minnesota) is an Assistant Professor of Communication and Gender Studies at the College of Saint Benedict and St. John's University. She teaches courses in gender and rhetorical history, gender and politics, rhetorical criticism, argumentation, public speaking, and communication law. Her research interests include gender in political campaigns, gender history, expanding the archive of women's voices, and the First Amendment.

Michaelah Reynolds (M.A., University of Arkansas) received her MA in Communication in 2019. She currently works as a Marketing and Publicity Account Assistant for Bond Theatrical Group in New York City after many years of experience within the theater community.

John Clyde Russell (Ph.D., Georgia State University) is a faculty member at Kennesaw State University in the School of Communication & Media. His research interests include whiteness, race, and public memory. His writing pays particular attention to the ways we remember our racial history through popular culture and the effects those acts of public memory have on contemporary political culture.

James Anthony Williams Jr. (A.B., Wabash College) is a 2020 graduate of Wabash College in Theater, with a minor in Digital Film and Media Studies.

Index

"Aaron Burr, Sir" (song) 36, 38, 40, 130
Action Comics #1 72
ad hominem attacks 148, 150, 154, 156
Adams, Abigail 56, 108
Adams, John 56, 92, 95, 108, 132
Adams, Louisa Catherine Johnson 109
Adelman, Joseph 117
Aden, Roger C. 49–50
African Americans 49, 55, 57, 62, 88, 166, 169
"Alexander Hamilton" (song) 24–26, 36, 40, 130, 136, 146, 169, 188
Alien and Sedition Acts 32
Allgor, Catherine 111–112
Amazing Fantasy #15 72
American Dream 5, 31–37, 39, 128, 136–137
American identity 19, 33, 88, 94, 98
American Revolution 18, 23, 107, 111, 127, 138
American values 3, 20, 130, 172, 181
Athens 180
  ancient 76, 180, 191
Aoki, Eric 48
Apollo Theater 165

Arendt, Hannah 138–139
argumentation 150, 154
  political 146–147, 149, 152–153, 156
Aristotle 71
Arnold, Carroll C. 186
art form 87, 168, 171–73
Athenian Democracy 180–181
audiences 4–6, 15, 17–27, 31, 33–40, 78–81, 88, 95–97, 106, 109–110, 117, 130–133, 135–136, 139, 145–146, 156, 164–168, 170–172, 179–182, 192
  members 6–7, 26, 117, 145–147, 150–151, 155–156, 167, 169–171, 173, 182
audionarration 47–52, 54–55, 58, 60, 62

Baker, Ella 175
Baptist, Edward E. 129, 139
Bates, Benjamin R. 167
Batman 75
Beard, Mary 191
Beer, Josh 180
Bell, Christopher 6, 20, 69–85
Benjamin, Franklin 56, 73, 92

Bennett, Michael 90
Benson, Thomas W. 146
Bill of Rights 92
BIPOC (Black, Indigenous, People of Color) 87, 89, 97, 99
Black History Museums 49
Black Lives Matter (BLM) 4, 17, 61
Blair, Carole 91
Bolton, John 3
Bond Theatrical Group 42
Bone, Jennifer Emerling 168
Bonilla-Silva, Eduardo
#BoycottHamilton 183–184
Boylorn, Robin M. 50
Brantley, Ben 1
Bring in 'Da Noise, Bring in 'Da Funk (musical) 152
Broadway 2, 17, 22–23, 105, 152, 171, 181, 184
Bronze Age 77, 79
Burke, Kenneth 33–34, 88
"Burn" (song) 24, 96, 111, 114–115, 116
Burr, Aaron 19–20, 26, 32, 35–36, 38–41, 52, 56, 59, 61, 75, 79, 81, 95, 130, 137, 145–146, 164–165, 169, 172
Bush-era individualism 34
Busta Rhymes 80

cabinet 110–41
"Cabinet Battle #1" (song) 6, 20–21, 60, 97, 113, 130, 131, 148–151, 154–155, 188
"Cabinet Battle #2" (song) 20–21, 148–151, 154
cadences 80, 113, 155
Cagan, Joanna 187
Cage, Luke 77
Cage, Nicholas 91
Campbell, Joseph 74
capitalism 25, 137
Captain America 77
Carp, Benjamin L. 2
casting 13, 21, 27, 70, 78, 88–89, 94–95, 99
  color-conscious 22–23
  choices 21–22, 97
Cato 23, 79
celebration 57, 62, 110–111, 118
characters 13–14, 35–41, 52, 58, 72–74, 77–79, 81, 88, 95, 105–106, 113–114, 170–171, 179

Chariots of Fire 34
Cheney, Dick 2
Chernow, Ron 32, 108, 111, 116, 129, 170
Chick, Daniel M. 156, 167
citizenship 88, 114, 137, 174
Civil Rights Movement 60
civil society 108
Civil War 60, 97
civility 145–148, 150, 153, 175
class 6, 21, 40, 153
Clinton, Hillary 31
Cocks, Joan 138
collectivism 33, 35–36, 38, 41
community 25, 34, 37, 40, 42, 49, 70, 147–148, 184, 190
  marginalized 153, 188–189
competition 33–35, 37, 39, 41, 154, 166
conflicts 3, 35–38, 40–41, 49, 57, 70
Congress 21, 69, 131, 133, 139, 148
Connolly, Joy 137
Constitution 19, 42, 59–60, 106, 133, 135, 139, 180
Constitutional Convention 59–60, 73
controversy 2, 62, 128, 153, 168, 171, 183
corruption 132, 135, 137, 153
cosmogonic myth 69, 71–73, 75–76
costumes 5, 37, 76–77, 117
Couldry, Nick 76
coverture 106–7, 110–12
Craft, Elizabeth Titrington 31
creation 15, 22, 26, 71–72, 106, 110, 130, 164, 168–169, 171
credit 133–135, 137
  public 131, 134–135, 139
A Crisis of Civility? (Lukensmeyer, Carolyn J.) 146
critical memory 14–16, 18–19, 22, 26
critical nostalgia 5, 14, 16, 19, 23, 26–27
critics 4, 33, 42, 49–50, 88, 128, 171, 175, 186, 189
critique 3–4, 16, 22, 32, 35, 41, 106, 110, 152
culture 14–15, 20, 48–49, 51, 54–55, 62, 69–71, 78–80, 138
  popular 2, 7, 33–34, 40, 87, 91–92, 109, 191
Cutting, Francis 107

Daughton, Suzanne 186
Davis, Patricia 49
"Dear Theodosia" (song) 95–96
death 40, 69, 72, 75, 110, 170, 180
debts 133–134, 137–139
    national 127, 129–130, 133, 149
Deckard, Sharae 25
democracy 3, 6, 148, 153, 164, 167, 174–175, 179–180, 189–191
depictions 19, 57, 95, 136
desirability 186, 188–189
dialogue 37, 131, 166–167, 175
DiAngelo, Robin 91
Dickinson, Greg 14, 48, 91
discourse 48, 99, 136, 147, 182
Disney 89
Disney+ 3
    streaming platform 2, 61
display 38, 48–49, 52, 55, 61, 116, 156
diversity 22, 37, 62, 88, 163, 166, 169, 172, 174
Dixon, Brandon Victor 2, 172, 179
Dolan, Jill 15, 19–21
Douglass, Frederick 90, 96
drama 180, 184
duel 32, 35–36, 40–41, 59, 61, 113, 136–137, 189
Drury, Jeffrey P. Mehltretter 1–10, 145–160
Drury, Sara A. Mehltretter 1–10, 47–65
Dyer, Richard 19

Early Republic 106, 111, 114, 116, 118, 129–130, 136, 139
Egan, Henry 1–10
election 32, 42, 172, 191
"Election of 1800, The" (song) 40, 110
elites 128, 137
Elizabethan England 76
Embodying Black Experience (Young, Harvey) 15
emotions 26, 76, 95, 113
enslaved persons 20, 53–55, 58, 96, 129
enslavement 54–55, 129, 139
entelechy 31
equality 7, 19, 42, 88–89, 163, 167, 172–173, 175, 192
Eustis, Oskar 3
evil 70, 93, 132, 136, 139

Executive Order 185
exhibition 5, 47–59, 61, 171

failures 75, 97, 111, 155, 170
fans 7, 62, 76, 155, 182, 187
"Farmer Refuted" (song) 113, 145, 148–150, 155, 188
Federalist 35, 132–133, 137
    debates 59–60
Federalist Paper #54 (Madison) 93
Federalist Papers 59, 69, 95, 109
femininity 112–13
feminism 118, 175
feminist criticism 106, 109, 118
films 34, 76, 91, 99
finance 133, 135, 149
First Amendment 184
Fisher, Walter 32–34
Floyd, George 3, 17
Foss, Sonja K. 163, 166
Foster, Hannah Webster 108
Founding Fathers 19, 21, 69–70, 73, 78, 80, 92, 95–96, 98–99, 116–118, 169, 171
founding generation 37, 107, 112, 115
Fox News 90, 183
Franklin, Benjamin 56, 73, 92
freedom 19, 56, 92, 96, 110, 130, 139, 167–168
Freeman, Joanne 32, 51–52, 62, 171
French revolutions 135, 138, 154
Freneau, Philip 132, 135
Frentz, Thomas 34
Funding Act 148–149

Gallagher, Victoria J. 49
Gastil, John 147–148, 150, 153
gender 5–6, 59, 105–106, 111, 118, 152
    coverture and separate spheres 106–107
    See also republican motherhood
genre 3, 61, 74, 98, 154
George III (king) 52, 56, 92, 111, 113, 169, 190
Giamatti, Paul 95
Gibson, Mel 91
Glassberg, David 88
Goldsberry, Renee Elise 169
Gordon-Reed, Annette 171
Graeber, Donald 129

Griffin, Cindy L. 163, 166, 168
Grimes, William 153
Groff, Jonathan 113, 169
Gross, Alan 94
Gusfield, Joseph R. 88

Hall, Edith 180
Hall, Stuart 128
Halperin, Elaine P. 72
Hamilton, Alexander 2, 13–15, 17, 47–51, 53–59, 61, 87–89, 91–114, 116, 125, 127–166, 168–179, 181–187, 189
  Caribbean identity 25
  cosmogonic origin story 69
  immigration stories 27, 32
  marital relation 20
  superhuman "powers" 79–80
Hamilton: An American Musical
  casting 22, 179–183, 185, 191
  central theme 47, 186–190
  connection to politics 2
  coverture in 110–112
  debt/trust 133–136
  depiction of the American Dream 32, 35–37
  entelechial nature of individualism 40–41
  feminist critique 105–119
  "Immigrants: We Get the Job Done" 3, 168–170
  indignity/virtue 131–133
  invitational rhetorical art form 168
  portrayal of women 109–112
  republican motherhood 114–116
  rhetorical artifact 3–5
  separate spheres 112–114
  theatrical phenomena 87–89
  2017 Hamilton Mixtape album 3
  uncivil political argumentation 147
  See also lyrics; Miranda, Lin-Manuel
Hamilton: The Exhibition 47–63
  rhetoric of space, place, and memory 50–51
  experiences 51–53
  analysis 53–54
  slavery, horrors of 54–55
  social history 56–59
  institutional turn 59–61
  story of America 61–63

Hamilton Education Program 2
Hamilton, Elizabeth Schuyler 6, 36, 52, 81, 96–97, 105–106, 108–117, 137, 171
Hamilton, John Church 117
Hamilton, Phillip 75
Hannah-Jones, Nikole 60
Harbert, Elissa 76, 32
Hariman, Robert 133
Harlem's Apollo Theater 165
#HAM4HAM 2
Hart, Roderick 186, 189
Hatfield, Charles 72
Hauser, Gerard A. 182, 190
"Helpless" (song) 113, 114
Hemings, Sally 22, 92, 112, 129, 136
Hemingway, Ernest 93
Henderson, Jeffrey 180
Henry, Patrick 130
Herbst, Susan 147, 150
Herrera, Patricia 61
hip hop 2–3, 37, 50, 61, 78, 80, 98–99, 106, 151–152, 166
"History Has Its Eyes on You" (song) 13, 79, 105, 118
Holler If Ya Hear Me (musical) 152
Horsey, David 37–38
Horton, Owen R. 75
Huell, Jade C. 5, 13–30, 79, 155
Huffington Post 169, 185
humanity 78, 88, 92, 94–95, 97
humanizing 70, 96, 98
Hume, David 133
Hurricane Maria 26, 42
hurricane 25–26, 96
"Hurricane" (song) 26–27, 96

ideals 15, 19, 22, 42, 76, 92, 106, 167
identities 14, 16, 25, 31, 37–38, 48–50, 58, 71–72, 91, 154–155
  political 107, 111, 174
ideologies 34–36, 38, 41, 79, 89, 91, 106, 113, 192
immigrants 13, 18–19, 23, 27, 31, 38, 168–169, 182, 185, 187–189
Inabinet, Brandon 6, 127–144
incivility 145, 147–50, 153, 156
inclusion 31, 57–58, 150, 163, 172, 188

individualism 33, 35–42
injustices 54, 105–106, 116
interpretation 4, 88, 94–95, 105, 118, 131
In the Heights (musical) 51, 152, 164
invitational rhetoric 7, 163–164, 166–69, 171
    exemplar of 172–173
    limitations of 168, 175
irony 91, 93, 110
Irony of American History, The (Niebuhr, Reinhold) 91
Isenberg, Nancy 18
"It's Quiet Uptown" (song) 96

Jackson, Andrew 54, 80
Jackson, Christopher 24, 47, 51, 62, 165
Jefferson, Thomas 19–20, 38, 40–41, 73, 78, 81, 95, 110, 112, 148–149, 169, 171
Jenkins, Lindsay A. 5, 13–30, 79, 155
Jewett, Robert 70
Johnson administration 33
Joker (film) 75
Jones, Cleve 168
justice 7, 19, 49, 72, 77, 90, 93, 185, 188, 192

Kaepernick, Colin 90
Kajikawa, Loren 31, 78, 155–1566
Katriel, Tamar 49
Kent, Clark 72–73, 77
Killmonger, Eric 81
King, Martin Luther, Jr. 90, 92
King, Rufus 132
Klotz, Kelsey 153–154
knowledge 5, 18–19, 79–80, 129

Laden, Anthony Simon 147–148
Lafayette, Marquis de 18, 38, 52, 57, 150
language 3, 110, 133, 166, 184, 188, 192
Larson, Jonathan 166
Laurens, John 38, 41, 52, 55, 57, 75, 80, 97, 111, 150
LaVally, Rebecca 186
Lawrence, John Shelton 70
leaders 57, 61–62
leadership 60, 171, 174–175
Lee, Charles 41

Lee, William 57–59, 61
legacy 17, 26, 39, 41, 47, 61, 109, 127, 154, 170
Legge, Nancy J. 7, 42, 179–192
Lewis, Helen 172
"Let it Go" (song) 112
liberty 15, 23, 42, 48, 62, 110, 187–188
Loewen, James W. 70
Louis, Winnifred 190, 192
Lucas, George 81
Lukensmeyer, Carolyn J. 146
Lunceford, Brett 50–51
lyrics 3, 5, 35–39, 41, 53, 57, 60, 109–110, 115–116, 118, 128–131, 134, 151, 185–186, 188–192

MacArthur Genius Grant 1
Maclay, Edgar S. 134
Madison, Dolley 109
Madison, James 19, 23, 26, 39, 56, 109, 114, 132, 149–151, 155
Maltby, Kate 31
Martinez, Theresa A. 152
masculinity 112–113
McAllister, Marvin 21–23, 25, 80
McCarter, Jeremy 80, 152
McMaster, James 116
Medhurst, Martin 33
"Meet Me Inside" (song) 80, 113
melodies 37–38, 115
melodrama 6, 127, 136, 139
Melville, Herman 93
memory 16, 19, 21, 26, 32, 47–50, 87, 91, 96, 98, 110
Merediz, Olga 51
metaphor 92–93, 133
morality 115, 132–133
    civic 128
Miranda, Lin-Manuel 7, 19–20, 25–26, 42, 79–80
    lived experience 13–14
    historical representation 14
    uses Shakespearian prologue 24
Monteiro, Lyra D. 32, 88
morality 115, 132–133
Morris, Robert 138
Morrison, Toni 93–94

Muddiman, Ashley 148
Mulligan, Hercules 23, 38, 79, 150
Murray, Judith Sargent 108
museums 48–49, 51, 53, 89
music 61–62, 80, 89, 94, 98, 115, 118, 152, 163–164, 166, 169
"My Shot" (song) 18, 38–39, 40, 80, 95, 185–186, 188–189
myths 5–6, 31–34, 40, 42, 69, 71–73, 75, 78–79, 81, 87, 92–93, 99

narrations 47, 51–56, 58–61, 117
narratives 5, 22, 49, 54, 73, 88, 90–91, 93, 116, 129
nation 3, 6, 22, 24, 59–60, 106–107, 133–136, 146, 148–149, 155–156, 170, 173
Native Americans 88, 171
negotiation 14, 131, 138
Neville-Shepard, Ryan 5, 31–45, 137
newspapers 132, 136
    news circulation 128, 135–136
Newton, Thandie 92
New York Orphan Asylum Society 109
Niebuhr, Reinhold 91
Nolte, Nick 92
"Non-Stop" (song) 33, 59, 111, 188
nostalgia 15–16, 19, 21–23, 25–26
Notes on the State of Virginia (Jefferson, Thomas) 92–93

Obama, Barack 2, 7, 31, 34, 87, 92, 146, 163, 165
Obama, Michelle 2
Odom, Leslie, Jr. 25, 165
"One Last Time" (song) 24, 62, 96
oppression 27, 109, 135, 153, 156, 163, 167, 182
Orbe, Mark P. 7, 42, 50, 163–179
Organa, Leia 81
origin 16, 57, 74, 79, 99
    character's 74
    stories 6, 19–20, 24, 27, 55, 72–75, 78, 99, 136
O'Rourke, Sean Patrick 148, 150
Ott, Brian L. 14, 48

Paine, Thomas 116
paintings 54, 56, 73, 95
pamphlets 53, 56, 81, 128
Panzica, Sofia 187
Parker, Peter 72, 77
Parks, Rosa 90
participants 20, 34, 76, 153, 179, 182, 186
participation 56, 95, 128, 190
participatory democracy 7, 179, 190–191
Pasley, Jeffrey L. 41–42
passions 22, 40, 132, 136, 153, 155
patriarchy 6, 105
    and subversive agency 106
patriotism 22, 107
Paulson, Michael 88
Paup, Emily Berg 6, 105–123
Pence, Mike 42, 168, 172–173, 181–183
Perelman, Chaïm 95
performers 23, 26, 76, 88, 155, 171
persuasion 134, 173, 175
Peterson, Carla L. 94
placards 55–57, 59–60, 62
Playing in the Dark: Whiteness and the Literary Imagination (Morrison, Toni) 93
Poe, Edgar Allen 93
poets 180–181, 191
politeness 130–131, 145, 147–149, 153
political agency 107, 109, 111, 164
political debates 6, 60, 107, 145–147, 150–151, 154–156
political discourse 3, 136, 147, 156
politicians 20, 108–109, 132, 149, 151
politics 2, 4, 49–50, 107, 110–112, 114–115, 132, 134, 163, 179–183, 191–192
    See also Founding Fathers
popularity 2, 7, 89, 99, 132, 165, 184
portraits 16, 22, 53, 56–57, 59–60, 95
portrayal 95, 117, 165
power 6–7, 25, 71–74, 76, 79, 105, 128, 130, 135, 138–139, 152–156, 173–175
    political 109, 132, 152–153
presentation 17, 48, 53, 56, 58, 112
privilege 49, 110, 136, 175
protestors 184–86, 188–190
protests 4, 184–192

public affairs 112, 128
public discourse 5, 148, 180, 192
public memory 3, 5, 11, 14, 16–17, 48–50, 53 87, 105
Puerto Rico 27, 42, 169

Raaflaub, Kurt A. 180
race 3, 6, 37, 49, 59, 87–91, 99, 105, 153
racism 21, 55, 61, 89–90, 98, 163
Raengo, Alessandra 99
Randolph, Edmond 132
rap battles 6, 81, 95, 98, 133–134, 146–147, 151, 154–155
rap music 146, 152–55, 164, 166
rappers 80, 154–155
Reagan, Ronald 33
realities 17, 19, 27, 54–55, 71, 73, 93, 105, 189–190
Reed, Ishmael 21, 128, 171
Remnick, David 166
reproductions 53, 55
republican motherhood 6, 106–107, 110–111, 114, 116
resistance 18, 152, 185, 188–190
retelling 37, 48, 88–89, 92, 110
Return of the Jedi (film) 81
Revington, James 56
revolutionaries 91, 113, 189
Revolutionary War 23, 47, 52, 57, 59, 108, 110, 114, 148, 189
Reynolds, Maria 6, 96, 111, 114–115, 127, 129, 131, 133, 135–136, 138
Reynolds, Michaelah 5, 31–46, 137
"Reynolds Pamphlet, The" (song) 114
rhetoric 3, 5–6, 50–51, 67, 125, 129, 138–139, 163, 166–167, 174, 192
    traditional conceptualizations of 166, 175
rhetorical history 105–106, 117–118
Richard III (Play) 22
Richard Rodgers Theatre 1, 172
"Right Hand Man" (song) 57, 80, 95, 189–190
Robbins, Caryn 118
Rocky (film) 34
Romano, Aja 21
Romano, Renee C. 42

"Room Where It Happens, The" (song) 3, 6, 24, 39, 130, 131, 137, 189
Roosevelt, Theodore 72
Ross, Betsy 99
Rose, Tricia 152
Rowson, Susannah 108
Rushing, Janice Hocker 34
Russell, John Clyde 6, 87–103
Ryan, Paul 31

San Juan, Puerto Rico 26, 42
"Satisfied" (song) 111
"Say No To This" (song) 96, 111, 114, 131
Scholz, T. M. Linda 168
Schudson, Michael 145
"Schuyler Defeated" (song) 111–112
Schuyler sisters 52, 81, 111–112, 131
"Schuyler Sisters, The" (song) 111, 116–117, 118, 185–186, 188
Schuyler, Angelica 38, 111, 115–116, 131, 137, 169, 171, 186
Schuyler, Philip 58–59
Schwarze, Steven 128, 137, 139
Scott, Robert L. 153
Seabury, Samuel 56, 81, 113, 145, 148, 150, 153, 155
self-determination 163, 167, 172–173, 175
self-starter 24, 36, 169
senate 111, 134
sexism 21, 55
Shakespeare, William 3, 76, 183
Shakur, Tupac 152
Skywalker, Luke 81
slaveholders 19, 22, 130
slaveholding 129–130
slavery 19–20, 54–56, 58, 60–61, 89, 92–93, 96–97, 99, 108, 110, 128–130, 134, 136, 171
slaves 19–20, 60, 92, 96, 137, 192
Smith, Donald K. 153
social change 3, 6–7, 90, 125, 147, 156, 163, 167–168, 174, 192
social media 2–3, 181–185, 192
society 21, 23, 31, 33–34, 38, 75–76, 78–79, 115, 182
Solomon, Martha 34

Sondheim, Stephen 166
soundtrack 53, 62, 97, 168
sovereignty 138
Spider-Man 6, 72, 77
Stamp Act 57
Star Wars (film) 81
Stark, Tony 77
status quo 153, 175, 189
"Stay Alive" (song) 189–190
Steuart, James 133
Stewart, Susan 21
storytelling 24, 89, 166
"Story of Tonight, The" (song) 188–189
"Story of Tonight (Reprise), The" (song) 98
Stuckey, Mary E. 148, 150
Styrt, Philip Goldfarb 14, 18
sublimations 130, 132, 136–137
Sugar Act 57
superheroes 6, 70, 72–74, 77, 80
symbols 16, 77, 110, 127, 138

"Take a Break" (song) 111, 115, 131, 155
tax 129
taxonomies 77
Tea Act 57
"That Would Be Enough" (song) 115
theater 7, 15–17, 23, 76, 80, 172, 179–180, 182–183, 191
　musical 4, 47, 117, 152, 170
　and politics 180–81, 183, 191
Thomas, Emma 190
threats 70, 113, 185, 191
tickets 76, 165, 184
Till, Emmett 90
"Tomorrow There'll Be More of Us" (song) 97
tragedy 35, 180
1778 Treaty of Alliance 149
Trump, Donald 2, 7, 27, 42, 165, 172, 179, 182–185, 190–191
　administration 2, 7, 27, 179, 184–185, 189, 191
trust 129, 133, 137–38

truth 54, 77, 150, 187
Twain, Mark 93
twitter 172, 182–183

utopia 13–16, 21–23, 26

Viertel, Jack 152
villain 40, 77, 81, 171
violence 75, 129, 138

"Wait For It" (song) 39
Waldstreicher, David 41
Warren, Mercy Otis 56, 108
War of 1812 75
Washington, George 19, 23–24, 51–52, 57, 73–74, 78, 80, 95–96, 99, 112, 165, 169, 171
Washington, Martha 59
"We Know" (song) 114, 115
"What'd I Miss?" (song) 95, 99, 112, 129, 154
White House 2, 151, 163, 165, 173
whiteness 6, 21, 89–91, 93–94, 96
　and (dis)comfort 90–91
　visceral nature of 91–99
　implications and ideological aspects 99
"Who Lives, Who Dies, Who Tells Your Story" (song) 5, 41, 48, 79, 105, 109, 115, 137
Wiles, David 180
Wiley, Kehinde 16
Williams, James Anthony, Jr. 5, 47–65
Williams Peter, Jr. 61
"Winter's Ball, A" (song) 52, 58
Women's March 184, 187
Woody, Rachel Cristine 58
"World Was Wide Enough, The" (song) 36, 40, 41, 61, 118

"Yorktown" (song) 18, 38, 78, 188
Young, Harvey 15
"You'll Be Back" (song) 113
"Your Obedient Servant" (song) 19, 81

Zarefsky, David 4

General Editors
Mitchell S. McKinney and Mary E. Stuckey

At the heart of how citizens, governments, and the media interact is the communication process, a process that is undergoing tremendous changes as we embrace a new millennium. Never has there been a time when confronting the complexity of these evolving relationships been so important to the maintenance of civil society. This series seeks books that advance the understanding of this process from multiple perspectives and as it occurs in both institutionalized and non-institutionalized political settings. While works that provide new perspectives on traditional political communication questions are welcome, the series also encourages the submission of manuscripts that take an innovative approach to political communication, which seek to broaden the frontiers of study to incorporate critical and cultural dimensions of study as well as scientific and theoretical frontiers.

For more information or to submit material for consideration, contact:

    Mitchell S. McKinney: McKinneyM@missouri.edu
    Mary E. Stuckey: mes519@psu.edu

To order other books in this series, please contact our Customer Service Department:

    peterlang@presswarehouse.com (within the U.S.)
    orders@peterlang.com (outside the U.S.)

Or browse online by series:
    WWW.PETERLANG.COM